MW01505791

THE CRISIS OF COLONIAL ANGLICANISM

MARTYN PERCY

The Crisis of Colonial Anglicanism

Empire, Slavery and Revolt in the Church of England

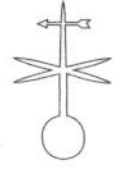

HURST & COMPANY, LONDON

First published in the United Kingdom in 2025 by
C. Hurst & Co. (Publishers) Ltd.,
New Wing, Somerset House, Strand, London, WC2R 1LA

Distributed in the United States, Canada and Latin America by
Oxford University Press, 198 Madison Avenue, New York, NY 10016,
United States of America.

A Cataloguing-in-Publication data record for this book
is available from the British Library.

ISBN: 9781911723585

www.hurstpublishers.com

Printed and bound in Great Britain by Bell & Bain Ltd, Glasgow

In Gratitude for Adam, Kate, Richard and Dawn

Clerici ad gentem, exempla curae pastoralis

‘The crisis you have to worry about the most is the one you don’t see coming.’

– Mike Mansfield

‘When great institutions decline they do not suddenly fall over a precipice; they simply slide down the slope, a little further each year, in a genteel way, making do in their reduced circumstances, like a spinster in an Edwardian novel.’

– Lord Baker, in a speech in the House of Lords, 2002[1]

'Look on my Works, ye Mighty, and despair!
Nothing beside remains. Round the decay
Of that colossal Wreck, boundless and bare
The lone and level sands stretch far away.'

– Percy Bysshe Shelley, 'Ozymandias', 1818

'To say that our Empire is "bone of our bone, flesh of our flesh", is not to express an opinion but to assert a fact. So long as Englishmen retain at once their migratory instinct, their passion for independence, and their impatience of foreign rule, they are bound by a manifest destiny to found empires abroad, or, in other words, to make themselves the dominant race in the foreign countries to which they wander.'

– Edward Dicey (1832-1911), quoted in
Lewis C. B. Seaman, *Victorian England: Aspects of English and Imperial History, 1837-1901*,
London: Routledge, 1973, p. 331.

'Imperialism is nothing but [a] larger patriotism.'

– Lord Rosebery, 1899, (speech,
City of London Liberal Club, 5 May 1899,
Daily News, 6 May, 1899)

'The empires of the future are the empires of the mind.'

– Winston Churchill, 1943, Speech at
Harvard University, 6 September 1943,
Onwards to Victory, London: Cassell, 1944

ADVANCE PRAISE FOR THIS BOOK

'*The Crisis of Colonial Anglicanism* is a provocative contribution to the scholarship and public debates about colonialism and the postcolonial world order. These processes and the realities they produced are too often discussed as economic and political phenomena. It is both challenging and productive to take (established) religion seriously as part of the analytical whole. And while Percy portrays the Anglican church, he also raises a mirror to Britain and its postcolonial malaise.'

— Miri Rubin, Professor of History, Queen Mary University of London and author, *inter alia*, of *Mother of God: A History of the Virgin Mary*.

'If you thought that the days of imperialism and empire were over, Martyn Percy's book shows that the long-term effects are still very much in evidence in the Church of England and that they continue to infect global Anglicanism. This is most apparent in contemporary divisive moral questions and how they are being addressed. Percy's careful and critical cultural study does not just lock up these questions in some poison cabinet, but puts the issues right in front of all of us to be dealt with. His book opens up entirely new perspectives. Ultimately, this is a book not only for Anglicans or about Anglicanism, but for all who are concerned about the long-term impact of white hegemonic male cultural supremacy.'

— Professor Angela Berlis, University of Bern

'A radical and, in many ways, devastating book ... Martyn Percy has examined how disestablishment has become more and more inevitable. Unlike Roman Catholicism the Anglican communion does not represent a universal church—the Archbishop of Canterbury does not have the same power as the Pope in Rome—and increasingly has been left with a series of individual churches organised country by country, and often disagreeing one with the other. The English Church can no longer function as a spiritual empire. As Percy makes clear in this book that all Anglicans worldwide should read, the game is over.'

— Professor James Carley, Distinguished Research Professor of Medieval History, York University Toronto and Fellow, Royal Society of Canada

'This is a significant but unsettling book in which Martyn Percy details the interlinking of the Church of England and Britain's colonial empire. Percy exposes the church's monarchical role in conquering and subordinating people the world over and its sacralised complicity with slavery, classism, racism, sexism and homophobia.'

— The Revd Professor Brian Douglas, Australian Centre for Christianity and Culture, Charles Sturt University, Editor, *Journal of Anglican Studies*

'Essential reading for all who truly want the Church to be a place of transformation and reconciliation.'

— Professor Greg Garrett, The Carole McDaniel Hanks Professor of Literature and Culture, Baylor University, Canon Theologian, The American Cathedral of the Holy Trinity, Paris

'For any global communion of churches founded in Europe, the question of our colonial past is one which cannot but be addressed. So many present-day issues which seem in some way to be dressed up in theological or ecclesial garb are so often, at root, outworkings of issues relating to colony, class and power. Martyn Percy offers a brave, honest and compelling account of the realities of the effect of colonialism on Anglicanism past and present. *The Crisis of Colonial Anglicanism* is a must-read book for any person with concerns for the Church, society and our global post-colonial situation.'

— Professor Tom Greggs, DLitt, FRSE, Director of the Center of Theological Inquiry, Princeton University

'That the Church of England and the Anglican Communion is in crisis is irrefutable. In *The Crisis of Colonial Anglicanism*, Martyn Percy reveals the origins of this crisis in the monarchical and imperial roots of English Anglicanism. Percy's book forces the question of whether the Church of England is willing, and able, to be transformed in the light of its past.'

— Professor Daniel Joslyn-Siemiatkoski,
Kraft Family Professor, Boston College

'In this important, well-researched, wide-ranging book, Martyn Percy gives an unflinching account of the Anglican Communion. Anyone who is rooting for the future of the Church of England—or Anglicanism in any region of the world—must face this exposition of its imperial and colonial entanglements squarely. As Faulkner warned us: "The past is never dead. It's not even past."'

— Professor Timothy Larsen,
School of Theology, Wheaton College, Illinois

'*The Crisis of Colonial Anglicanism* is an extraordinary exploration of the complex entanglements between the Church of England and the British Empire. Percy critically examines how the Anglican Church served as both a spiritual arm and a moral justification for imperial expansion while grappling with its enduring legacy of complicity in slavery and colonialism. This book challenges readers to confront uncomfortable truths and invites a reckoning with the past. Essential reading for anyone seeking to understand the intersections of faith, power, and history is a compelling and enlightening work that promises to shape the understanding of Anglicanism and its future in the modern world.'

— Rev. Prof. Derrick Lemons,
Department of Religion, University of Georgia

'For those of us in the Catholic Church who owe much to the nearly 500-year history of the Church of England, the approaching anniversary might have been an occasion for celebration of distinctiveness and hope for further rapprochement. That it is not is in no small measure due to factors brilliantly explored in Martyn Percy's book, *The Crisis of Colonial Anglicanism*. The rejection of ecclesial catholicity at the root of the Anglican project meant that its fortunes would always be ineluctably tied to that of England and its imperial project. Percy's book charts the intensity of the colonial hangover and suggests that it is no longer possible to sustain the pious fiction of a global Anglicanism. In its stead we are left with yet another Protestant denomination unable to exorcise the ghosts of its past.'

— Revd. Professor Stephen Morgan, Rector,
University of Saint Joseph, Macao

'In *The Crisis of Colonial Anglicanism*, Martyn Percy offers a powerful and insightful analysis of the Church of England and Global Anglicanism. This is a challenging, disturbing and necessary book traversing history, ecclesiology, culture and politics in an informed, fluent, and sustained argument. For Percy, a Christian future for the Church will have to be forged from the ground up, with a leadership fit for such a task.'

— Rt. Revd. Professor Stephen Pickard,
Charles Sturt University

'A searching use of history for a pre–post-mortem on the Anglican Church that was tied to monarchy and empire from its origins under Henry VIII. It flourished with empire as the spiritual arm of that Victorian public school mission. Unflinching in its challenging scholarship, this book is full of arresting comparative insights into long-term legacies infusing current confusions and differences. For example, monarchic Anglicanism spread Henry VIII's 1533 ban on same-sex relationships across the globe, whereas in those countries colonised by the French there was no state interest in such private acts according to their Penal Code of 1791.'

— Simon Szreter, Professor of History and Public Policy, University of Cambridge and co-author of *Sex Before the Sexual Revolution*

'Martyn Percy explores the undisguised classism and unaccountable hierarchy of colonial Anglicanism in new ways. This is a compelling, original, fresh perspective on privilege and the imposition of a self-serving worldview. Ultimately, he shines a searchlight on the contorted governance of episcopacy since Henry VIII.'

— Sir Iain Torrance PhD, President Emeritus of Princeton Theological Seminary and Pro-Chancellor, University of Aberdeen

'My move into the Anglican Church of Southern Africa, having been expelled from my church in 1983 for being too political, was because of ACSA's commitment to the political struggle against apartheid. Here my political commitments were welcomed, here was a home for my socially engaged spirituality. However, in the decades since, I have become increasingly uncomfortable, no longer feeling "at home" in ACSA. While ACSA's theological engagements with gender and sexuality have been particular ruptures in my sense of 'home', forcing me to analyse my church more deeply, it has been Martyn Percy's superb historical and sociological analysis of our "Mother Church", the Church of England, which has given me an understanding of why it is so difficult for ACSA to move beyond a theology of "control", a recurring concept in Percy's profound analysis.'

— Professor Gerald West, School of Religion, Philosophy and Classics, University of Kwazulu-Natal

CONTENTS

INTRODUCTION

IMPLOSION

The Crisis of Colonial Anglicanism explores the expansion, gradual retraction, decline and fall of an empire and national church. More specifically, it seeks to examine the role played by the Church of England as the spiritual arm of the British Empire. This is a story of national and spiritual hubris, expressed in a shared desire for pre-eminence across the global stage. Yet by regarding the rest of the world as somehow lesser than themselves, both the British Empire and the Anglican Church slowly moved from domination and expansion into a state of degeneration resulting in a loss of place, status, respect and reputation. A body that is degenerating, whether human or socio-political, such as the Roman or British Empire, or the Anglican Communion, is one that is showing its age, and can no longer stave off its internal collapse and external threats. For Anglican churches, such threats are simultaneously internal and external, and include secularisation, consumerism, the information revolution, decline in authority and respect, and more besides.

The process of degeneration is cyclical, natural and normal. It is also something that an individual or society can bring upon themselves. Here we are concerned with how an empire and a national church have broken down and fallen apart. In the post-Second World War era, which is also the post-colonial era, that degeneration has been rapid. So fast, in fact, that those still inclined to succumb to the mystique of empire have found the speed of British decline to be traumatic. After 1945, Britain was reduced to the role of a missile base for the United States and, in terms of trade, was overtaken by Japan, the European Union, and, slowly but surely, China and India. Today, the empire is no more, and Britain no longer great.[1] In this book, we seek to explain how the fortunes of the British Empire and the Church of England were always in lock-step, and show how the decline of one led to the deterioration and decline of the other.

Much of what happened to the empire can also be seen in the fortunes of the Church of England. The Anglican Communion is a kind of quasi-ecclesial 'commonwealth' that has been riven apart by factionalism between wings representing liberals and conservatives, progressives and traditionalists, Anglo-Catholics and evangelicals. Disputes about gender, sexuality, authority, order and autonomy are part and parcel of the post-colonial life and legacy of the Church of England, and it has hardly begun to take account of its history and responsibility for the era of empire. The structure of the Anglican Communion itself has been reduced to an opt-in body on issues and policies but with few mechanisms to exclude others, discipline, or censure for dissent. Whereas a bishop in some far-flung overseas colony defying the Archbishop of Canterbury a century ago would have seemed inconceivable, it is now so routine as not to even merit so much as a comment in the media or indeed a word from Lambeth Palace.

However, this book is not concerned with the long-term palliative care of the Church of England or the wider global Anglican Communion. It is more concerned with sketching an account of the church's role, both supportive and independent, of

England's conquest and subordination of peoples the world over, its effective endorsement of slavery and the financial benefits derived from the slave trade, and its imposition and transmission of hierarchical world-views and practices especially in relation to race and class. The Church of England has till recently evaded scrutiny and transparency in respect of these actions through its pre-eminent position as the established church. In so doing, it has been long opposed, historically, to democratic accountability and open governance, preferring instead to stay within a privileged monarchical pattern of control over clergy and laity that merely pays lip service to egalitarian and elected assemblies.

This book advances a number of bold claims. It highlights the shocking legacy of slavery, which is part and parcel of the DNA of the Church of England, and which has been transmitted to most of the familial extensions across the worldwide Anglican Communion. In so doing, it carries the coding of classism, racism, sexism and homophobia—and even eugenics. The book shows how such beliefs and practices were sacralised legitimisations of the social, economic and ethical drivers within the British Empire.[2]

The book also argues that the unresolved tension in the foundation of the Church of England in 1534, between local congregation Presbyterian polity and quasi-regal episcopal polity, is now forcing it apart at the seams. Appeals to synodical government (i.e., quasi-democratic but relatively ineffectual) and claims of catholicity (i.e., lodged in quasi-regal episcopal authority) are more of a fudge than a middle way (or the *via media*, as most Anglican apologists prefer to term it). Being neither Protestant nor Catholic, the Church of England and wider Anglican Communion are slowly being sucked into becoming a global network that has far more in common with Presbyterianism or Lutheranism.

Furthermore, the book argues that just as empires fall apart, being unable to overcome their internal insurgencies, and eventually implode, so can denominations. English Anglicanism can often present itself as authentic and pastorally grounded in local parishes and chaplaincies. But in its national leadership and structures, the Church of England has often been revealed as a form of sacralised manneredness, thereby confirming classism, elitism and the status quo in social hierarchy. This is also part of the DNA coding of the Church of England. However, it has proved to be an insufficient glue to bind the wider Anglican Communion together. Over the decades, it has seen its structures deteriorate, collapse and ultimately implode.

The once-dominant parent of global Anglicanism has struggled to assert itself in a post-colonial and anti-imperial era. Much of the imperialism with which this book is concerned amounts to an English cluster of values, practices and outlooks. As Edward Said made clear, 'imperialism' represents those attitudes and practices of domination that demoted and subjugated the world-views of other people. Plainly, even after empires fall and a post-colonial era emerges, imperialism can persist in the practices, perspectives and positions taken by the inheritors of empire, so that the indigenous rulers pick up where the conqueror left off. Freedom and independence do not necessarily rid a newly founded nation of its subtle indoctrination in empire.[3]

In terms of the Church of England and the wider Anglican Communion, elitist English imperialist attitudes have remained in place well into the post-colonial era. While the specious attractions of the evangelical or Anglo-Catholic wings of the church may have camouflaged some of the impetus of English entitlement for a season, the underlying ecclesial culture has remained steadfastly aloof and presumptuous within its upper echelons. Even when the Anglican churches of former British colonies have managed to secure their own ecclesial autonomy, an imperialist drive has persisted in the ordering and organisation of the churches. This plays out in mercurial imperialist—some may say quasi-regal or monarchical—decision-making and governance within Anglicanism, where bishops and senior clergy treat the rest of the church, and the wider world, as a kind of subjugated 'other'. The lack of accountability, transparency and integrity in the clerisy of leadership flows from this. There are rulers, and there are subjects. God has ordained it so, and the hierarchy has no need to explain itself to the people.

What is being offered in this book is a new critical cultural theory of the British Empire as an overwhelmingly English construction and the role therein of the Church of England, which has presumed to act as and benefit from being the spiritual arm of that English enterprise, through its inchoate adoption of imperialism and the attendant attitudes and outlooks it carries. The English Anglican polity has become what I term a character within its own 'serious fiction'—the major player in a drama of empire and church. Indeed, it has become a prisoner within an opera of its own composition. Edward Said called this 'the empire of [the] imagination'.[4] Consequently, there needs to be a different kind of reckoning with the worldwide Anglican Communion. I argue that the worldwide Anglican Communion is morally problematic in both theory and practice, since it was but the Church of England hitching a ride on the expansion of the British Empire. Operating as a spiritual wing, the church inevitably capitalised on and gained from British expansionism, which was itself driven by commerce and conquest.

The approach to historiography taken in this book is one that is intentionally critical and moral. According to Friderich Nietzsche,[5] critical history refuses to revere the past. In fact, it rejects such constructions of reality and valorisations of the past, precisely in order to inaugurate those processes that can create something wholly new. Plainly, the danger is that one will be unfair to the past. Nietzsche was alive to the danger of failing to appreciate how elements in our past cultures, which we might now despise, were in fact necessary, as they were among the very elements that formed us.[6] In defence of Nietzsche, his primary concern was to cut through the excessive superfluity of knowledge that clouded critical judgement. In modern idiom, we might say he was arguing that 'less is more', especially if what is now less is shaped by critical attention that leads to a far more astute, self-aware and progressive culture. However, Nietzsche asserted that only critical history, and not monumental or antiquarian history, could provide life and moral direction—much as liberation theologians might claim for churches and communities. Of course, the first three types have the capacity to metastasise in any body politic, and threaten the pulse of critical history.[7]

Following Mark C. Taylor,[8] I have opted not to make the argument in this book into a theological treatise. Taylor's strategy in many of his works was to write about religion and theology, but to do so with the more 'indirect' economic, social, political and historical evidence that more fully illuminates the context in which religions and theologies gestate. In a similar vein, the earlier, ground-breaking work of George Lindbeck approached and interpreted theology and religion as a cultural-linguistic phenomenon. Lindbeck viewed theology and religion as 'regulative' for culture, devising rules and codes that enabled religious institutions to navigate and avoid, or resist or adopt, cultural norms.[9] Taken as a whole, the approach and method adopted in the book is one of critical cultural theory. As readers will therefore appreciate, this book takes a critical cultural approach to the favoured (historical) story of worldwide Anglicanism and the Church of England, and to the story it tells itself ('serious fiction') and the wider world.

In *The Crisis of Colonial Anglicanism* we contrast the model of 'Old World' Anglicanism with that of the 'New World' democratic entity that quickly evolved in early America, thereby giving us two complementary but quite different forms of polity. The two worlds had entirely incongruent outlooks. The Old World believed in the pre-eminence of God-willed monarchical authoritarianism. The Church of England and wider Anglican Communion was rooted in such foundations. The New World, on the other hand, believed in an inalienable right to democratic equality. The Old World offers monarchy—even if benign, kind and good, its citizens were still *subjects* of a realm. 'Subject' here meant deference to those who were born or made to rule over others. The New World, by contrast, is democratic, and governance and government can be changed by the consent and will of the people. All are equal. There are no subjects, only citizens.

No Archbishop of Canterbury could ever possibly appease such a breadth of theological, political and moral viewpoints. That this has even been attempted is hugely problematic and doomed to failure. The book explains this lost cause and writes the eulogy. In short, those in power who only propose reforms will ultimately fail in their monarchical rule, and conservative or radical revolution will succeed in its place. Reform is of the Old World; revolution is of the New.

Readers on either side of the Pond (i.e., the Atlantic Ocean) will also note that I have used the terms 'Anglican' and 'Episcopal' interchangeably.[10] As we shall see, these are essentially two sides of the same coin. While American Episcopalians became unavoidably committed to democracy and the theological rationale for that, and English Anglicans remain inclined to reformed models of monarchy, also with a theological rationale, it is but one faith. It just happens to have been practised in two different worlds for 250 years.

Ultimately, the rejection of monarchy and the embrace of democracy will be the fate of the Anglican Communion. The seeds of ecclesiastical insurgency might have been slow to fruit, but they were inevitable. Furthermore, their advent now marks the end of the Church of England as we know it. It cannot be reformed any further. Only a revolution can save it.

1

THE RISE AND FALL OF A GLOBAL CHURCH

As a people, the English face innumerable challenges from within, and yet persist in struggling—vainly and hopelessly—to retain the sovereign position they once held in the world. Fear of losing pre-eminence is a very English vice. The same impetus lies within the DNA coding of English Anglicanism. How could other faiths or denominations possibly be superior? Surely this English religion is 'Best in Show', even if not the largest or strongest? It may be smaller than its competitors, but overall it sees itself as top dog. One can easily note how English Anglicanism talks itself up as one of the world's largest and most influential denominations, often placing itself third (by number of adherents) behind Catholicism and Eastern Orthodoxy.

But it isn't; this is just more of its own 'serious fiction'. The global numbers for Anglicanism are hyperinflated to around 80 million. Over recent decades Anglicans have developed a largely unchallenged narrative of global growth (for orthodox and evangelical Anglicans) and decline (for liberal and broad church Anglicans). The story narrated tells of Anglicanism's success being largely due to growth in the developing, post-colonial nations which, according to the narrators, are conservative, traditional and orthodox, and unstoppable in their growth. The same narrative claims First World, mostly post-modern nations have seen a steep decline in church membership and attendance due to their liberalism.

The truth is somewhat different. Daniel Muñoz[1] has researched the numbers and crunched them, showing that claims of steep rises in Anglican affiliation in the global South are prone to significant exaggeration. Nigeria, for example, claimed as of 2016 that it had a membership of over 18 million out of a total Nigerian population of 180 million. But such figures ignore variables, including the practice of many Christians of being affiliated to several denominations at once. The Church of England claims 25 million members, though the average Sunday attendance is now under 0.5 million. Despite the English having colonised one third of the world, the statistics for 21st-century Christianity offer a more sobering narrative. The Orthodox and the Pentecostal churches each account for around 300 million followers worldwide. Baptist, Methodist, Lutheran and the Reformed churches make more reliable claims for followers than those of global Anglicanism. Roman Catholicism can claim 1.5 billion followers. One can see here that, based on the statistics we have, Anglicanism would be a relatively middle-ranking denomination, were it not for the history of entwinement with the British Empire.

Status: Keeping Up Appearances

Fear of losing pre-eminence continues to shape the deep anxieties of successive Archbishops of Canterbury, who cannot face a post-imperialist, post-colonial world in which former subjects are now equals or may even enjoy greater leverage over the denominational parent. In terms of the global Anglican Communion and the Church of England's most senior leadership, the anxiety drives every attempt to maintain the serious fiction of still being *primus inter pares* (first among equals) and cling to the remnants of degenerating unity as a means of keeping some pre-eminence. The status quo is defended with tenacity and determination—and the emphasis is firmly on status here.

The same fear lay behind the desire for monarchical pre-eminence of Henry VIII. Henry feared inferiority in wealth, power and influence, and sought to have the English at the top table of European dynasties. However, in the 15th and 16th centuries, compared to the major nation-states of Holland, France, Spain and Portugal, the English were decades behind the curve in acquiring wealth, power and lands abroad. As the historian Peter Frankopan astutely observes, Henry VIII was positively embarrassed by the accumulation of wealth and power enjoyed by Dutch, Spanish, French and Portuguese monarchs, who commissioned 'explorations' of the world, often under the thinly veiled guise of Christian mission to the heathen, that resulted in boats returning laden with treasures. As a highly competitive individual, Henry did not enjoy being left trailing in the European wealth league.[2] But the king's organised programme of asset stripping of the English religious houses changed all that. It was nationalisation on an epic scale: lead stripped from church roofs; stone dismantled from monasteries, priories and convents and resold as building materials, along with their lands and revenues; gold, silver, priceless books and paintings sequestrated, and kept or sold.

In challenging the Pope to grant him an annulment of his marriage to Catherine of Aragon, Henry inadvertently picked a fight with Europe's richest man, Charles V, Catherine's uncle, on whose approval the Pope depended. Henry lost. But the English Reformation that followed and the birth of the Anglican Church reversed the result, and the rapid programme of religious asset stripping in England gave Henry a triple win. He got a new wife; he got his wealth; and he broke the power of Rome to interfere in England.

The new wealth also paved the way for the commercial expansion and exploitation of overseas territory. Over the next few centuries the entwinement of commerce, civilisation, Christianity and conquest would enjoy the services and support of the Church of England as the spiritual arm of empire. In turn, the church directly and indirectly benefited in wealth, extent and reputation.

The costs of such exploitation were reprehensible, and their legacy continues to this day. From 1757, Robert Clive, the first Governor General of Bengal (later Lord Clive of Plassey), was able to combine the military and commercial muscle of the East India Company (founded in 1600) to intervene in local civil wars, and amass enormous wealth and power for his employers and sponsors. By 1770, Clive had become one of the richest men in the world by virtue of taking over the taxation of Bengal. The exploitation that followed was one of ruthless greed. £2 million in revenue (which would amount to tens of billions today) was appropriated and redistributed to East India Company officers. The price of food soared, inflation rocketed, and famine followed, with millions dying of starvation—possibly up to a third of the population. This was an entirely English-made disaster.[3]

Then karma followed. Within Indian religion, karma refers to the universal causal law by which good or bad actions determine the future of an individual. It is a kind of spiritual irony. The Bengal famine caused a huge labour shortage, which led to a rapid decline in productivity. Revenues quickly collapsed, prompting a run on the shares of the East India Company. The English government had to intervene with a banking bailout, and by 1773 the only way to steady the nerves of investors was the tax on tea imposed on the American colonies. The rest, as they say, is history.

Throughout this period, hundreds of English Anglican clergy served the East India Company militia and the colonial administrations as chaplains. The chaplains were overseen by English bishops and were clearly seen as key personnel in the protection of the East India Company's interests. Humphrey Prideaux (1648–1724), who was Dean of Norwich, argued that the wealth and success of the Dutch East India Company was entirely down to God's favour, as colonies founded by the Netherlands had been actively furthering Christianity. Prideaux urged the East India Company to adopt Church of England chaplains, so as to establish sound Protestant belief and oppose Popish ambitions. Churches and schools were duly set up and run by the Company, with Church of England chaplains presiding over the foundations.

Church of England interests were deeply embedded in the monopoly held by the East India Company. Church of Scotland (Presbyterian) ministers were only reluctantly allowed to minister in India from 1814, when the East India Company was forced to renew its charter. The Company had also strongly discouraged evangelicals and missionary societies from working in India, on the grounds that Christianising the indigenous population would affect the economic interests of the Company and also interfere with slave labour. In the end, parliamentary legislation had to be brought forward in the early 19th century to enable permits and licences to be issued to missionaries seeking to serve in India. Nonetheless, for more than a century, the Church of England's own interests had been furthered through its collusion with a commercial monopoly, backed by armed militia.[4]

The havoc wreaked upon India was to continue well into the 20th century. Winston Churchill argued that India had to be held on to at all costs if the British Empire was to remain a serious entity.

Churchill's fear of losing India was rooted in his conviction that for Britain to *look* great, it needed substantial imperial domains, and the labour to serve the empire. Even when a cataclysmic famine took hold of Bengal (again) between 1943 and 1944, British reputation was privileged above political reform and welfare. It is estimated that between 1.5 and 3 million Indians died.[5]

The Business of Slavery

It is precisely this kind of double-think that kept English slave colonies such as Bunce Island in business. Bunce Island, located in Freetown Harbour, Sierra Leone, was settled and fortified from around 1670 by English slave traders, who sold captives to the American and Caribbean plantations. The island was run by London-based firms, including the Royal African Company, which again could call upon the Church of England. Slaves on Bunce Island did not benefit from the 1807 Act that banned the slave trade. As they were already the property of their owners, the Act of Parliament did not apply to them, nor to other British slave-owning colonies. Banning the slave trade did not free those who were slaves already.

In neither the New World nor the Old World was slavery considered criminal or immoral. Slavery was part and parcel of the social ordering of society and the social and theological construction of reality. Churches understood themselves to be divinely appointed, and the followers of Jesus to be entitled in their subjugation and ownership of others, especially those from a different race, continent or ethnic background. Had God not sanctioned such things in the Old Testament? Had anyone in the New Testament so much as condemned the practice of slave-ownership?

The question of slavery was intensely debated from the 17th to the 19th centuries. However, few today can easily relate to the nuances and complexities of a phenomenon that was commonplace across societies. Those inclined to defend slavery on the grounds that it is not condemned in the Old and New Testament could expect to be met with counter-biblical arguments stressing the human dignity, equality and worth of all in God's sight. One could go further and deduce that if we behaved towards our kith and kin as commanded, there would be no slaves at all, as we would all be serving one another, and not counting ourselves as superior to anyone, but, rather, humbling ourselves.

In so saying, one cannot relativise or minimalise the reality of its criminality. However, contextualising it is different. North African Barbary pirates were raiding Europe for slaves well into the late 18th century. British subjects were only protected, relatively speaking, from such raids with the strength of the Royal Navy. The American Navy (marines) came into existence as a result of their losses in shipping and personnel to this kind of raiding. By 1783 the United States made peace with the British monarchy. In 1784, an American ship was seized by Barbary pirates, and within a decade a dozen American ships had been captured, plundered and everyone enslaved. In response, the United States created its first proper navy in 1794, but the Barbary raids continued, eventually resulting in the first and second Barbary Wars of 1801–5 and 1815 respectively. Unprotected citizens were tempting low-hanging fruit for pirates still engaged in the slave trade. In 1815, the United States was spending as much as 20% of its revenue on payments for ransomed Americans. Some European nations entered into contracts with the Barbary pirates, and were still paying ransoms well into the 1830s.

The picture in continental America was no less complex. The Illini people (from which we derive the state name of Illinois) traded in slaves commercially and also as a means of terrorisation. Their enemies, the Sioux, Pawnee and Chickasaw, were no different. Indeed, from the top of what became Canada to the tip of South America, it would be hard to find a community or ethnic group that did not engage in slave-ownership. The so-called discovery of North and South America by 16th-century European settlers did not introduce slavery to otherwise Edenic civilisations. Rather, the settlers worked closely with indigenous populations to mutual advantage.

As North and South America became contested territory for the imperialist expansion of the British, Dutch, French, Portuguese and Spanish, indigenous groups were used as surrogates to fight proxy wars, settle vendettas, or conduct atrocities that the European sponsor could subsequently claim were regrettable savagery but had nothing to do with them. We see something of this in James Fenimore Cooper's historical romance, *The Last of the Mohicans: A Narrative of 1757* (published in 1820).

Set in the Canadian War between the British and the French, the book tells how the British forces under Lieutenant Colonel George Monro, based at Fort William Henry, were besieged by French forces led by Major General Louis-Joseph de Montcalm. The British surrendered but, under the terms struck with the French, were permitted to remain lightly armed and march home, leaving the fort. However, the Huron tribe, allied to the French, massacred the retreatants, taking many of those captured as slaves (including women, children and British slaves). The Huron scalped the British casualties under the care of French doctors, who were made to look on while the slaughter took place.

Whether this action took place with the tacit complicity of the French or was an unstoppable vendetta perpetrated by an enraged tribe cannot be known to this day. However, as all the colonial powers effectively used their tribal allies to perpetrate the very worst war crimes, by licensing their Native American allies to massacre others the colonial power could still claim plausible deniability. Here, the French would have been acting no differently from the British. Slavery, rape, kidnap and torture, all used as weapons of terror, were part of the day-to-day collateral damage of European proxy wars conducted on American lands.

During the American Revolution, British colonialists competed with patriot forces for the loyalty and service of indigenous tribes. In 1779, George Washington ordered that the Iroquois be eliminated as they were allied to the British, having enslaved captured patriots and engaged in proxy massacres on behalf of the English military. Equally, tribes keen to secure some advantage over their more long-standing indigenous rivals were often to be found wooing colonists in order to gain military superiority over their neighbours. Land could be exchanged for armaments, and people (slaves) operated as a kind of human currency from earliest times.

Some may argue that the racism, slavery and abuse of the past were just part and parcel of the times in which people lived. Yet at the time, with the Enlightenment—driven by writers, reformers, philosophers and inventors—well under way, the importance of liberty and the necessity of equality were becoming more morally and politically urgent. Philosophers such as Edmund Burke were arguing that true liberty was not a matter of some selfish personal freedom but, rather, an authentic social freedom secured by well-constructed institutions.

With the right to freedom, equality, political voice and reform so clearly on the agenda, the relative lack of attention to systemic, economic and punitive racism remains today shocking beyond comprehension. George Washington was a slave-owner. Many Episcopalians north and south of the Mason–Dixon line were slave-owners too. Yet in encountering such difficult history today, and its systemic legacy in racism and generations of economic detriment, there are few signs of genuine remorse, reparation and change. Yet the past is hard to escape if one looks closely enough.

For example, I recall some years ago preaching in a beautiful historic Episcopal church that would have sided with the

Confederate forces during the American Civil War (1861–5). The church still contained an upper gallery with benched seating that was inferior to the pews on the floor of the nave. The seating arrangements clearly indicated a slave gallery. Lest English readers feel a twinge of smugness at this point, many parish churches had similar seating arrangements based on servitude or class or on pew rents. Enclosed pews were reserved for the gentry; they were often equipped with heating and could even provide alcoholic refreshment during services. Inferior benches were for the servants and the working class.

As a whole, this book is therefore concerned with the legacy of the past, especially of empire and slavery, and the moral injury that has inflicted a long-standing and near-fatal soul wound on large segments of humanity. Christianity and civilisation ought to be two forces for the benefit of all humanity. As we shall see, the church and empire, while laying claim to that mantle, in actual fact did the very opposite. Their combined legacy left communities and nations in tatters, and peoples in despair, with millions of souls left in anguish—yet with a torment that still finds no kind of recognition or rapprochement from the perpetrators. Racism continues, with slavery treated as some unfortunate oversight in an otherwise distant past. The present work of reform and redress, moreover, has simply not reckoned with the pain of the past. Just as post-colonial Britain has collective amnesia about the age of empire, so likewise the Church of England fails to reckon with its role in the export of its nascent cultural values and outlooks.[6] These include classism, racism, sexism, homophobia and views on society and politics that are essentially counter-democratic.[7]

As William Faulkner famously noted in *Requiem for a Nun*, the past is never dead—it is not even past.[8] The past is always with us. Likewise, George Orwell observed in his dystopian novel *Nineteen Eighty-four* that whoever controls the past controls the future, and those who control the present control the past.[9] If English history is in the hands of those who valorise and bowdlerise the past, the present and future are unavoidably corrupted. To authentically engage with the present, however, would require the agents and conduits of harm and suffering to face up to their past and its consequences in the present. That must mean humility, repentance, contrition, respect for all and courageous compassion.

Most of those who suffer serious moral injury seek to be empowered, valued as equal, respected, and ultimately become at home with the culture that inflicted degradation, trauma and degeneration upon their people and places. It is precisely this kind of elegiac 'soul repair' with a vision for spiritual, social and political integration that one finds in the speeches of Martin Luther King Jr, Desmond Tutu, Nelson Mandela and Mahatma Gandhi. Their answer to deep moral injury is not to repay in kind. Rather, it is to shine nothing less than the light of truth on the degeneration that led to and still perpetuates the multiple betrayals of inequality.

Churches: The Origin of Species

It pays to remember that most churches and denominations like to imagine they have gestated *in vitro* (as it were) within the heart of God, only then to be born into the world. In fact such bodies owe much in their origins to the social, cultural and political forces of their time. Churches are hybrids of earthly powers and spiritual compulsions, and social historians still have much to teach theology about the cultural drivers that gave rise to distinctive doctrinal emphases in any given era. Put simply, churches and denominations adapt and evolve.[10] Unless we understand the social and historical factors behind such commonplace notions as Anglican comprehensiveness or universality, there is little chance of understanding the (unsurprising) advent of its unravelling.

For example, it may come as a surprise to learn that the Anglican Communion evolved entirely by accident. The Communion has its origins in Bermuda, which was wholly unintended, and later in Aberdeen, which simply vindicates the saying that 'necessity is the mother of invention'. Perhaps it is a caricature to state that the Anglican Communion is the unintended consequence of merchant adventurers in their exploration and exploitation of resources overseas. This would include spices, sugar, precious metals, and, of course, from very early on, human cargo—slaves and prisoners. In both America and Australia, the first settlers were often exiles or prisoners, and the settlements were penal colonies. The first Anglican church services taking place outside the British Isles merely followed in the wake of the advancing commercial stepping stones and secure outposts for trading.

Nonetheless, Bermuda can lay claim to being the oldest continually inhabited English settlement in the New World. This was an accident waiting to happen. In 1607 the British had begun a colony in Virginia—Fort James, later known as Jamestown. Conditions were so harsh that the colony was briefly abandoned in 1610. But in 1609 a British ship, HMS *Sea Venture*, en route to Jamestown came to grief on one of Bermuda's perilous reefs. The shipwrecked crew and passengers declined to move on, once they heard of the conditions in Jamestown, and argued that they had the right to establish their own government. This was not taken especially seriously.

Nonetheless, by 1612, St George's Town, Bermuda, was the first English capital city of the New World, albeit comprising little more than a labour camp, penal colony and trading post. In 1612 St Peter's Church in Bermuda became the first parish church outside the British Isles. The Church of England had thereby expanded its boundaries. Even today, Bermuda is an extra-provincial diocese of the Archbishop of Canterbury, and not part of either the Episcopal Church of the United States or the Province of the West Indies, and it only separated from the Church of England in 1978. By 1639, the first Church of England building in America had been constructed—built of brick in Jamestown, Virginia.

All of this was in place long before the first attempts at establishing a code for conduct and unity (i.e., the Lambeth Conferences) were made in a suggestion by the Bishop of Vermont, Henry Hopkins, to the Archbishop of Canterbury in 1851. It was to take another sixteen years to gestate into the first gathering of 1867. Here, I hold that by stressing the social, political and cultural origins of the Communion, we can better understand how individual provinces came to possess their distinctives and also reassess the landscape of contemporary schism.

For example, the Archdiocese of Sydney has been deeply supportive of the Reformed Evangelical Anglican Church of South Africa (REACH). Previously known as the Church of England in South Africa (CESA), it originally separated from the rest of the Anglican Church over high church practices. But in the 20th century it evolved an anti-liberation theology stance on a range of issues. The apolitical position of CESA, and its previous pro-apartheid stance, including an archbishop (Stephen Bradley, in office from 1965 to 1984) who backed the government of apartheid, have placed CESA outside the Anglican Communion, although, curiously, its ordinations are recognised by the Archbishop of Canterbury. (A somewhat similar stance was taken by the Episcopal Church towards the single Confederate bishop consecrated during the American Civil War.)

In contrasting the model of the 'Old World' Church of England (post-revolution and a reformed monarchical establishment) with that of the 'New World' democratic entity that quickly evolved in early America, we begin to understand two complementary but quite different forms of ecclesiastical polity. Modern European democracies that have retained monarchies have recalibrated the role of the ruler into sacred-symbolic and other functional duties. This creates the space and conditions for the democratic processes to work without the intervention of arbitrary and unaccountable power.

One can hear archbishops and bishops talking to their churches and synods in similar terms. The assumption seems to be that the people cannot be left to themselves. Autocracy, however, is rarely a resource of resolution for the reconstitution of society.[11]

It is here that both the Old World and New World orders depend on the rule of law: judges and courts to keep those in power in check. Threats to a fair and just social order occur when courts and judges are persecuted or manipulated by politicians or rulers, or the politicians and rulers are the possessors, implementers and arbiters of the law—as still happens in Old World state churches under its leaders (ecclesiastical law). Much as the story of ancient Israel unfolds in the Old Testament, monarchy carries risks, not least because monarchy, as well as certain models of episcopacy, always carries theocracy within its DNA. Any religion or church of the state that has the power to anoint and proclaim the monarch will play a significant part in the ecology of unaccountable power.

When Richard Hooker, one of the finest Anglican theologians ever, wrote his *Lawes of Ecclesiastical Polity* at the end of the 16th century, he was seeking to outline a form of social order that was fair, just and tolerant. His work subtly crafts arguments for loyal dissent, liberty of conscience, and a form of thinking and acting that does not capitulate to the forces of totalitarian religious or political rule. Over several volumes, Hooker's *Lawes* offer a kindly critical vision for order that remains keenly alive to the threats posed by theocratic power—whether by monarch or church leadership.[12]

As time has gone on, the Old World order has declined in power and value, and the New World has become a more globally accepted norm. In some respects, this may also help us understand why Americans insist on the separation of church and state (unlike Europe), but are at the same time much keener on religion mixing in politics (unlike Europe). Once we understand what the state represents (e.g., monarchy, unaccountable power), and what politics can be (e.g., democratic, not autocratic), then faith in public life evolves differently. But to be clear, this is still one faith, albeit in two different worlds. The parallels with 'two nations divided by one common language'—a dictum often attributed to Oscar Wilde, George Bernard Shaw and others—will be striking. How can it be that one faith is responsible for the origin and authenticity of two quite different worlds?

Much of what the future holds for churches and mainstream Protestant denominations, of which Anglicanism is a major example, depends on whether democratic accountability is allowed to function and flourish. I contend that it is not Anglican faith that is falling apart. Rather, this is a story of two worlds slowly drifting apart following the split between the world of monarchy and the emerging world of democracy. In this, the Old World has passed through its phase of empire, become post-colonial, and is ceding its last residual powers to the new normal of democratic liberalism. In this, the New World continues to ascend.

2

FAITH IN AN AGE OF CRISIS

The latter part of the 18th century has been dubbed the Age of Revolution, with the American and French Revolutions being the stand-out events of this age. But there is another revolutionary moment of that time of which most people are unaware, which was to have profound implications for the Anglican Church. This was the consecration in 1784 of Samuel Seabury as the first bishop of the Episcopal Church of the United States. Significant here were both the manner of his consecration—by Scottish Episcopal, not Church of England, bishops—and its decisive impact on the form and ethos of Anglicanism in the New World, one that was anti-monarchical and democratic in character. This would set the New World of the Anglican Church against the Old World of the Church of England, establishing different poles of attraction and influence that would have, and still continue to have, lasting repercussions on Anglicanism worldwide. The revolutionary event of 1784 thus deserves our closer inquiry.

Prior to 1784 the story of the implantation of Christianity, and in particular the Anglican Church, in the New World took several different forms. Back in the 17th century across Europe, there was no separation between church and state. So just how Anglican was the New World? The British commercial licences granted by the crown in the 17th century required the merchants and business leaders to take the oath acknowledging the monarch as Supreme Governor of the Protestant Church of England, to renounce the authority of the Pope, and to accept the Book of Common Prayer as the only authorised liturgy.

Early settlers in Jamestown, Virginia, were required to attend Morning and Evening Prayer daily; on Sundays sermons were preached and the catechism taught. The penalties for dissent could range from loss of food rations to jail, and even execution—the last was used sparingly for blasphemers and those who dared to challenge the authority of an authorised minister. In the New World, social order meant religious order. Dissent and disorder were punished harshly.

But, of course, the colonies of east coast America were settled at different times, for different reasons, and by different groups. For the hundred settlers aboard the *Mayflower* in 1620, it was their Puritan faith, which had been nurtured by separatist Dutch Reformed theology, that prompted the pilgrims to seek a new Promised Land in America. It is important to understand that the Christianity of the *Mayflower* passengers was unwelcome in England, and subject to penalties. The Puritans took the Geneva Bible with them, in contrast to the settlers of Virginia, who were equipped with the King James Bible and a pre-Elizabethan Book of Common Prayer.[1] To the uninitiated, the choice of Bible by colonists might seem a trivial matter. But this is not so. The Geneva Bible of 1560 was a translation by Protestants who had fled to Geneva during the reign of Mary I (1553–8). The translation was the first mass printing of the Bible available in the English language and included cross-references and notes. It contained over forty references to 'tyrant' and 'tyranny' in the translation.

The King James version, in contrast, forbade the use of these words. It was the Geneva Bible that Oliver Cromwell's soldiers marched with, that Shakespeare used for his plays, and that *Mayflower* pilgrims took to their Promised Land. The longing for freedom from monarchy and tyranny underpins the most basic fracture and fissure in the worldwide Anglican Communion. The right to self-determination, and to democracy, flows from this. Escaping or overthrowing tyranny remains to this day an abiding deep trope in American culture and can be cited in indictments against foreign regimes, city and state governments, and even federal rule from Washington DC.

The Scottish Aspect

The early experiments in the colonisation of the New World were largely English-led and exclusively for the furtherance of the Protestant cause. Ireland fell into this category as well: it was already proving to be fertile ground for new waves of English settlers, sponsored by the crown, who were driving ancient Irish landlords from their holdings and, in so doing, establishing the united crown of Britain as a Protestant bulwark against the continued encroachments of European Catholicism. This was a continuous endeavour throughout the 17th and 18th centuries.

When the Protestant Elector of Hanover ascended the British throne as George I in 1714, the Protestant faith may have seemed secure at this moment. However, there was an attempted rebellion in 1715 by Edward Stuart, son of James II, who had been deposed in the so-called Glorious Revolution of 1688 and replaced by the Dutch Prince William of Orange. The first Jacobite uprising was followed in 1745 by a second, led by Edward's son Charles Stuart, more usually known as Bonnie Prince Charlie. As we shall see, the Jacobite cause had more than an indirect bearing on the birth of the Episcopal Church of the United States.

Following the accession of William III in 1689, the Presbyterians in Scotland restored the fullness of the earlier Scottish Reformation. So-called high church practices were outlawed, bishops were deposed, and the Church of Scotland—the Presbyterian Kirk—became the national church. Episcopalians found themselves in an invidious position. Successive gestures (Acts of Indulgence) in 1693 and 1695 allowed Scottish Episcopal clergy to retain their livings if they accepted the monarchy. If they were unwilling to do so, they were deposed and deprived. Around one hundred Episcopal clergy took advantage of the offer, conditional upon swearing the oath of allegiance to the new Hanoverian lineage. The remainder declined. It was only in 1711 that Scottish Episcopalians, through an Act of Parliament, were able to gain a very small degree of autonomy and modest respectability. However, the problems for Scottish Episcopalians had barely begun.

When George I came to the throne in 1714, the vast majority of Scottish Episcopalians chose to side with Edward Stuart, the son of James II, as the rightful monarch. By not recognising the reign of the Hanoverians, the Scottish Episcopalians consigned themselves to decades of marginalisation and penalisation until the death of Charles Stuart in 1788. In 1719, any Episcopal congregation or church meeting that would not pray for the new king was closed. Episcopalian bishops dwindled in number—death and the deprivation of livings reduced their number to just one by 1720. To meet the challenge, so-called qualified chapels for Episcopalians began to emerge in Scotland. They literally did 'qualify', as they adopted the Church of England's Book of Common Prayer, and their congregations were led by English or Irish Anglican clergy, loyal to the Hanoverian line. There may have been three dozen such congregations at their height, but the number of deprived Episcopalian congregations would have been far greater.

In the political culture of 18th-century Scotland, Episcopalians, being considered loyal to the House of Stuart and to the Jacobite cause, faced the real possibility of fines, imprisonment and deportation if more than four of them were to gather in a single room. They were not allowed to use their churches and chapels for worship. Never before has a denomination taken the words of Jesus—'where two or three are gathered in my name, there I am amongst them' (Matthew 18:20)—as a set quota that should not be exceeded. To all intents and purposes, Episcopalians in Scotland were akin to some form of underground church. In response, they devised novel ways of getting around the restrictions imposed on their meetings. For example, it was not unknown for a minister to stand in the hallway of a makeshift 'house church' (barely permitted), and preach and teach to all the rooms of the house, none of which could contain more than four people. This helps to explain why Samuel Seabury was consecrated in 1784, not in a church, but only in an upper room of a hall, off a busy street in the city of Aberdeen, with only three other bishops present to witness this.

Samuel Seabury (1729–96) was born into a moderately prosperous slave-owning family from Connecticut. Seabury's father was originally a Congregationalist minister but had become a priest of the Church of England in 1730. Samuel was raised as an Anglican and, before going on to study theology at Yale College, was a medical student at Edinburgh University from 1752 to 1753. During this time, he was ordained a deacon in the Church of England by the Bishop of Lincoln and, some months later, a priest by the Bishop of Carlisle. Seabury thus returned to America in 1754 as a qualified medical doctor (after just a year of study) and an ordained Church of England minister (following three years of study).

In common with many Church of England clergy in America, when the War of Independence broke out, Seabury was loyal to the British and fled to the city of New York, eventually enrolling as chaplain for the King's American Regiment in 1778. For much of the war, he was a noted opponent of Alexander Hamilton. When the War of Independence finally ended in 1783, he opted to stay in America and was loyal to the new government. The newly independent colonies needed clergy, and for that they needed bishops who would ordain them. After being elected by Episcopal clergy as their bishop in Connecticut, albeit as second choice, with the preferred candidate declining for reasons of health and infirmity, Seabury travelled to England in genuine hope and serious expectation of consecration.

But the reception he met with from the Church of England bishops was, to put it kindly, polite but cool. He spent the better part of a year trying to negotiate for American episcopal orders but found himself being passed from pillar to post and treated with a mixture of bemusement and studied indifference. As he would be unable to swear the oath of allegiance to George III and his successors, no Church of England bishop would contemplate making any American a bishop. Exasperated, he considered taking episcopal orders from the Danish Lutheran Church. Was it to be, or not to be?

It was the intervention of Dr Martin Routh, a very young president of Magdalen College Oxford, that dissuaded Seabury from this path. Instead, Routh suggested, why not look north—to the Episcopal bishops of Scotland? He had been persuaded that Danish bishops were not of the 'apostolic succession' kind, and that if the serious fiction of ontological lineage was to be maintained in the New World, then consecration at the hands of Scottish Episcopalian bishops was the only option. The stage was therefore set. American Episcopalians, in 1784, might have turned east and claimed Lutheran orders. But they turned north, and to Scotland.

A Gradual Split

Samuel Seabury was not consecrated, as he might have wished, within the Church of England. Instead, on 14 November 1784 he was consecrated by three Scottish bishops who were so-called non-jurors—they did not recognise the authority of the reigning British monarch, which was hardly a problem for an American republican. It did mean, though, that some of the still wavering Americans who thought that British rule might still be restored were not necessarily likely to receive or recognise 'foreign' episcopal orders.

In abdicating responsibility and postponing a decision (a trait present to this day among the episcopacy in England), the English bishops were in the end left with no choice, save to accept a fait accompli, and recognise that Anglicanism was now one faith but operating in two quite separate worlds.

For the American Episcopal Church the irony is striking, since it rests on not one rebellion, but two: the Jacobite uprising with its claim to the British throne, and the American War of Independence involving a revolution against the British throne. It is these that have helped to create an Episcopal church founded on revolt against monarchy and the beginnings of a polity rooted in democracy. (In noting this, we must bear in mind, however, that the Jacobites were hardly democrats, since they were championing an alternative rival monarchy with very different theological sympathies.)

For the global Anglican Communion (which only came about in formal terms a century later), the single innocuous act of Seabury's consecration carried the seeds of the downfall of the worldwide Anglican Communion. All of the schisms, spats, rows, divisions and gradual collapses that have taken place since then are mere aftershocks following a barely noted earthquake in a backstreet of Aberdeen, Scotland. That first fissure led to all the later fractures that now herald the break-up of the global Anglican Communion. For what split the Anglican Communion before it even started was the separation of the Old World (Europe, and specifically Britain and the Church of England) and the New (Continental America).

In many respects, what we see here is the emergence of two contrasting though at times complementary forms of polity; two worlds with entirely incongruent outlooks. The Old World believed in a pre-eminence of God-willed monarchical authoritarianism. Even if it was benign, kind and good, its citizens were still 'subjects' of a realm—implying deference to those who were born or made to rule over others. It was on such foundations that the Church of England and the wider Anglican Communion were built. The New World, on the other hand, believed in an inalienable right to democratic equality. Here, governance and government can be changed by the consent and will of the people. All are equal; there are no subjects, only citizens.

What this meant within the worldwide Anglican Communion is that, while all shared the same faith, Episcopalians became unavoidably committed to a democratic polity and the theological rationale for this, while Anglicans remain inclined to benevolent models of monarchy, also with a theological rationale. Today, many believe that an Old World autocracy cannot survive in public life (save as some symbol for the legitimate rule of law and an elected government), nor can it survive as a model of governance in ecclesial life.

Meanwhile, the Church of England has attempted to have its cake and eat it, with synodical structures that mimic the democratic powers of Parliament. In truth, this seldom works. The Church of England's General Synod does not exercise any meaningful governance or oversight over the church or its bishops. Synodical processes are controlled by a small elite of autocratic lawyers, bishops and a cadre of courtiers, with democratic decisions regularly undermined. For example, the voting for women priests (1992) and bishops (2014) in General Synod was diluted—delayed and qualified—by an executive compact of senior church officials, lawyers and bishops, who argued that democratic decisions were insufficient for those who held different theologies and ecclesial outlooks. Alongside this habitual modus operandi in the Church of England, fair, open and democratic governance has been further undermined through bureaucratic processes that effectively valorise management and leadership. That said, I suspect that an autocracy pretending to be a democracy has a limited lifespan. The New World order is the future.

Futurescape

As social historians know, all nomenclature is inherently partial. 'Civil War' is the terminology of an uneasy state still hedging its bets. The English Civil War ultimately ended with the 'Restoration' of Charles II, and was consolidated by the 'Glorious Revolution' of William III. The English, it seems, like to read their history through an ongoing fondness for monarchical authority. When it comes to revolutions, the English are squeamish about the term and prefer to avoid it. Revolutions are for foreign countries. If they really must be applied to events on home soil, then the industrial (18th century) or social (e.g., swinging sixties) might just be countenanced; or possibly a political one (the 1788 Glorious Revolution, an anti-Catholic pro-Protestant coup).

The difference between a rebellion and a revolution all depends on who wins the wars and battles and gets to write up the history. Rebellions tend to be local and isolated, with specific grievances that don't draw wider support. More often than not, they are mercilessly suppressed (e.g., Irish, Jacobite, etc.). A rebellion is the terminology applied to those who are revolting but are crushed by victorious regimes.

Historians agree that for a revolution to take place, several conditions have to be met. Acute economic depression, widespread alienation of social groups, opposition from elites, a shared rhetoric of resistance, and favourable international conditions need to be in place. They also require the military to stand aside or change sides. Yet from the collapse of the Roman Empire to the Renaissance (i.e., almost a millennium), there were remarkably few revolutions in Europe. Their city-states, countries and provinces were ruled by monarchs who were able to draw on claims of divine right. The Renaissance tipped the balance against such hegemony.

A revolution is a concept with inbuilt insecurity. The modern word for 'revolution' comes from the Latin *revolvere*, referring to the frequent rotations of power between competing groups locked into a cycle of constant change. Perhaps the best way to see it is in terms of an observed mass mobilisation for institutional change and a movement that is driven by an ideology birthed in a vision for social justice. Revolutions do, therefore, involve the forcible overthrow of regimes or ideologies through mass mobilisation, with the intention of creating new social and political states of being.[2]

The post-colonial revolution has seen plenty of bloody and brutal episodes, and plenty of attempts to suppress rebellion or attempts at reform. But in the end, the legitimacy of the conquering colonial power has been checked, resisted and ultimately forced to withdraw. The colonial right to rule has been set aside. Globally, the Anglican churches that have emerged in the post-colonial era have also set aside the historical hegemony of the Church of England. Although this has been a slow revolution, albeit punctuated by 'spiritual warfare' (e.g., over gender, sexuality, power, authority), it marks a discernible movement in polity; namely, one towards a democratic republican pole, and away from the monarchical. Indeed, the Latin term *res publica* means 'public affairs', implying that decisions that affect everyone are no longer just matters to be settled by an elite, entitled monarchy or their advisers. Rather, public concerns are for the public to debate and decide upon.

Meanwhile, and across the world, most Anglicans have moved on from being mere subjects of a colonial church to becoming global citizens with opinions, rights, powers and leverage. And yet the Communion, like its parent church, is quickly coming apart at the seam which stitched together two organic skins of ecclesial polity, which were ultimately bound to reject each other. The tension that Elizabeth I and her *via media* project once appeared to have pulled off does not look like it can endure for an eternity. The tension rests between a model of authority in the church that sees prelates ruling over plebeians, on the one hand, and the devolved power of Presbyterianism, where authority primarily rests with the local congregation, on the other.

The bishops and their burgeoning legions of ecclesiocracies sit in the middle of this, hoping to maintain control over two models of the church that are rapidly bifurcating. The quasi-monarchical episcopal model that conflates deity with domination is now exposed as an unaccountable, elitist, entitled and aloof brand of Laudian ecclesial governance—much as an early Stuart monarch might have assumed a divine right to rule over Parliament and all subjects, and promoted its divine right and absolutism in decision-making. Rather like James II and Charles I with Parliament, the present archbishops and bishops consider that the proroguing of a diocesan synod or even General Synod is wholly in their gift. In the 21st century, this cannot be an effective or ethical system of governance.[3] Meanwhile the Presbyterian-republican model of polity, with its inherent democratic accountability, is resisted at all costs, since it has little need for bishops nor much time for centralised infrastructure.[4]

The English, and the Church of England, are captive in the myth of its dangerous memory. Gripped by nostalgia—an emotion that at one time was thought to be potentially fatal—the church is in danger of self-imprisonment through false memory and perilous emotion. Nostalgia can become a displaced social repository for collective feelings of regret, dislocation and belonging, distorted desires for the past, dissatisfaction with the present, and naive visions for the future. Nostalgia can be a vehicle that tries to carry a community through the uneasy conditions of modern and contemporary life, and the politics of fear and anxiety. It is unlikely to complete such a journey.[5]

The English have too easily forgotten—or erased—their memory of a brief republic, which, were it not for the turn of a few events, might easily have lasted several decades or some centuries or even endured to the present. That past may now be hard to see. Yet that past remains present. Like the French Revolution of the 18th century, the English Revolution of the 17th century has had an impact that is still being processed and yet to be fully understood. The results and legacies remain unclear.[6]

The Church of England's leadership has not found this post-colonial era to its liking, and continues to struggle with basic democratic processes. In many respects, the leadership treats its synods, committees and professional advisers much as Henry VIII or Charles I took advice from Parliament. Ecclesial-monarchical leadership expects deference and presumes it cannot be held accountable. Rule is by right.

In return, bishops occasionally condescend to listen but otherwise will not yield to the will of the people and their elected representatives. True, there are three meetings per year for the Church of England's General Synod, but these gatherings are carefully choreographed and their agenda wilfully manipulated by quasi-monarchical machinations. The leadership reigns without accountability and will only act on advice that chimes with its own interests, but otherwise ignores dissent and overrides resistance.

Yet monarchical authority in the Church of England has had its day. There is both rebellion and open revolt under way across the Anglican Communion and plenty within the Church of England itself. Conservative evangelicals and Anglo-Catholics are peeling away. New Wine Networks are threatening secession. Liberals and broad church groups are also creating enclaves to retreat into, or just standing their ground and stubbornly resisting the tsunami of imperious episcopal-ecclesiocratic initiatives. The rebellions and quiet revolutions against monarchical English Anglicanism at home and abroad have been happening for more than three centuries, and can no longer be contained or just glossed over.

Yet it will not be the wars over sexuality or gender that mark the end of the Communion. It is what has been resisted in the Church of England since late medieval times, namely democracy. A recent report for the Church of England's General Synod bemoans the lack of trust and confidence in the church, and lays some of the blame at the door of social media.[7] It is a puzzling argument, since social media, much like printing, puts power in the hands of ordinary people by giving them access to knowledge that is not controlled by elites. Knowledge is power. It is also a fundamental cornerstone of democracy.

As noted in George Orwell's *Nineteen Eighty-Four,* pronouncements that come from the so-called Ministry of Love can be treated with some healthy scepticism. The public are rightly wary of the theocracies favoured by bishops. The 21st-century communication revolution is an important counterpoint of resistance against those who previously controlled the flow of information. Though not without its ethical and political problems, social media remains a positive asset in furthering free speech and social democracy,[8] even though the sheer quantity can often occlude the quality.

It is hardly a surprise that the Church of England finds this problematic. Unable to cultivate external or internal trust and trustworthiness through exercising soft authoritarian control, the church comes across as despotic, evasive and unaccountable. Such appearances are not deceptive. Furthermore, in the post-colonial era the Church of England's leadership has not been able to accept the growing dysphoric mood within its ranks and the wider public disenchantment. Recent attempts to reignite ecclesial euphoria—a coronation, good news on finance and mission, or perhaps some new public relations scoop—usually fail to produce the necessary spark. Indeed, they are more likely to register indifference, weariness or even cynicism among core members, congregations and clergy.

The dysphoria spreads in proportion to the weakening of power and agency for clergy and congregations at the hands of the leadership. So, if one were to predict a future at all here, it would be that the Communion will cease to exist in all but name well before 2034—the last edifice of an English Empire now long gone, and the English finally tiring of their unaccountable quasi-monarchical leadership. The future of the Communion lies in a Presbyterian polity that holds bishops to account, and in which congregations and clergy can regulate their own mood and work together democratically and faithfully for their future ministry.

Ultimately, what will be left of the Church of England by 2034 is a question left hanging in the air. Scottish Episcopalians and their American cousins are more inclined to the Presbyterian model of polity than that of English prelature. As the Church of England's 'command-and-control-central' culture continues to collapse under its own weight, congregations will increasingly assume authority and responsibility for local ministry. The

Church of England will eventually become what most English Protestant Reformers had originally intended it to be, almost 500 years ago. That said, and despite its continuing fragmentation, ongoing dissolution and creeping disestablishment, one may still dare to hope for good and faithful local churches, with their ministers continuing to serve the communities around them. That will always be worth something. Finally, the sum might become greater than the parts.

3

EMPIRE, CHURCH AND MORAL GEOGRAPHY

I was standing in St Thomas' Cathedral in Chennai (India) some years ago and puzzling over an age-old hypothetical question. Suppose Christianity had travelled east, not west? Suppose the spread of this new religion had been nurtured not in Asia Minor, Rome and Jerusalem, but instead in modern-day India, China and the eastern lands of the Russian Federation? We cannot know what it would have become, but it is reasonably safe to conjecture that the doctrinal debates that were to consume Western Christianity would have been addressed differently in the East. Polity, practice, governance, liturgy and belief would have been, well, different.

Can any of this be mapped, perhaps especially in relation to moral or religious geography? Moral geography, as a term, is in some respects similar to the implied meaning of a moral landscape. That is to say, some moral outlooks have spatial and temporal identities or boundaries that are rooted in local, regional or national notions of what constitutes good, bad, valued and unacceptable beliefs and practices. For example, the ethics of care—for close family—may hinge on factors such as social mobility and diversity, or on social continuity and stability.[1]

Maps are narratives that simplify complex data and skate over diversity through unifying symbols. What we all call a 'country' from the outside isn't necessarily true on the inside, on the ground—just ask the Swiss. Some years ago I was shown some of the very first maps of America. There was a hesitant, feint sketch of the Eastern Seaboard, which looked like educated guesswork based on some travel, yet long before Columbus set sail. In other maps there was no South America or Canada or California. In another old map, California was thought to be an island. Many of these maps were a blend of the reasonably accurate and the purely speculative.[2]

What these maps showed is what we ought to remind ourselves of in the study of religious belief. Namely, that there is a relationship between the world around us and the God whom we think is behind this world—or above, beneath or wholly beyond it. Maps illustrate—to a scale, and using signs and symbols—what people think they know; but they also reveal what they don't know. Some maps—a bit like some beliefs and theologies—are decent educated guesses. But they are of their time. So what are maps? The answer is not as simple as some might suppose. They are not simply about navigation. Rather, they are also about orientation, imagination and innovation. They are aids to reflection and potential ways of seeing.

Maps reveal not so much a world that might be encountered but, rather, how the cartographer chose to view and guide us through the world. Scale, symbol, demographics, topography, geography—indeed, any number of factors—play their part. The mapmaker, in many ways, is a narrator and a guide, and tries to attempt something similar to the sociologist or anthropologist of religion, every time they venture into the field.

Now, there are many and various ways of mapping the Anglican Communion. Many Anglicans will be familiar with a world map that puts Britain at the centre and shades much of the rest of the world in a fetching rose colour that bears a remarkable resemblance to the British Commonwealth. A less easy map to reckon with is the nations of the world the English or British have never invaded or occupied in the last 500 years. You may be surprised to learn that of the almost 200 nations on the planet, the British have clocked up an astonishing 89.5% strike-rate of coverage. The British have spared such small fry as Luxembourg, Andorra, Liechtenstein and Monaco. The British have never invaded the Vatican or Sweden. In America, only Guatemala, Bolivia and Paraguay have been left undisturbed. Yet our concern here is not with accuracy, but rather with the narrative it offers.

Maps as Narratives

What stories do our cherished maps tell us? For Anglicans, it is plainly one of extensity, global coverage and prestige. The Anglican Communion boasts 65,000 congregations in 164 countries. The emerging British Empire—not formed until the second half of the 19th century—is partly what enabled the Church of England to move from being a national church to becoming a global Communion. The expansion of Anglicanism was both an ordered and untidy affair, simultaneously systematic and unsystematic.[3]

But—and it is a big 'but'—what other overlays could be placed on the map described above? I ask this because I think there is a real danger of taking the 'serious fiction' of the Anglican Communion at face value. I also think that the maps of the Communion we are often shown can be unhelpful and unreliable, and give the reader a highly partial and distorted account of what the Anglican Communion consists of. For serious fiction to function as a helpful and authentic narrative, one does need to amass a wider range of facts.

For example, there are 54 countries and around 30 small states in the British Commonwealth. One might assume the Commonwealth is the acceptable face of the British post-colonial legacy. That as the sun set on the British Empire of Queen Victoria, and moves for independence and autonomy grew (in India, Africa and elsewhere), the Commonwealth was some kind of successor to the empire. Not quite. The Commonwealth did not come into existence until 1926.

Furthermore, of the 54 countries in the Commonwealth, countries such as Gabon, Namibia, Togo and Eswatini were never within the curtilage of the British Empire. Samoa was only really under the control of New Zealand, and Vanuatu was jointly administered by an established Anglo-French governance arrangement. It is worth remembering that many of the countries in the Commonwealth are republics. Quirkily, though Fiji is a republic, its motto is 'Fear God and honour the King'.

Not all countries that are former colonies are members of the Commonwealth—notably the United States. Gibraltar is not a member of the Commonwealth of Nations in its own right, and is represented by the United Kingdom, but was granted associate membership of the Commonwealth Foundation in 2004. Yet Gibraltar has competed in the Commonwealth Games since 1958. Gibraltar is not a sovereign state: its formal international relations are the responsibility of the Government of the United Kingdom. Since Brexit, it is not part of the European Union, but it is a participant in the EU–UK Trade and Cooperation Agreement.

There are around 2.5 billion Muslims in the world today. The vast majority of countries that the Anglican Communion claims to be present in and ministering to within are nations containing many millions of Muslims. The amount of energy expended by the Church of England in engaging with global Islam is, however, negligible. Many of the countries that are shaded on maps of the Anglican Communion have negligible numbers of Christians. True, one can find Anglicanism in Moscow, Mongolia, Ethiopia, El Salvador, Bahrain, Belgium, Finland and Fiji. But shading in such countries as somehow coming within a curtilage of an Anglican province is, to put it mildly, misleading. In terms of coverage across continents, one could liken the Anglican Communion, perhaps, to a couple of small pats of butter spread over several large loaves of bread. The coverage would be thin, at best.

For example, a current map of the Diocese of Cyprus and the Gulf will chart post-empire interests and spheres of influence (mostly through chaplaincy). It is not a map that can help the reader determine the number of Anglicans on the ground, as there will be very, very few. A similar map of Nigeria might tell a more accurate story about the numerical strength of Anglicans.[4] A map of England wholly shaded as Anglican is unlikely to be a reliable guide to the numbers attending church on Sunday, which is below a million, and nothing close to the 40 million adherents the Church of England lays claim to. Maps of Anglicanism in South America, Japan, Korea, India and Pakistan also require heavy qualification. In short, maps can be serious fiction, but more fictional than one might think.

Charting Confusion

Then we come to other puzzles in Anglican cartography. Overlapping episcopal jurisdiction has been around for a long time. Italy, France, Germany and Switzerland all have Church of England and Episcopal Church (of the United States) churches. The American Cathedral in Paris has existed since the 19th century and falls under the American Bishop for Europe. The origins of the American Cathedral of the Holy Trinity in Paris date back to the 1830s when American Episcopalians began to meet together for services in the Hôtel Matignon. Naturally, however, the Episcopal Church bishop doesn't have jurisdiction over the churches of St Michael and St George, which are under the Church of England, and whose bishop, though based in Brussels (which is a member of the European Union), has his episcopal seat in Gibraltar (which is not in the EU). Portugal and Spain have native Reformed Episcopal churches as well as Church of England chaplaincies. One faith, two worlds is an Anglican reality in Paris, Portugal and the other places mentioned. The American churches are funded and governed in line with the New World order, and the Church of England's with the Old World order.

In fact, the more one travels around the Anglican Communion, the more one begins to understand how culture has shaped global Anglican polity. Taiwan is under the US Episcopal Church (as the island was handed over to the Americans at the end of the Second World War), but Hong Kong, until 1997, was under the Church of England. The ethos and governance of these territories reflect the differences and, of course, the historical reasons for Americans and British being present in China.[5] In Australia, the Anglican polity still reflects its roots in the Church of England. Haiti draws from its American Episcopalian roots. Thus, in some places, residual empire and gradual decolonisation are factors in Anglicanism. But others—the Philippines, Korea and Japan, for example—are more in debt to post-war American expansionism.

So what of the moral geography in the Anglican Communion? In Amy DeRogartis's fascinating study,[6] the author invites us to consider how Christian expansion has divided the world and redrawn our sense of moral imagination, influence and outlook. In the case of Anglicanism, for example, we might ask how

African nations could have come to acquire punitive legislation on same-sex relations without the prior teaching provided by Anglican missionaries and churches? More specifically in terms of national culture, what exactly is the English legacy throughout the former colonies, in terms of social hierarchies, normativity and other expectations? The landscape is far from obvious.[7]

There is also the awkward question of inter-denominational missionary competition to consider. This was extensive in Africa, India and parts of the Pacific. In New Zealand, entire settlements—now cities—derived their identities from denominational roots. Christchurch is Anglican, while Dunedin (Otago) is Presbyterian, and Wellington and Auckland have significant concentrations of Roman Catholics. The inter-denominational competition was hardly friendly. Anglican clergy such as Samuel Marsden combined the role of chaplain with that of magistrate for the new colonies of Australia and New Zealand from 1794 to his death in 1838. Marsden thought Roman Catholic convicts were inherently depraved through their beliefs ('wild, savage, ignorant ... destitute of every principle of religion and morality'), and his attitude to administering punishment to them (e.g., frequent floggings) was as baffling as his insensitivity in trying to evangelise the Māori.

In terms of ethnicity, the settlement of New Zealand, involving the historic and ongoing subjugation of the Māori, and systemic racism against Polynesians, led to the creation of the Tikanga system within Anglicanism. There are the three bishops who share the title of Primate and Archbishop of Aotearoa New Zealand—Māori, Pasefika (Polynesia) and Pākehā (representing those of European heritage). Each Tikanga is largely independent, and the areas they cover reflect either indigenous native or European settler boundaries. Technically, this means a person can be in one place yet find themselves located within three different Tikanga—each with its own kind of governance, authority and accountability. In the foreseeable future, a fourth Tikanga for Asian settlers seems likely.

As for the Caribbean, even the name 'Province of the West Indies' is potentially awkward for colonial and post-colonial identities. From 1958 to 1962, there was a short-lived country called the Federation of the West Indies composed of ten English-speaking Caribbean territories, all of which were (then) British dependencies. The West Indies cricket team continues to represent many of those nations. The very name of the Anglican province reflects this experiment in post-colonial organisation.

Missionary Positions

Anna Johnston's work explores how Christian missionary activity was central to the work of European colonialism, providing British missionaries and their supporters with a sense of justice and moral authority.[8] It offered the wider public a model of 'civilised' expansionism and colonial oversight of communities and plantations. At the same time, it afforded governments, traders and explorers a platform, exploiting the aura of ethical responsibility offered by Christian civilisation to the 'heathen', which became attached to every endeavour of British colonial expansionism. The Church of England played a key role in this imperialist colonisation.[9]

John Darch's *Missionary Imperialists?*[10] examines the frontiers of empire in tropical Africa and the south-west Pacific in the mid to late Victorian era. Darch shows that the role played by Church of England missionaries, including chaplains, unavoidably elided imperial development with missionary endeavour. There was continuous interaction between the missions and those in government, in both London and the colonies. Covering Nigeria, Gambia and the Pacific (e.g., Fiji), Darch shows that where Church of England missionary agencies, chaplains and clergy aided imperial development, the church's role was substantial, though largely incidental. In effect, the Church of England functioned as the spiritual arm of the British Empire in outcomes rather than specific intent.

In practice, there were significant numbers of missionaries who saw little distinction between the virtues and necessities of imperialism and evangelism. Many missionaries presumed that the future of their particular mission and its people would be most secure under British jurisdiction. Even those who had little appetite for the export of the Christianity–Culture compact were disinclined to resist imperial development. The debates on slavery in the Church of England sat within this paradigm. Overall, missionaries continued to see themselves as bearers of moral and spiritual values, bringing civilisation and Christianity to peoples and places that were lacking. Church of England missionary societies and their clergy were, therefore, effective agents of imperialism, even when the extension of Christianity served only incidentally and unintentionally as a vehicle for imperialism.

The links between slavery, empire, colonisation, Christian missionaries and the expansion of Anglicanism are entwined. But a reckoning with moral geography demands that such history be faced.[11] The Society for the Propagation of the Gospel in Foreign Parts (SPG) was incorporated under Royal Charter in 1701. As a Church of England organisation, it was highly active in the original colonies of North America. The SPG was not initially intended as a pastoral mission to the colonists, but rather as an evangelistic mission to the 'heathen'.

Much of the funding for the several hundred missionaries at work in the colonies came through an endowment bequeathed by Christopher Codrington, a planter, government official, merchant, entrepreneur and estate-owner in Barbados. Codrington's father was a Royalist who had fled England before the outbreak of the English Civil War. Codrington made his money from sugar plantations, silver mining and mercantile trading. His business interests included acquisitions in Antigua, Dominica, the Leeward Islands and other Caribbean territories. To work the land, the Codrington family owned thousands of slaves. Like his father, Christopher Codrington was effectively the acting governor for the territories they controlled commercially, thereby ensuring that the law there was administered by the same family gaining from the business interests, including that of human cargo and capital. In 1710, when Codrington died, he bequeathed at least 300 slaves to the SPG to continue its missionary work in the New World colonies.[12] The SPG even branded its slaves on the chest with the word SOCIETY to show whom they belonged to.

It is something of an irony that the SPG's first missionaries, George Keith and Patrick Gordon, graduates of the University of Aberdeen, sailed from England for North America on 24 April 1702. Gordon died of fever almost as soon as his ship docked at Long Island, and little is known of him. We know more about Keith, however, who was born in Peterhead and, as a Quaker in 1693, had been party to the publication of *An Exhortation & Caution to Friends Concerning Buying or Keeping of Negroes*—possibly the first tract of its kind to make a Christian call for the cause of abolition. Keith left the Quaker denomination over doctrinal differences and was ordained in the Church of England. It is ironic that such a noted abolitionist ended up being funded by the SPG on the proceeds of slavery.

It is also something of an irony that the first public protests and riots against American slavery were held in Aberdeen. The shoemakers and weavers were at the forefront of lobbying for change. At the same time, the Free Presbyterian Church was still the beneficiary of slave-trading. One of the complications in city and civic wealth in British cities lies in their decidedly mixed pedigree when it comes to politics, economics and social justice. To a large extent, location for trade was a significant determinative factor in political and theological views on slavery, and a city like Aberdeen, with so little exposure to slave-trading, took a different trajectory from that of Glasgow.

By the time the American War of Independence ended in 1783, there were dozens of English missionaries funded from the proceeds from slavery. John Wesley, the Anglican cleric and later founder of Methodism, was one, although there is some dispute as to whether Wesley was ever funded by SPG or simply held an SPG-approved chaplaincy. Whatever the case, Wesley and other SPG missionaries were nicknamed 'Anglican Jesuits' for their singleness of mind, zeal and dedication to the cause of mission and conversion of the heathen.

Ending Slavery—Slowly

Slavery ended in the colonies partly for moral reasons and owing to some religious, social and political campaigning. But in reality, for the British government, another primary driver was economic, not ethical. The plantations—frankly little more than forerunners of Nazi slave labour death factories—were expensive to run and prone to inefficiency, and suffered from regular revolts that were increasingly costly to suppress in terms of military resources.

Slavery's abolition came about because of economic changes and moral concerns. And the ending of slavery between 1807 and 1833 was a delicate matter of political decision-making, and adjustment to economic realities (machines were cheaper to run), not just a debate on moral principles. In the first quarter of the 19th century, British colonies produced over half of the world's sugar. When slavery was abolished, the price of sugar increased by around 50%. Perhaps anticipating the price hike and its potential political consequences, more slaves were shipped by the

British between 1821 and 1833 than at any other time since the 1780s. When the slave-owners were paid off for the purposes of passing the 1833 Slavery Abolition Act, the £20 million cost represented over 40% of the Treasury's annual budget. Even then, the enslaved on St Helena and Ceylon (Sri Lanka) owned by the East India Company were excluded by the legislation, and not freed. The £15 million loan that the British government took out to pay off the slave-owners was not finally settled until 2015, hard though this may seem.

Most British people today, as two centuries ago, had little direct experience of slavery. The slaves worked on the plantations of the Caribbean and the vast estates of the deep American South. Yet Britain's deep economic entwinement with the slave trade was baked into everyday life. British trade and goods depended on slavery. Companies, families and individuals invested in the slave trade and in ownership, with mortgages, loans and insurance all raised against the commodification of enslaved people.

One notable family involved in slavery were the Gladstones. John Gladstone was a plantation owner in Demerara, British Guiana (now called Guyana). As it happens, he was the father of William Gladstone, a four-time Liberal prime minister of Great Britain in the 19th century. In August 1823 the slaves on John Gladstone's estate rose up against the brutal regime he presided over, in which rape, torture, brandings, beatings and executions were daily occurrences. The revolt incited around 13,000 Africans to revolt on more than sixty plantations across the region in what has become known as the Demerara Uprising or Rebellion. On 20 August 1823, 200 slaves were shot dead when British troops opened fire on a gathering of 2,000 protesting strikers, who were refusing to disperse. The leaders of the revolt were tortured and decapitated, and their heads speared on spikes as a warning to others. John Gladstone, at the time of the revolt, owned over

2,500 slaves outright by purchase or through mortgage loans. As slaves were property, a mortgage loan was perfectly normal.

The Black Lives Matter movement can trace its origins to atrocities like these. They were and are crimes against humanity. The legacy of such evil lives on, however. Modern Guyana is divided ethnically between the descendants of the enslaved from Africa, others from India whom John Gladstone began importing (numbering over 230,000 by the end of the 19th century), and the indigenous peoples of the region. European settlers barely accounted for 4% of Guyana in 1833, yet they were substantially compensated for the loss of all their 'property'—slaves—when slavery was finally abolished in the British Empire in 1833. Yet even after emancipation, the slaves were forced to continue working—for free, and for a further six years—as 'apprentices', and only when their apprenticeship was completed would they secure the actual award of their freedom.[13]

As John Lennon and Paul McCartney sang in their song 'Revolution' in 1968, a year of huge international turbulence, we all may want to change the world, a constitution or institution, but whether we put faith in evolution or revolution, nothing can happen until some change has taken place inside our heads. That is why paying attention to the details of commerce and capitalism are so important. They may seem obvious and necessary to some readers, but probably not to all. So I hold that to ignore such history is perilous, since it has a vital role to play in how we now understand our national and ecclesial stories and the present state of affairs. We cannot escape the past, but we can reckon with it.

Thus, the Anglican Church in Hong Kong (Sheng Kung Hui) cannot be understood apart from the British interventions in China, and specifically the trade-led Opium Wars (1839–42 and 1856–60). The military advantage of the British (and their allies) forced China to accept unjust 'treaties', involving damaging concessions on trade, reparation and territories. For China, this resulted in 'a century of humiliation'. 'Guns and gospel' were united under English imperialism.[14] Today, Hong Kong Anglicans continue to address the legacy of this history through significant ongoing investment in pioneering mission and ministry.[15]

Colonial Exploitation in Non-Colonial Territories: Money, Sex and Power

British commercial interests in China during the eighteenth century had led to two Opium Wars (1839-42 and 1856-60), the sequestration of Hong Kong, and the subjugation of the Qing Dynasty. But for many British men in the Victorian and Edwardian era, the commercial opening up of China and its military and political emasculation was seen as an opportunity for missionary work and the spreading of the gospel. The issues raised in Mark O'Neill's book (*Frederick: The Life of My Missionary Grandfather in Manchuria*)[16] also shed interesting light on false memory syndromes regarding Protestant missionaries and identity issues. While O'Neill provides moving details on the hardships faced by most pioneering Protestant missionaries from the nineteenth and twentieth centuries, he also notes that:

> ...the missionaries' attitudes to marriage was similar to that of the wider foreign community in China...many had Chinese mistresses or girlfriends [but] chose women from their own countries when it came to the question of marriage.[17]

For example, the diplomat Sir Robert Hart, probably the most significant British civil servant under the Qing Dynasty, kept a Chinese mistress who bore him three children. It was common practice for unmarried Englishmen resident in China to keep a Chinese girl. In October 1854, Hart noted following his purchase of a teenage sex servant that "some of the China women are very good-looking: you can make one your absolute possession for 50 to 100 dollars and support her at a cost of only 2 or 3 dollars per month". Hart purchased women for sex as he like to "have a girl in the room...to fondle when [he] please[d]". His purchase of Chinese sex workers occurred over a twenty-year period.

When it came time for Hart to wed, he chose Hester Bredon, a woman from an impeccable British family. She was eighteen when they married in 1866, and with Hart being thirty-one, this represented an unremarkable and quite conventional age gap in the colonial era. Hart paid off the Chinese woman with $3,000 and sent the children to Britain so they would not embarrass him in Shanghai with their presence. Hart communicated with them through his lawyer for the rest of his life, though he was later forced to acknowledge his paternity. Married to Hester, Hart did not resume purchasing Chinese sex workers until after Hester returned to England with their children in 1876.

Hart's conduct would not have been out of kilter with other British missionaries at that time, and nor would he have attracted much criticism for his domestic arrangements. This was a case of "what goes on in China stays in China", amounting to a working assumption in the ex-patriot community. Christian missionaries were abroad to convert the natives, not police their fellow countrymen.

Hart was the epitome of British colonial organisation and entrepreneurialism. He established rules and regulations in China for taxation, customs duty, import and export, the civil service and local organisation. He received numerous honours, including several knighthoods, honorary doctorates, decorations (e.g., Norway, France, China, Denmark, etc) and a baronetcy (Kilmoriarty, County Armagh). There are roads named after him in Tsim Sha Tsui (Hong Kong), Beijing, and Shanghai, as well as a school in Portadown and a rare Chinese species of lizard.

The British colonial exploitation of China in the late nineteenth and early twentieth century often plays second fiddle to the story of slavery and racism in the eighteenth and nineteenth centuries. Few remember – except perhaps in China – that the severe shortage of male manual labour during the Great War led the British to recruit the Chinese Labour Corps, whose role it was to clear the battlefield of corpses, mines and live ammunition. They also loaded and unloaded cargoes, built railway lines and aerodromes, dug trenches and filled sandbags. The British hired close to 100,000 Chinese labourers during the war, and in the months following the Armistice, their role was to dig graves, bury bodies, roll up barbed wire, and search for and unearth unexploded shells.

The British also hired tens of thousands of Egyptians, Indians, black South Africans and many people from the Caribbean to undertake this work, but the Chinese Labour Corp was by far the largest. The Corps were paid a small fraction of the rate for ordinary soldiers. Furthermore, they were made to live in conditions more closely resembling concentration camps and permitted to send home only two letters a month. The three-month journey by sea from the Franco-Belgian theatre of war proved too much for many, who chose to commit suicide by drowning themselves at sea. Those who did return home to China received no recompense or recognition from the British, other than a small gratuity if they had been wounded. In contrast, the Chinese working for the French, who had already acquired the same rights as French citizens, were allowed to stay, and many chose to do so. The British did not officially recognise the contribution of China to their war effort. In a further act of betrayal, German interests in the Chinese region of Shandong were handed over as concessions to Japan (Article 156 of the Versailles Peace Treaty), an ally of the British during the Great War.[18]

***

Mapmakers do not just reproduce the world they see. Indeed, they can never do that. In their drafting they *create* some view of that world—constructed through their sifting of information, values, boundaries, territory, assets and ownership—drawing lines, selecting colours and tones, devising symbols, and choosing scales and relations, and then invite viewers to share in that construction of reality. A map always manages and imagines the reality it is trying to convey.

No map can ever perfectly capture the territory it purports to survey. There is too much to see and take in; too much to weigh and discern; too much to be interpreted and then refracted back. All maps are partial interpretations of reality. So if there is to be a critical moral geography of the post-colonial Anglican Communion, a modern map will be needed that deals with the past. It will have to chart the social realities of ethnicity, gender, inequality; show how little millions of black lives mattered to the churches only a few centuries ago; and reveal how, even today, continued social inequalities and racism question whether black lives matter to those who still preside over the Anglican Communion.

If black lives matter, and those who are discriminated against on grounds of gender, sexuality and class are to be treated as equals, Anglicanism will need new maps to be accurate, ethical, honest and candid. The maps that claim to narrate a sweeping story of global Anglican expansion spreading civilisation and Christian faith are a serious fiction from the Old World. They belong to a history that salves the consciences of those organisations and institutions which, even today, retain the wealth and power they inherited through oppression. The 21st century requires new maps to chart a quite different future—one that is firmly directed towards seeking truth, justice and equality for all.

4

TIPPING POINTS

To some extent, the clue to the identity of a person or an institution will lie somewhere in their name. And as with most acts of christening or naming, the newborn has no say in how they will become known. It is rare for denominations to choose their own name. Unless of course they choose to merge with or marry into another denomination (in which case they can hyphenate or rebrand), they are stuck with what they were called at birth. The United Reformed Church of England (URC) is a marriage of Congregationalists and Presbyterians. They plighted their troth in 1972, and have just celebrated their golden jubilee after fifty years of relative wedded bliss. (Not being part of their relationship, I can hardly speak for either party—but they seem happy enough together.)

But the URC is the exception and not the rule. Roman Catholics did not choose the prefix 'Roman', which is a post-Reformation addition foisted upon them by those who were not of that ilk. 'Anglicans' is also a post-Reformation nickname, intended to suggest the Englishness of the faith. Methodists did not choose their nickname; nor did the Baptists. All Orthodox churches like to think of themselves as the one Orthodox Church but are unable to avoid their rivals prefixing their name with qualifiers like 'Russian', 'Greek', 'Georgian' or 'Ukrainian'. Prefixes such as 'Open' (Brethren), 'Closed' (Brethren again), 'Primitive' (Methodists) and 'Free' (various and numerous) were added by third parties, and only later adopted internally.

We hardly give names a second thought. A term like 'Communion' (as in Anglican Communion) sounds like a body with unity, coherence and familial-like belonging. But in reality, 'Communion' has more equivalence with 'family', one separated centuries ago by emigration, multiplication and diversification. Kinship yielded to more distant kithship many moons ago, with friendship and acquaintance providing the social glue for a globally stretched denomination. There are few legal, fiscal or structured ties of authority to hold the federal body together. In plain terms, there is no United States of Episcopalianism. Worldwide Anglicanism—as a global network—largely adopted the 'Communion' nomenclature with the spread of the British Empire (which in turn carried the Church of England). In the post-colonial era, Episcopalians do not need—it is not a necessity—to keep the Anglican/English name or even remain in the Communion. Independent identity can be asserted—and, increasingly, has been.

A term like 'Communion' probably does far too much heavy lifting for what amounts to a tense and contested sense of belonging. Likewise, consider the word 'united' prefixed to a nation. The United Kingdom is not as united as it likes to think, and the very name presumes a mode of being when division or separation between the nations was normal, as indeed it was.

Anglicans, globally, have already begun to stop doing things together. A family reunion every ten years (i.e., a Lambeth Conference) cannot sustain the familial relations that are required to knit together a global Communion. There is no common liturgy. There is no common theological training or education. Evangelical and Catholic wings of the Church of England promote different proclivities, and missionary endeavours in the past tended to produce different Anglican emphases. There is much diversity. But although there is a single Christian faith, divisions are often exacerbated by a lack of depth, and cultural differences quickly acquire an unhelpful theological varnish that can breed mistrust.

In South America, large parts were cultivated by the Church Missionary Society (CMS), an evangelical body within the Church of England. To this day, many of the South American Anglican congregations are biblically conservative and low church. Anglicans in Uruguay, for example, do not ordain women and self-identify as conservative evangelicals. But the CMS did not cultivate the whole of South America: the most notable exception is the Anglican Episcopal Church of Brazil (in Portuguese, *Igreja Episcopal Anglicana do Brasil*), where Anglicans constitute the oldest non-Catholic denomination.

Like much of the expansion of Anglicanism through English imperialism, Anglicanism in Brazil arrived as the result of a trade treaty; this one between Portugal and Britain, signed in 1810, granting mutual benefits in terms of trading and movement. The treaty made specific provisions for the Church of England to establish chapels in Brazil, but with the Napoleonic Wars in full swing, not a lot happened. This changed in 1890 with the arrival of American Episcopalian missionaries. Unlike the few English missionaries, the Americans adopted Portuguese as their language and began to work with the local populations. Brazil became a missionary district of the US Episcopal Church, and in 1965 gained its ecclesiastical independence as a province in its own right. Brazilian Anglicans carried the US Episcopal Church DNA with them. They ordained women before the Church of England. They preach a social gospel and work in areas such as domestic violence, homophobia, racism, domestic violence and gender justice. The Brazilian Anglican Church could hardly be more different from its neighbour in Uruguay.

Compare and Contrast

Historians, sociologists and theologians might puzzle over how it is that Roman Catholicism manages so much diversity and yet still maintains its unity. To some extent, the answer is Papal and episcopal authority. But to a larger extent, it is the amount of time that all clergy and religious (i.e., monks, nuns, etc.), no matter where they serve, spend in training, formation and education, and what they are required to know. Typically, their theological education takes place over at least five years in residence. Furthermore, there is something like an agreed common corpus of theological material that will be studied, no matter where the vocation to serve is offered. There are variables, of course: Jesuits, Dominicans and Benedictines will incline their study to the emphasis their tradition offers. But it is hard to imagine a Jesuit priest who will not have read the *Rule of Benedict*, or a Benedictine who will be unfamiliar with the *Spiritual Exercises* of St Ignatius of Loyola.

There is no equivalence with Anglicanism here. Many Anglican provinces do not subscribe to the Thirty-Nine Articles. Growing numbers of clergy training across the Communion, now in a post-colonial era, will not have studied European history and will therefore have little or no knowledge of the 16th-century religious wars from their schooling or higher education. It is essentially impractical to presume to educate Anglican seminarians of the global South on the finer points of English history and theology in Europe. No matter how idealistic one might be about the potential for a core Anglican curriculum for every Anglican seminary across the world, the means to resource and impose such an endeavour do not exist. Furthermore, Anglicanism, more than most Protestant denominations, would not be able to agree on the theological and ecclesiological essentials, never mind the blends of moral reasoning within pastoral theology.

One way of characterising the difference between Anglicanism and Catholicism may be to say that the former has been weighed and found wanting, and the latter weighed and found hard. That said, the lack of Anglican clarity does not necessarily lead to anarchy. Anglicanism knows that scripture, tradition (including liturgy), reason and culture (or episcopal ordination) is a kind of sacred–social bonding agent. In any case, Anglican theology is inherently broad, hybrid and reflexive in character. Clergy training for ordained ministry in Uruguay might not share any common reading with their neighbours in Brazil. But it does not follow that they cannot relate as equal but different.

The unity in Anglicanism is therefore rather fluid. In Australia, Anglican churches that used candles on the altar were extremely rare until the early 20th century. Australian bishops did not habitually wear (or own) mitres until the Book of Common Prayer revisions in 1928. The unity of Anglicanism is rather opaque, and it rests on the relational method. Anglicans agree that they process and practise their faith through a quadrilateral: scripture, tradition, reason and culture (some replace culture with the historical episcopacy). There is warrant for this method in the writings of Richard Hooker.[1] Frankly, it is hard to disagree with the quadrilateral as a proposition. But as a paradigm, all it can ever be is an interpretative template, which in itself is subject to debate and dissent. Furthermore, it is hardly unique to Anglicans since Methodists and several other denominations also deploy variants of the same paradigm.

Presumably to provide further indemnity for unity, the Anglican Church also cites the Office of the Archbishop of Canterbury, the Anglican Consultative Council and Meetings of the Primates, and the Lambeth Conferences as traditional guarantors of unity and a distinctive *via media* polity. Yet in the post-colonial era, this has deteriorated to the point of being in tatters. The Lambeth Conference family reunion scheduled for every ten years does not help, especially if around a third to a half of the Communion boycott it. And the purple-clothed remnant that do gather all spend their time together discussing the things that keep them apart and make any future gatherings even more awkward. Some who do come feel that they cannot be seen to worship together in the same space. It is a bit like travelling thousands of miles for a family reunion but boycotting the main dinner and letting everyone know that you'll be eating and holding court in a restaurant over the road.

Seeds of Sedition

The seeds for this habitual sedition and separatism were planted long before the Anglican Communion existed or could articulate itself. To some extent, this is an American story or, rather, a story about what the English tried to do with America, yet failed. The failure left American Episcopalians with autonomy and their independence. But released from monarchical and episcopal authority, American rationalism of the Enlightenment kind and reasoned pragmatism came quickly to the fore. The tipping point for the future of Anglicanism is still to be found in the turns of events and the slings and arrows of fortune embedded within the War of Independence—and what emerged in its wake.

Yet even in 1784 the colonies still remained closely linked to the British crown. Even with American Independence declared in 1776, many of the settlers still expected the republic to be a short-lived experimental fad, and that British rule with its laws and order would be restored. The British, it would seem, were just as presumptuous. In 1787 the Church of England appointed

Charles Inglis as the bishop for all of North America. There is a certain hubris to be found within imperialism.

Thus, in 1814, only thirty years later, during an attempt by the British to retake America, a Bishop of Calcutta was appointed (for all of India, no less), and, likewise in 1824, two bishops for the West Indies. In 1836, Australia gained its first Church of England bishop. By 1840, there were ten colonial bishops presiding over the mission and ministry to the colonies and countries of the entire British Empire. They were effectively episcopal chaplains to the expatriate settlements.

The social stock from which Church of England bishops were drawn was white, male (obviously), elite, upper class, public school and Oxbridge-educated. A middle-class Victorian bishop would have been a rare creature, and a working-class episcopal appointment unknown. Class depends on wealth and privilege, and in order to understand the economic and social drivers over the past 250 years since the American Revolution, one needs to have some grasp of how differentiated society was during the early era of the British Empire.

Generally speaking, Anglicanism has undergone similar sociological patterns to those experienced by most other Protestant denominations, such as Methodism or Presbyterianism. Numbers of churches and adherents grew significantly in the developing world as the result of earlier missionary endeavours. The growth of capitalism and the spread of empire in the 18th, 19th and 20th centuries led to the emergence of a mercantile and mobile middle class. Significant numbers found their way into professions such as medicine and law, while others swelled the ranks of the clergy, eager to contribute to the demands of mission and ministry.

The New World also wrestled with different issues, which were racial rather than classist. Bishop Payne Divinity School was founded in Petersburg, Virginia, in 1878, to train African Americans for ministry in the Episcopal Church of the United

States. When Bishop Payne Divinity School closed in 1949 and merged with Virginia Theological Seminary, the latter institution inherited its records and its heritage. The merger led to a richer culture of formation and training; hymnody changed, and new commemorations and events were celebrated.

These post-civil war racial tensions in the United States were also replicated in South Africa during the apartheid regime. St Bede's College, in Mthatha in the Transkei, existed to prepare black ordinands to serve in the 'native reserves', black townships and rural areas of South Africa. The constitution of St Paul's College, Grahamstown, contained a clause restricting students to 'Europeans' for some years, although two bishops did send black students to St Paul's in the 1960s. St Paul's appointed a black chaplain in 1973, with the first 'coloured' (mixed race) students entering in 1976 and the first black African students in 1978. St Bede's and St Paul's eventually merged to form the College of the Transfiguration.

In New Zealand, the separate formational seminaries that had catered for Polynesian, European-descended (Pākehā) and Māori students came together as a single college, following the Reeves–Beck report of 2010. There is a principal (or Manukura) in overall executive charge of St John's College, Auckland, and three deans, one for each Tikanga (or cultural/ethnic identity) of the church. This means that some ethnic streaming for training, education and formation still continues. The Pākehā students (which ethnically can include Melanesians, Chinese, Indian, Fijians and other Asians), Māori students (which can include ethnic Pākehā), and Polynesian students therefore make up a rich ethnic group of seminarians, who are trained and formed both together and apart.

In the Church of England, numerous schemes have sought to extend and shape theological training for ethnic groups and working-class people. The Simon of Cyrene Institute in London was augmented in the 1980s (later merging with the Queen's Foundation, Birmingham) to encourage more ethnic minority vocations to the ordained ministry. Initiatives such as Industrial Mission have sought to connect the cares and concerns of the working class with the mission and ministry of the church.

In each of these examples, Anglican churches have attempted to address the issues presented to them through factors relating to ethnicity and class, and in turn address the needs for greater and more diverse representation in leadership for parishes and congregations. So what of class and ethnicity? Sociologists such as Max Weber were clear that class was not a specific 'entity' with a 'membership'. The division between so-called mass and elite society is an interpretative rather than descriptive perspective.

To account for the persistence of factors of class and race in shaping North American religious affinity, we can cast an eye over the demographics of the colonies. As David Hackett Fischer notes in his fine book *Albion's Seed: Four British Folkways in America*,[2] East Anglian Puritans settled in what became Massachusetts, Quakers from the Midlands went to Pennsylvania, while Royalists from the southern counties fled to Virginia. All brought to their fledgling 'New World' communities their own ideas of how to live as a citizen. The strong markers of identity that drove those people to seek out unknown territory in which to freely forge unfettered ways of living left traces of their cultural DNA in subsequent generations of churches, denominations and wider communities.

We can find some illustration of this in the history of festivity in the New World. The development of new communities afforded the freedom to keep or dispense with traditions, especially those rooted in religion. Cromwell's staunchly Puritan English republic had looked to end the celebration of Christmas with the threat of fines. This was replicated in the New World. So, the early American Puritans, in keeping with their outlook, frowned upon celebrations and, if they were permitted, ensured they were kept low-key, frugal and prudent affairs, expunged of frivolity and hedonism. Puritans purged the calendar of seasonal festivities too. Months became numbered instead of named, and the Sabbath or Sunday became known as the 'first day'.

In contrast, the decadent exiled and transported Cavaliers who had been forced to decamp to Virginia to escape Cromwell were keenly and extravagantly observant of the full Christian calendar. Christmas, Whitsun, Shrovetide, Hocktide and Twelfth Night were richly celebrated with feasts and festivity. Fischer's account paints a picture of a jubilant society that embraced 'parties, dances, visits, gifts and celebrations', with accompanying delicacies such as fried chicken and fricassee. The Cavaliers were wealthier, too, and brought hares, foxes and stags to hunt, and servants to help. Hunting was primarily for sport, but it also functioned as a way of asserting power over the indigenous communities. For example, early-17th-century English settlers in Ulster were encouraged to hunt and kill 'wood kern' (i.e., native Irish living in the forests and foraging off the land), just as Indians were hunted in the Virginia colony and beyond, and as Aboriginal natives in Australia would be from the late 18th century onwards.[3]

One could pause at this point for some self-justification, and claim that that was then and this is now, and we would certainly not allow such things in our culture, society and time. I beg to differ. Considering the role of major business corporations in the Second World War, we can observe how companies such as Bayer and Porsche, or Kawasaki and Mitsubishi have had to work hard since then to address their use of slave labour and profiteering during the war, gaining wealth through oppression. We are probably less comfortable with putting Ford in the same group, even though Henry Ford was a known Nazi sympathiser and virulent antisemite. Very few British institutions or organisations—in commerce, insurance, shipping, banking or raw materials, for example—have faced much, if any, scrutiny about their past. On the other hand, many cities, churches, museums and some educational institutions have acknowledged their past role and issued retrospective apologies.

With the recent recovery of African American histories, it is only now that Christians are coming to terms with their systemic and deliberate collusion in privileging white male normativity. Not many people today have seen a copy of the Slave Bible, specifically published for educating slaves in the early 19th century. Its full title was *Select Parts of the Holy Bible for the Use of the Negro Slaves in the British West-India Islands*. Such Bibles had all references to freedom and escape from slavery excised, while passages encouraging obedience and submission were emphasised instead. It was a kind of racist *Reader's Digest* version of scripture—in which the editors served up just 10 per cent of the Old Testament and around half of the New Testament. Among the excluded passages was Galatians 3:28 ('There is neither Jew nor Greek, there is neither bond nor free ...'), which was thought to have potential for inciting rebellion. Passages such as Ephesians 6:5 ('Servants, be obedient to them that are your masters according to the flesh, with fear and trembling, in singleness of your heart, as unto Christ') were retained.

What lies behind such initiatives is the sense of society as being divinely ordered. Few in England have ever sung the third verse to Mrs Cecil Alexander's well-known Victorian hymn, 'All Things Bright and Beautiful', written in 1848 as part of her collection, *Hymns for Little Children*:

> The rich man in his castle,
> The poor man at his gate,
> God made them, high or lowly,
> And ordered their estate.

The hymn reflects similar theological notions of divine providence ordering the hierarchy of society and sustaining it as part of creation. Alexander was, interestingly, Anglo-Irish, and her hymn very likely reflects her view of the Irish peasantry whom she would have known as a wealthy landowner. It was also written at the height of the Irish Famine, the worst year of which was 1847, yet the hymn both sacralises and affirms the existing social order. Percy Dearmer, the Christian socialist and hymn-writer, expunged the third verse from his *English Hymnal* (1906).[4] He took exception to the implicit inertia and passivity the verse expressed in the face of such devastating social inequality, and openly opined that the hymn reflected the world-view of a wealthy woman brought up as the daughter of a land agent on an Irish estate. The apparent lack of Alexander's familiarity with the story of Dives and Lazarus (Luke 16:19–31) also struck Dearmer as rather odd.[5]

Warnings from History

As a consequence of their past history, Germany and France (both republics, it needs to be said) have long outlawed the collection of data regarding a person's ethnicity. It is illegal for the government or any commercial enterprise to identify a person by some kind of racial profile. That is one small step towards levelling the playing field of normativity. People are just people. But in the 18th century, English Anglican churches, together with bodies such as the evangelical London Missionary Society (LMS), saw the world more literally in terms of black and white. The LMS arguably had the best of intentions, viz., to evangelise 'pagans, living in cruel and abominable idolatry' and 'to spread the knowledge of Christ among heathen and other unenlightened nations'.[6] On slavery, an LMS pamphlet of 1795 instructed its missionaries about to venture abroad:

> Some of the gentlemen who own the estates, the masters of slaves, are unfriendly towards their instruction. Not a word must escape you in public or private that might render the slaves displeased with their masters or dissatisfied with their station. You are not sent to relieve them from their servile condition, but to afford them the consolation of religion and to enforce upon them the necessity of being 'subject, not only for wrath, but also for conscience sake' (Romans, 13:5; 1 Peter 2:19). The holy gospel you preach will render the slaves who receive it the most diligent, faithful, patient and useful servants. It will render severe discipline unnecessary and make them the most valuable slaves on the estates. Thus, you will recommend yourself and your ministry even to those gentlemen who may have been averse to the religious instruction of the Negroes.[7]

Of course, there were abolitionist activists in Britain. Women were especially involved, although this is also a neglected history in the campaign to end slavery. Yet even here, political, economic and class interests frequently led to calls for compromise or gradualism. Today, it is not hard to see how the reaction to the brutality of the British authorities in suppressing the Demerara slave uprising of 1823 in British Guyana might prompt a pamphlet entitled *Immediate, Not Gradual Abolition*, written by Elizabeth Heyrick in 1824. Gradualism was a common response to slavery.

Gradualism was a common response to slavery. William Wilberforce and John Newton were both of the 'slavery must end, but not just yet' school of thinking. Evangelicals like to remember John Newton's dramatic conversion to Christianity, after having been a slave trader and captained many ships carrying slaves. Evangelicals like to link Newton's conversion to his abolitionist position though they are less keen to engage with the ten-year gap between these conversions.

While we might be tempted (or groomed?) to suppose that the churches were at the vanguard of reform, the picture is more subtle and shaded in tone. Such was the indebtedness of foreign mission to the proceeds of slavery, that it was as difficult then as it is now to split the formation of the Anglican Communion from the money that rolled in through slave-trading. For example, slave-owners—the newly moneyed of their day—enjoyed public prominence as patrons of the arts and education and as builders of new chapels and churches. In the 1790s, the Hibbert family owned a 3,000-acre estate in Jamaica and a cotton factory in Manchester. On Sundays, George Hibbert habitually worshipped at Holy Trinity Clapham—the same church attended by William Wilberforce, Henry Thornton and other members of the pro-abolitionist Clapham Sect. Hibbert contributed substantially to the new chapel built by Holy Trinity. Plaques to slave-owners who helped to establish and build new churches can be found across the Anglican Communion. Evangelical, Baptist and Methodist churches were also beneficiaries.

In the Church of England hierarchy, the closeness between proponents of abolition and those favouring its continuation was common throughout the 18th and 19th centuries. The Anglo-Irish writer Laurence Sterne, author of *Tristram Shandy* (1759), produced some publications to support the cause of the abolitionists. Sterne was a leading Church of England clergyman, powerfully connected to some of the very highest-ranking clergy and consequently highly influential in the debates on slavery. Yet at the same time, and in his later years, Sterne also enjoyed a very close personal relationship with the heiress Eliza Lumley, whose considerable wealth derived directly from the East India Company, which owned hundreds of thousands of slaves as part of their commercial enterprise.

Consequently, gradualist approaches to slavery and oppression were a common device in managing change, as the goal was to protect economic interests and maintain power structures. In the past, Anglicanism has seen this with native clergy, women bishops and LGBTQ+ causes. The elite are very practised at saying 'let freedom and equality reign' but whispering under their breath 'just not in my time ... we are not ready yet'. Abolitionists were split on strategy and tactics. Some saw befriending the planters and slave-owners as the best means of achieving change. In such thinking, proponents of gradual abolition championed mitigation of the cruelties and evils of enforced bondage. Others could only see immediate, total emancipation as the goal.

By paying proper attention to slavery, class and social polity (e.g., whether monarchy or democracy, etc.) as part of the spiritual engine of growth of the Anglican Communion, we cannot miss the failures of function and performance in its present situation. Slavery, rooted in racism, is part of the present legacy of post-colonial Anglicanism. For sure, today's white, male leaders will claim that they no longer deliberately discriminate as their forebears did. But the inadvertent racism needs just as much serious energy and purposeful expunging for it to be removed. We simply don't see much appetite for that in the current leadership of the Church of England.

What seems to keep things ticking over at the present time is what sociologists refer to as Pournelle's iron law of bureaucracy—named after Jerry Pournelle, an American scientist, essayist and philosopher. Pournelle theorised that organisations or institutions consisted of two kinds of staff. First, those devoted to the goals, purpose, vision and ethos of the organisation. Second, those dedicated to the organisation itself, who would regard the goals, purpose, vision and ethos as subordinate to the existence of the organisation itself. In every case, noted Pournelle, the iron law states that the second group gains control of the organisation or institution, and will ultimately go on to determine who succeeds in power and authority.

With all of the key roles and tasks eventually secured by the second group, the organisation morphs into being run as an ontologised executive. Churches, universities and other institutions can all bear witness to such a trajectory. Pournelle's iron law is at home in both the Old and the New World, and it can take advantage of monarchical or democratic polity. But it will be less visible and accountable in monarchical systems of governance, precisely because of the lack of transparency and the 'mystique' of those who rule.

Thus, tokenism can reign supreme in a culture where valorised gradualism is part of the ecology of establishment and monarchical hierarchy. Even today, tweaks and reforms are still the favoured responses, just as they were in the 18th and 19th centuries. Modest gradualism and reform are the eternal friends of monarchical power, as they require micro-tweaks to the current arrangements. Only modest, mild adjustments to the present need be made. The agenda is to retain the majesty and power of the Steady State and its ruling elite. And the courtiers will see to it that Pournelle's iron law delivers now and in the generations to come. Perhaps that is why the endless English Era of Reform is due for the disruption that only an Age of Revolution can usher in and finally deliver.

5

SLAVERY, CHURCH AND COLONIAL RACISM

While some might take great pride in the British being the first to outlaw slave-trading (1807) and slave-ownership (1833), it is equally important to remember that Britain never passed a law legalising slavery. There were a handful of legal cases that highlighted the cognitive dissonance in national consciousness. In 1569 the English courts ruled against a man named Cartwright, who had been reported for savagely beating a man, which in law would have amounted to a battery and assault. Cartwright claimed through counsel that the man was a slave whom he had brought to England from Russia, and thus such chastisement was not unlawful. The courts ruled against Cartwright, arguing that slaves did not exist in England. England's Magna Carta of 1215 and common law had long declared that one might be a villein (or serf) in England, 'but not a slave'.

In terms of English law, the picture was mixed for the colonies. The colony of Virginia in British North America prohibited slavery within the colony, and in 1766 a legal case had established that there were no slaves in the state, only indentured servants. Legally, the same was true for the other twelve states of British North America, the passing of whose laws required the consent of England's king. This did not change at the end of the American War of Independence, after the peace treaty was signed in 1784. The Virginian legislature continued to uphold its colonial charter adhering to English law, and enact nothing 'repugnant' to it. But like bootleg liquor and alcohol prohibition in the early 20th century, slavery, though illegal, certainly existed.

Slavery: Normal Service Resumed

Slave-trading existed, and persisted, largely owing to ongoing shortages of labour. The New World depended on such labour. This accounts for the jaw-dropping statistics that reveal the scale of the transportation of the enslaved. An investor in slave-ownership could typically expect an annual return of 6%. Between 1600 and 1800, the estimated number of slaves transported to the New World numbered 12.5 million. Of those, 4.8 million were sent to Portuguese America; 3.3 million were transported to British colonies; France took 1.3 million; the Dutch around 0.5 million; the Americans 0.3 million; and the Danish 0.1 million. Of the 12.5 million transported, only 10.7 million arrived, with 1.8 million dying of disease or dysentery during transportation, or by suicide, shipwreck or execution following an uprising. With almost 15% not completing the journey to the New World, it is further estimated by scholars that 33% would die within one year of disembarkation because of disease or working conditions. Portuguese slave-trading accounted for almost 40% of the total, and British slave-trading almost 30%, with the majority of those enslaved being put to work on Caribbean plantations.

None of these figures take account of enslaved peoples under the British Empire from China, the Indian subcontinent and elsewhere. Between 1904 and 1910 some 64,000 Chinese labourers were shipped by the British to South Africa in order to work on the gold mines. Tens of thousands of labourers were shipped from India to British Guyana and other parts of the Caribbean to shore up the labour supply there after the abolition of slavery. Mention must also be made of the Irish, who were periodically enslaved in workhouses or forcibly transported for labour. Following the Great Famine of Ireland (1845–52), it only took until 1861 for New York to become the most Irish city in the world. Ireland had a population of eight million in 1845, of which one million died and two million emigrated during this seven-year famine. The Irish population has only recently recovered and begun to exceed (slightly) the population level of 1845.

European religious attitudes towards slavery and migrants had, in any case, been riddled with duplicity for centuries. Even when the Roman Catholic Church and the Holy Roman Emperor outlawed slavery, religious orders (like the Jesuits), convents, monasteries, clergy and laity in Central and South America retained slave-ownership. While the global expansion of Anglicanism was indebted more indirectly to slavery, churches were built on the profits and proceeds from slave-trading, as were missionary societies, such as the SPG through Caribbean sugar plantations. When slave-ownership was finally ended under British law in 1833, the Bishop of Exeter, Henry Phillpotts, was one of the appointed trustees acting in the estate of the Earl of Dudley, who owned 665 slaves.

For many Europeans in the 18th and 19th centuries, slavery was only visible to those who might travel to the colonies and their plantations. In the early developmental days of the British slave-empire, most slave-holders lived abroad and played a direct role in the management of their estates and plantations. But as profits boomed, slave-owners could afford to buy or develop large estates in Britain. They left their plantations as mini-enclaves or exclaves in the newly formed colonial territories, with their estates functioning, to a large extent, outside the law. Back home, the plantation owners could afford to endow public works, including libraries and other facilities, and become patrons of charities, the arts and civic bodies. Contributing to the upkeep of churches or the building of new places of worship or helping to finance foreign mission was also well within budget.

Under slavery, capitalism and Christianity found their interests conflated. The headline justification that brought these interests together was 'civilisation'. Capitalism, exploitation, enslavement and catechesis might be justified if some greater good could be claimed for those forced to endure the miseries of the slave trade. 'Civilisation' was that justification. The merchant class grew wealthier, and the owners of slaves and plantations gained substantial profits. From 1760 to 1800, a slave-owner could bank on a 9.5% annual return on investment, compared to a 4.5% return on property lettings or loans. Sugar, at wholesale, returned between 6% and 11% profit in this forty-year period.[1] Even poorer British citizens gained materially from the slave trade.

To most upper- and middle-class British citizens, slavery and its economic rewards constituted a plain and simple means to an end. The favoured commodities produced through slavery enjoyed a growing global market—coffee, tea, rum, sugar, tobacco and cotton being the principal goods. These were as vital to the economy of the American South as they were to Britain or to New York. Yet as Hanoverian and Victorian missionary endeavour worked with capitalism to expand the British empire and, with it, the basis for the later Anglican Communion, there were niggling questions around African slaves converting to Christianity.

'Plantation churches' developed early on in the Caribbean and Americas, but they were generally treated with suspicion, if not harshly suppressed, by plantation owners. The fear of these gatherings lay in the possibility of slave congregations fomenting dissent, sedition, riot or revolt. Moreover, a distinctive (Negro) spirituality developed early, with songs, hymns, rituals, prayers and liturgies that reflected the hardship of slavery and the suffering of the congregations. Despite slaves converting to Christianity (and becoming Anglicans in Virginia, the Caribbean and other colonies), they remained in bondage, and were subjected to intense cruelty. Lambeth Palace library holds letters from Anglican slaves petitioning for freedom, dating from the early 18th century.[2]

It is most likely that the Belmont Plantation (Virginia) revolt of 1831 led by Nat Turner was planned from his plantation church. Turner was an educated preacher and one of 56 enslaved people put to death for the revolt—still one of the most significant uprisings in American history. As a result of the revolt, legislation was passed prohibiting the education of enslaved people and free black people. Furthermore, it restricted the rights of assembly and other civil liberties for free black people, and required white ministers to be present at all worship services. One cannot help observing that if China were to implement such censorship and control on church services, most Americans would be outraged. But less than two centuries ago, the state of Virginia passed laws restricting the freedom of worship—based on the colour of a person's skin.

The legacy of English slave-trading continues to this day. Queen Anne's Bounty was a charitable foundation established in 1704 to augment the stipends of poor Church of England clergy. The charitable foundation invested significant sums in the transportation of slaves to the Americas. In turn, the grants the foundation gave were not direct payments to the clergy but, rather, were spent on the acquisition of land for the petitioning parishes, which could then be turned into rental or agricultural income. Furthermore, in order for parishes to draw down such financial support from Queen Anne's Bounty, it was often a requirement for the parish to find a wealthy patron or benefactor—a third party—who would provide matching funding.

There had been earlier versions of such arrangements to support poorer clergy. The church burgesses of Sheffield were granted around 150 acres of land and the income from them in order to support the development of the town and its churches. Under a charter issued by Mary I in 1554, the twelve burgesses drew the income from this endowment. However, rather as with Queen Anne's Bounty 150 years later, the endowment provided by the monarch was closely related to the new plantations that Mary I had established in Ireland, confiscating lands to give to favoured English settlers. Mary I also benefited from Spanish trade, which included slavery, through her marriage to Philip II of Spain. Then, perhaps as now, it was hard to find 'clean' money from complex investment portfolios.

In the early 18th century, newly moneyed slave and plantation owners were often called upon to provide civic support. Edward Colston, who endowed charitable and Christian causes in Bristol, is just one example. William Beckford inherited over a dozen plantations and 3,000 slaves in Jamaica in 1737. Beckford went on to be twice Lord Mayor of London, supported city and guild churches, and used his slave-based wealth to advance political causes and champion candidates for political office. Robert Walpole was a beneficiary. Beckford's willingness to cultivate political friends and gain influence often led to profligate spending: infamously, one dinner to entertain peers and nobility reportedly cost £10,000. Beckford was instrumental in suppressing the Jamaican slave rebellion of 1760. Over 400 slaves were killed, and the leader burned alive 'as an example'.

Reparation and Making More Mythology

Queen Anne's Bounty and the wealth of the Ecclesiastical Commissioners were merged together in 1947 to create the Church Commissioners, whose current net worth is estimated at around £12 billion. In January 2023 the Church Commissioners announced that they were setting up a fund of £100 million to be spent over the next nine years on addressing the church's historical links with slavery. The figure of £100 million may seem considerable, but it amounts to 0.83% of the Church Commissioners' estimated wealth, and there is still no indication of how this fund will be used for reparations, if at all. Similarly 'generous' figures have been offered by the Church of England to victims of sexual abuse—£150 million—which is a minuscule sum for the estimated 5,000 victims, and a fraction of the payouts made by Anglican provinces in Australia and Canada.

While £100 million may seem generous, the historical amnesia of the Church of England continues to be deeply troubling when it comes to a moral reckoning with its colonial past. Cynics and critics were quick to point out in the media that £100 million was not very much, given how much the Church of England had benefited from slavery. The Church of England's communications team promptly declared that the amount ought to be £1 billion. But looking more closely at the announcement, all that the Church of England was proposing to do was 'set aside' £100 million, the interest from which would be directed to future applications from post-colonial communities seeking aid for development. The Church of England was not giving away £100 million. More risibly, the £1 billion 'target' was something that was being suggested as 'a catalyst to encourage other institutions to investigate their past and make a better future for impacted communities', but the missing £900 million would have to come from other institutions, not the church.[3]

Queen Anne's Bounty was established in 1704 to support poorer clergy. A 2023 report by forensic accountants at Grant Thornton found that by 1739, when the South Sea Company stopped its actual slave-trading, the bounty held annuities issued by the company valued at just over £200,000—equivalent to about £440 million today. However, the South Sea Company continued to invest in slave-trading, and the value of the annuities was over £400,000 in 1777, roughly equating to £725 million today. Grant Thornton also estimated that the Church of England received around £360,000 from individuals with 'very high or high likelihood' of being linked to the slave trade—roughly £485 million today. Small wonder that many former colonies and communities exploited by the Church of England's former investments feel they are being short-changed.

While missionary endeavour can appear to act as the proverbial straw man or pantomime villain in any discussion of imperialism and colonialism, there are those who will still defend its legacy, and with vigour. At the beginning of the 20th century, the Church Missionary Society could boast that of its 9,000 missionaries, more than 8,000 were African—or 'native agents' as they were known. Samuel Ajayi Crowther, who was the first African Anglican bishop, and a former slave who had converted at the age of sixteen, brought his own Yoruba translation of the Bible and the Book of Common Prayer to the numerous communities along the Niger River because he saw it as his calling to 'make all men wise unto salvation' and to 'fight manfully under Christ's banner against spiritual enemies'. No one did more to bring Anglicanism to Nigeria, or to make Anglicanism distinctively African.[4]

But critics will point out that the entitled hegemony of English Anglicanism also resulted in a multiple forms of 'epistemicide'—the denigration and destruction of local knowledge (e.g., oral, not written traditions), valued practices, rituals and rites of passage, and even the wanton annihilation, confiscation or theft of precious artefacts. The suppression or devastation of local knowledge would lead to famines and other shortages across the world, leaving indigenous communities with European farming and cultivation methods that simply did not work in Africa, India, Australia or the plains of North America.

In November 2023 Lloyd's of London announced it was 'deeply sorry' for its links to the slave trade and pledged to invest £52 million in helping affected communities. The 335-year-old insurance firm had played a significant role in enabling the transatlantic trade. Lloyds formed an essential component of 'a sophisticated network of financial interests and activities which made the transatlantic slave trade possible', according to an independent report conducted by academics at Johns Hopkins University in Baltimore (funded by the Mellon Foundation). The Scott Trust, which owns *The Guardian* and *The Observer*, apologised for the founders' involvement in slavery and pledged to invest over £10 million in restorative justice. The Bank of England revealed in 2022 that it had owned enslaved people in the 1770s. The National Trust found links to colonialism or slavery in a third of its properties. Greene King apologised for its links to chattel slavery in June 2020.[5]

Just as Lloyd's of London profited from the slave trade, so the Church of England, both at home and abroad, was also a significant beneficiary through the profits derived from traded goods in the plantations, and from the patronage of slave-owners in their benefaction of churches. As Alex Renton notes, taking account of the past, in terms of slave-ownership, the Church of England needs to embark on a moral, political, ecological and financial reckoning of epic proportion.[6] But the church has not even begun such work for the substantial rewards it accrued from across the British Empire.

Social Engineering

Another legacy of empire that continues to impact on the Church of England is race theory and attitudes to ethnicity, which once fed the fiction of imperial supremacy. It is unlikely that many readers will have come across the Galton Institute. It was formerly known as the Eugenics Society from 1907 until 1968, and it published an interdisciplinary journal, the *Eugenics Review* (1909–68). Named after the Victorian polymath Sir Francis Galton (a half-cousin of Charles Darwin), it drew on Galton's speculative theories of racial origins and purity, and his 'social Darwinism'. Leaving aside the problematic period when Nazism appropriated the term 'eugenics' (an understatement, if that is possible), the Galton Institute and its forerunners have always existed as a not-for-profit learned society seeking 'to promote the public understanding of human heredity and to facilitate informed debate about the ethical issues raised by advances in reproductive technology'.[7]

Looking back on previous issues of the *Eugenics Review* and the work of the Society makes for uncomfortable reading today. In 1910, the Society's own Committee on Poor Law Reform tried to persuade a Royal Commission that poverty was rooted in the genetic deficiencies of the working class. The committee suggested that genuine paupers might best be detained in workhouses, under the authority of the Poor Law Guardians, in order to prevent their breeding. Some in the Society genuinely believed that there were 'pedigrees' of impoverished families, and that the nature of poverty was therefore hereditary.

In 1916, Leonard Darwin (son of Charles) published a pamphlet entitled *Quality not Quantity*, which sought to encourage the 'professional classes' to have more children. To help them, he proposed tax incentives for the middle classes. Parliament, to its credit, did not rise to the bait. Undeterred, the 1920s and 1930s saw the Eugenics Society campaigning for a graded Family Allowance Scheme which would have rewarded wealthier families with more funds for having more children, thereby incentivising fertility in the middle and upper classes.

It followed that lower grades of family allowance were proposed in order not to 'reward the breeding of individuals' who were deemed less desirable.

The pre-war and post-war years saw the Society consumed with concerns relating to a range of social issues, including interracial marriage, immigration, racial purity, class differences in marriage, changing rates of fertility, the working classes, the (so-called) 'feeble-minded' and the 'mentally deficient'. As late as 1954 the North Kensington Marriage Welfare Centre was offering couples a consultation and pamphlet on *Eugenic Guidance* for those worried about passing on their 'weaknesses'. An organisation known as the British Social Hygiene Council had close ties with the Eugenics Society, and also helped found the Marriage Guidance Council.

One year after the Lambeth Conference of 1958, the Revd Dr Sherwin Bailey (at the time research secretary of the Church of England's Moral Welfare Council) published his reflections on the Lambeth Conference resolutions on the family in the January 1959 edition of the *Eugenics Review*.[8] Older readers might recall that of the 131 Lambeth Conference resolutions passed in 1958, numbers 112–31 were on the topic of 'The Family in Contemporary Society'. That comes to 19 resolutions. So the family, marriage, breeding, children and sexual relationships consumed a good deal of time at the Lambeth Conference of 1958. To put this in perspective, at the same conference, there were a few dozen resolutions on the Bible, two for Ceylon, two regarding Methodists, several on 'missionary appeal' (i.e., have we got it, and if not, can we get it?), eleven on global conflict, and then one apiece for the task of the laity, post-ordination training, Roman Catholicism, and (the intriguingly titled) 'the contribution of women'.

The 1958 resolutions on the family were wide-ranging, and were the biggest category. The Anglican Communion was struggling with cultures converting to Christianity that still affirmed polygamy. The Lambeth Conference of 1888 had already agreed that 'the wives of polygamists could be admitted to baptism subject to local decision', but not the male party, who could only receive 'Christian instruction'. As late as the Lambeth Conference of 1920, these issues were referred to as 'missionary problems'. By the time of the Lambeth Conference of 1958, however, things had moved on. Anglican bishops had twigged that there might be a socio-economic dynamic underpinning polygamy, which was 'bound up with the limitations of opportunities for women in society'. At the 1968 Lambeth Conference the clauses and resolutions on polygamy were dropped, following pressure from the African bishops, who had talked of the 'great suffering' caused by 'abrupt termination' of polygamous marriages.

The Lambeth Conference of 1988 resolved to welcome and receive '[any] polygamist who responds to the Gospel ... [and wishes to be] baptised and confirmed with his believing wives and children'. On the whole, Lambeth Conferences have steered clear of polygamy since then. But what of Resolution 41 at the Lambeth Conference in 1908—the 'artificial restriction of the family'? The 1908 gathering regarded artificial contraception as 'demoralising to character' and 'hostile to national welfare'. It went further, and decreed that artificial contraception was 'repugnant to Christian morality' and constituted the 'deliberate tampering with nascent life'. Even with the trauma, social upheaval and diseases (especially venereal) that came in the aftermath of the Great War, the bishops approved Resolution 69 at the Lambeth Conference of 1920, which rejected the use of prophylactics, seeing them mainly as a means of increasing the potential for vice.

By the time of the Lambeth Conference of 1958, and again in the aftermath of a major global war, the language of vice, restriction, control and censorship had shifted to that of 'responsible parenthood'. Nevertheless, Sheridan Bailey's article in the 1959 *Eugenics Review* noted with approval that many bishops argued that vasectomies constituted 'a major and irrevocable abdication of an important area of responsible freedom, a violation of the Body that is God's gift and not ours to dispose of as we will and a step fraught with unknown physiological and psychological consequences that could only be countenanced as a useful family planning device suited to poor and illiterate peoples'.[9]

Although the status of divorcees was largely left to individual provinces to determine at the 1948 Lambeth Conference, it is again worth noting the gradual progressiveness of Anglican attitudes. At the 1908 Conference, even the innocent party in a divorce was forbidden to remarry or be blessed in church. The Lambeth Conferences of 1958, 1968 and 1978 all saw resolutions passed expressing 'pastoral concern' for divorcees. The one from 1978 spoke of 'ministries of compassionate support to those suffering from brokenness within marriage'. Across the Anglican Communion, each province varied on admitting divorcees to Holy Communion or permitting them to be ordained. As things currently stand, 40% of the world's population have legal access to equal or same-sex marriage or to civil partnerships.

The 1968 Lambeth Conference committed Anglicanism to testing the teaching of scripture against the results of emerging scientific and medical research in respect of homosexuality. Bishops were encouraged to have 'pastoral concern' for and 'dialogue with' homosexuals. It is against this background that current Anglican 'difficulties' should be understood. The lack of definition regarding 'pastoral responses' to such 'difficulties' remains highly problematic in English Anglican ministry, as practised by its leadership. For the most part, many bishops assume that simply 'listening' in itself constitutes pastoral care, and therefore nothing further need be done. Their assumption is that their obligation to an individual seeking help is limited, namely, to sacrifice some time for the person in need, in the belief that all a despairing interlocutor really wants is to get the relevant matter off their chest.[10]

Church leaders often lack agency, or refuse to accept it, in resolving pastoral crises. Many in authority within the church sincerely believe that they have somehow 'done' something (and have 'done enough') by simply listening to, or receiving, the complaints of abuse victims, and that they have therefore fulfilled their perceived side of the presumed pastoral bargain. And because they have 'listened' or 'heard', they not only need do no more, but can then tick that box, and concentrate on priorities such as church growth. Yet few things are more frustrating to anyone in despair than being 'listened' to by people who are not really *hearing* what is being said and who, in any case, will not take action. Clergy in authority who listen but do not hear, or vice versa, are often unaware of the further trauma this is likely to cause to victims. The culture of the church is empathetic, mild, expedient, reactive and pragmatic, but also pastorally sluggish and risk-averse. The biblical reasoning, such as it is, will usually consist in sprinkling a selective veneer of scriptures onto some issues, hoping somehow that meaning and relevance will germinate afresh.

Naturally, in all this, the bishops have remained oblivious to how their views were shaped by their own social constructions of reality from the 18th to the 20th centuries, including early 'race theory', which also influenced attitudes on ethnicity across the British Empire and fed the fiction of imperial supremacy.[11]

6

CROWNING GLORY

In British coronations, the meanings are multiple. The sovereign will be presented to, and acclaimed by, the people—in a kind of nod to egalitarian society. He will swear an oath to uphold the law of the land. Yet coronations manifest more. The ceremony is presided over by the Archbishop of Canterbury and the Dean of Westminster Abbey. Traditionally, there is no explicit mention of other branches of the Christian faith, let alone other religions.[1]

The coronation is something of a crowning glory for the Church of England and at times is referred to as its eighth sacrament. Sacramental materials—whether bread, oil, wine, water or words—are recognised by theologians as instruments that signify the transforming power of God entering the life of the world. What was previously an ordinary piece of bread is now regarded as hallowed and a channel for blessing.

The occasion almost resembles an ordination or the consecration of a bishop. Like a priest or bishop, this monarch is chosen and anointed by God—and has been endowed with significant spiritual–sacred–sacramental power. Even the medieval Latin hymn *Veni Creator Spiritus* (Come, Holy Spirit), used in ordinations, is prayerfully chanted before anointing the monarch, who is clad in robes.

The monarch therefore becomes a single conflation of *opus dei* and *opus hominum*: embodying both godly and human power. Charles I knew exactly where his divine right to rule came from: God. For him, defying the king was tantamount to defying the deity. He went to his execution believing that God was being usurped just as much as his kingship was. Oliver Cromwell, during his short-lived republic, saw things differently. He presided over the realm as Lord Protector, transforming it from a monarchy to a theocracy. The rule of privileged genealogy was usurped by a regime founded on religious orthodoxy. Charles II was more circumspect and knew he was reliant on permission from Parliament. Charles III will rule by consent more than by right. The king may be the head of state but is otherwise dependent upon and subject to the sovereign body in the Palace of Westminster. Democracy will not be replaced by the claim to divine inheritance.

Coronations in the Present

In David Nicholls's *Deity and Domination*,[2] he discusses how notions of dominion, majesty and might in the secular-public sphere are still theologically freighted. Imagery, symbols, words, roles, offices and rituals combine to reinforce hierarchical patterns of dominion, in which the state appeals to God for legitimacy in hegemony. King, Lord, Judge—the monarch and Church of England bishops combine all three—make it possible for theocratic and theological constructions of reality to impose themselves on civil society.

The uncomfortable truth for the Church of England in the 21st century rests on its inescapable identity as a Protestant established church, which was anti-Catholic in character and culture, and formally enshrined in law. The coronation service in the present reflects that, with the monarch promising to uphold the Protestant faith of the Church of England. It was Parliament that resisted the authority of the Pope and those forces loyal to the concept of a European Holy Roman Empire. Then, as now, the English had a somewhat inimical attitude towards the rest of Europe. Their myth-memory is that England saved Europe and so is not about to be subject to it.

There is much irony here. In the 'Glorious Revolution', it was James II who found himself cast as the dangerous foreigner and William of Orange as the safe insider. In this epoch, Catholic meant foreign, and Protestant meant domestic and familiar. Perhaps it was no surprise, then, that the coup against James II was essentially a family affair. James's daughter, Mary, had married William of Orange, a Protestant. Mary was raised as a Protestant and Anglican, while her parents (James and Anne) had converted to Catholicism. Anne bore James eight children, but only two survived—Mary and her younger sister, the future Queen Anne. James remarried Mary of Modena, a Catholic. Two children from this relationship survived, the eldest of whom, Edward (known as the 'Old Pretender'),[3] led the first Jacobite rebellion in 1715 against the crown, with the second led by his son, Charles, in 1745. The emergence of the Jacobites (Jacobus being the Latin for James) and their defeat by 1745 were widely seen as the end of Roman Catholic claims to the throne.

William III (r. 1689–1702) and Mary II (r. 1689–94) were offered the throne as joint monarchs on condition they agreed to a Declaration of Rights (later a Bill). The Bill limited the Sovereign's power, reaffirmed Parliament's powers over taxation and legislation, and provided guarantees against the abuses of power which James II and the other Stuart kings had committed. England was now a Protestant kingdom, and the monarch was required to maintain the Protestant religion in the coronation oath. The 1689 Toleration Act granted freedom of worship to Nonconformists but withheld it from Roman Catholics.

This history is how the present coronation service and its arrangements arrived. It is a blend of English Protestant assertion and quasi-mystical symbolism. That said, every coronation marks a subtle step in social and cultural evolution. For example, the coronation liturgy was only translated from Latin into English for the first time for the crowning of James VI of Scotland as James I of England in 1603, since the law now required liturgical services to be understood by the English people. James II, in 1685, opted for an abbreviated liturgy. As a Roman Catholic, he felt the (Protestant) Eucharist was superfluous to the ceremony, presumably ineffectual in any case, and so it was omitted. His successors were Protestants, and they restored it.

The Latin text made a comeback in 1714 for the coronation of George I. But this was no sop to the Catholics. As he was German-speaking, Latin was the only common language for king and clergy. George III's coronation was marked by numerous errors and baffling gaffes. George IV's coronation in 1821 was grotesquely expensive and lavish. In contrast, in 1831 William IV had to be leant on hard to have a coronation at all. It eventually went ahead, costing just tens of thousands of pounds—compared to the £230,000 spent by George IV in 1821—and without the customary banquet, thereby ending six and a half centuries of tradition. Traditionalists sneered at what they dubbed the 'half-crown nation', and threatened a boycott. But the new king stuck to his guns and wore his military-issue uniform (as an admiral). These economising measures set a precedent for future monarchs.

Victoria was crowned in 1838, and her coronation largely followed the pared-down model set by her uncle. Perhaps the simmering clamour for reform led by the Chartists in the same year led courtiers and government to be more circumspect about seeming to lavish expenditure on coronations. Even so, the coronation service was apparently under-rehearsed, arrangements for the music in the abbey heavily criticised by the press, and the ceremony, in an echo of George III's, marred by mistakes.

Coronations usually conclude with a procession, and in recent times it has been customary for the royal family to appear on the balcony of Buckingham Palace. There is nothing new under the sun, and the paradigm set in the last century was for the pageantry to parade national and Commonwealth diversity. The 20th century—perhaps setting a pattern for the 21st—sought to blend innovation with tradition.

Coronations have not always required the Archbishop of Canterbury. William the Conqueror was crowned by the Archbishop of York, and Edward II by the Bishop of Winchester. Mary I was not crowned by the (Protestant) Archbishop Cranmer, who was locked up in the Tower of London; she also chose the Bishop of Winchester. Elizabeth I was crowned by the Bishop of Carlisle, but only because the other bishops were dead, too old and infirm, unacceptable to the queen, or simply unwilling. The Archbishop of Canterbury refused to recognise William III and Mary II, so the joint coronation was conducted by the Bishop of London.

Anglo-Saxon monarchs were relatively flexible about their coronation venue, with Bath Abbey, Winchester Cathedral and even Kingston-upon-Thames favoured as locations. Henry III chose St Peter's Abbey, now Gloucester Cathedral, but also opted for a rather statelier coronation at Westminster four years after his first. An ancient court, known as the Court of Claims, is traditionally used to hear petitions from those who seek to perform a service at the event. It was used for Elizabeth II's coronation and heard claims from the Lord High Steward of Ireland, who wanted to carry a white wand, and from the Duke of Somerset, who wanted to carry the orb or sceptre.

The Dean of Westminster advised the queen on the coronation in 1953, as his predecessors had done. The *Liber Regalis*—a kind of medieval manual for coronations kept by Westminster Abbey—contains guidance and advice on how to run the event. Perhaps this guidebook helped to shoehorn the 8,000 guests into the Abbey in 1953. That was quite a feat, with many attendees given a seat just 45 cm in width, making social distancing pretty tricky.

The Coronation Oath Act of 1688 laid down a statutory formula for the taking of the oath. In 1953 the queen promised to 'govern the Peoples of the United Kingdom of Great Britain and Northern Ireland, Canada, Australia, New Zealand, the Union of South Africa, Pakistan and Ceylon'. The archbishop then asked the monarch:

> Will you to the utmost of your power maintain the Laws of God and the true profession of the Gospel? Will you to the utmost of your power maintain in the United Kingdom the Protestant Reformed Religion established by law? Will you maintain and preserve inviolably the settlement of the Church of England, and the doctrine, worship, discipline, and government thereof, as by law established in England? And will you preserve unto the Bishops and Clergy of England, and to the Churches there committed to their charge, all such rights and privileges, as by law do or shall appertain to them or any of them?

Granted, the monarch also swears a separate oath to preserve ecclesial governance in the Church of Scotland. But this oath is taken before the coronation, and the liturgy affirms the position, power and privileges of the Church of England, which parades itself as established by the power of God and Parliament. As repeated in 2023, this made for a rather uncomfortable moment in our multi-faith and increasingly secular United Kingdom.

Coronations have evolved into a spiritual, civil and moral matrix for mutual affirmation. In an economically depressed Britain, limping on with post-Covid wariness, Charles III's coronation was an occasion for celebrating communities and the civic values that bind them. Yet we are left with awkward issues and nagging questions that no amount of pomp and pageantry can camouflage.

Questioning Establishment

The coronation was meant to be a crowning glory for Charles III. Yet coronations, even dressed-down versions, risk the glorification of glory itself. Arguably, the hierarchy of the Church of England needed a grand coronation more than the monarch. Ecclesiastical leaders doubtless hoped that a national celebration might provide temporary respite from the internal and external problems the church faced. But beyond providing nostalgic distraction, it is unlikely to have made much difference.

For the Church of England, the time may be ripe to 'level up' and share ecclesiastical power and privilege. If proof of the problem were still needed, the recent national census, with its statistics on religious affiliation, made for uncomfortable reading. For the first time in a census for England and Wales, less than half of the population (46.2 per cent, or 27.5 million people) described itself as Christian. This represents a 13.1 percentage point decrease from 2011. As the *Church Times* noted, Christianity is now a minority religion in England.

The paradox for members of the Church of England—and, remember, Anglican congregations can be found in more than 160 other countries—is that while the population of England is primarily pro-equality and pro-democracy, the established church remains rooted in monarchical theocratic hierarchies. The coronation offered a potential occasion for national renewal and presented a chance for the Church of England to begin setting aside its privileged positions and hierarchies, and fully embracing equality and solidarity with all of its people.

This was a moment crying out for authenticity, integrity, and disinvestment in patrimony. It could have been a genuine opportunity for change. But it wasn't to be. Like hundreds of millions of people watching the coronation, I found myself caught up in a complex web of sentiment. The music was beautiful and in places was spine-tingling. Slow-paced stately grandeur is an aesthetic, but also a kind of politics. The appearance of progress—on the day and over time—comes through small but welcome advances. But appearances are all it is.

The presence of other faith leaders, and the visual complexion of the event (far less ermine, and welcome representatives of civic, social and charitable causes), reminded us of how much Britain has changed. Greater ethnic diversity better reflected contemporary society. The lengthy back-catalogue of Conservative prime ministers inevitably provided a silent comment on the state of the nation.

Newly commissioned music ranged from aria and anthem to a gospel choir. You could say that the bandwidth of the coronation service moved effortlessly through a repertoire of fare to suit audiences from Public Broadcast Radio and Fox News (US) or Radio 2, 3 and 4 (UK), bracketed by pre- and post-processional commentary that was more in tune with Radio 5 Live (UK) or US talk radio. As national liturgies go, this one seemed to tick every box and could be safely chalked up as a minor triumph.

Yet my reaction was tempered with profound unease. Britain is not secularised, but it is spiritually and religiously diffuse. Faith finds itself poured out and spread thinly across society. Religious salience and affiliation are nothing like as powerful as they were during the last coronation in 1953.

In the months leading up to the coronation of 2023, consistent surveys and polls showed little appetite for the event among the under-thirties. Along with other religiously disaffiliated sections of society (which now cover more than 50 per cent of the UK population), very few among the emerging generation turned to religion or spirituality for support through the trials of the Covid pandemic and the country's current economic tribulations. Instead, they have found more dependable comfort in material and social and familial palliatives.

Coronations have previously been occasions for national spiritual renewal. What the British people were served with in the coronation of 2023 was a kind of cake (or perhaps coronation quiche), made with the ingredients of nostalgia and paternal sincerity, and baked together with quirky pageantry and atypical liturgy. For some, this was a banquet to savour. For others, it resembled the proverbial curate's egg.

The dissonances the coronation service could not overcome were rooted in the symbols and words that can only have any meaning if carefully explained and pleaded. Without the lengthy elucidations, we—the subjects—would be left to puzzle over the point of the objects. To be sure, Penny Mordaunt's sword-bearing has already become the stuff of legend. But what did the sword symbolise?

The golden sword only dates back to King George IV's coronation in 1821. It is entrusted to the monarch upon the order that 'it should be used for the protection of good and the punishment of evil'. So, it is a symbol of defence, but also attack; protection, but also assault. The bearing of the sword is unavoidably linked to the armed forces—present in large numbers at the coronation—with the powers of state coercion and lethal force also affirmed in the symbolism. (One can imagine the media brouhaha if a president of the United States was inaugurated holding a Bible in the left hand and a Magnum revolver in the right.)

Explanations for the symbols appeared in the liturgy, the pre-coronation PR warm-up and the media commentary for the day. One could jest about the orb, sceptre, robes, glove, spurs and other 'ancient' artefacts. But I suppose it was better than having cufflinks of conformity, a tiepin of togetherness, or shoe buckles of sobriety. Symbols have to mean something: more than the sum of the token or object.

As the eminent sociologists Émile Durkheim and Edward Shils both observed,[4] national symbols are a kind of currency, and their value depends on taking their meaning on trust. Although Durkheim did not directly address the issue of monarchical sovereignty in his writings, his theory of religion and society highlights the likely collapse into irrelevance, and the 'serious fictions it depends upon for its survival'.[5] But if you are explaining your symbols, you are already acknowledging their receding value. Moreover, as these explanations become increasingly remote from the lives of most people, the risk of loss of meaning, value, form and function looms larger.

The coronation of Charles III was an opportunity to read the sign of the times and present the United Kingdom with a more holistic vision for the monarchy, society, the people and the world. Greater sensitivity to religious diversity added some granularity and complexity, but, alas, the Church of England still retained a virtual monopoly over the event, ensuring that what came through any superficial nod to other faiths was a determination, through clenched teeth, to assert that Anglicanism was still the Top Denomination in the land.

This grated with many onlookers. There were far too many male bishops with high visibility yet minimal functional or even symbolic tasks in the coronation. The PR attempted to distract us from this by inviting us to be in awe at the presence of women bishops as some kind of breakthrough moment and marvel of modernity. Yet the Church of England remains aloof from modern social norms, with exemptions under the Equality Act permitting it to discriminate in ways other institutions cannot.

Handel's haunting 'Zadok the Priest' would have given even the most hardened atheist goosebumps. Yet we forget that the anointing of Solomon (I Kings 1) was conducted by both Zadok and Nathan the prophet. The act of making a king for Israel was performed by a hereditary priest and a non-hereditary prophet. Yet the coronation liturgy has almost eliminated the role of the prophetic. This leaves us with a ritual celebrating theocratic power, but without its necessary prophetic challenge.

'No Zadok without Nathan' might have made a pretty decent crowd chant on the day of the coronation, though its pointedness would have been lost on most. Thus, the liturgy gave us far too many bishops and priests, but few prophets anywhere in sight. Perhaps—and it is a stretch to suggest this—the prophet of climate action and ecological concern was the one being anointed and crowned?

Yet the anointing of a monarch is done once, and once only. Prophecy, in contrast, is a thankless daily task and lifelong vocation. The function of prophets in the Old Testament was to keep rulers honest and accountable, and call them out when they failed the people and God. Prophets were raised up to level down the rulers.

But the Church of England is hypnotised by the faith of the managers. It knows it is under some spell, and even in some state of induced trance, bordering on coma. But it cannot break free. It has promised its future to nostalgia, and is constantly captivated by its own (erroneous) sense of the past. This places the institution at the mercy of those who either promise to restore 'the good old days', or appear to represent the best route to returning to them. As such, the church is inclined to swoon over charismatic leaders (in the Weberian sense of the word) and their latest programmes, or ecclesial demagogues and autocrats promising shortcuts to success.[6]

Part of what holds the Church of England back is the fear of facing its past with clarity, integrity and honesty. The quasi-regal power of its episcopacy sits uncomfortably with the kind of governance that Thomas Hobbes inclines to in *Leviathan*. Writing between 1642 and 1651—the English Civil War—Hobbes argued that power rested on what or who was sovereign, and the process by which such power was acquired was delivered through representation. To be sure, Hobbes was no democrat, and he certainly thought that sovereignty was best represented in a single person, who was the decision-maker, namely a monarch. But *Leviathan* also left the door open for Parliament to be sovereign too. Those who accept the Sovereign—whoever or whatever they are—will be more likely to accept the peace that comes with accepting such rule.[7]

The Marriage of Monarchy and Episcopacy

The coronation ritual was one of scintillating splendour—dazzling and deifying. Yet despite the enchantment, the ritual remains opaque. The density of the liturgy is impenetrable to the vast majority of the public, and that risks rendering the whole event incomprehensible. Unlike that of 1953, the 2023 coronation essentially failed as an effective public ritual. If those watching the coronation need to have everything explained, and can no longer make affective and effective connections between words, rituals and symbolic actions, then the freighted weight of religious meaning is no longer understood. Too much is lost in translation. Those explaining it are losing.

Next time—assuming there is a next time—ushering in a new reign could be achieved more simply. The monarch could pledge a civic oath of allegiance and service to Parliament and the people in the Great Hall of Westminster, before being consecrated in a religious service at Westminster Abbey. This would not require a Eucharist. The symbols of monarchical power—military and sacred—could be blessed on the high altar, but vesting would not be necessary.

The suggestion that a monarch reigns only by the grace of God is outmoded and risible. That such rule should also include supreme governorship over the Church of England—a small minority of the English population—renders the case for continuity even weaker. The nature of the Church of England's 'establishment', which is defended by the monarch under oath, grants privilege, power and patrimony which now undermine its purpose and identity. The 26 unelected bishops who sit as of right in the House of Lords is a further snub to the rest of the United Kingdom. Bishop-barons are only there by virtue of residual ties to the vast swathes of land and incomes that they enjoyed under the Norman and Tudor monarchs.

For all the liturgical and ritualistic camouflage provided by the coronation, it is not hard to see the failings. Even the briefest touching of the bread and wine by Charles III before the Eucharist provided confirmation of the sacramental status the monarch then assumed. Anointed, consecrated, vested in a stole which he wears as a priest or bishop might: the symbolism is all there to emphasise Charles's royal priesthood.

Churches and denominations typically resist change because they lack a vision for the future of society, and can only anticipate any change to rituals as yet another step in diminution, dilution and marginalisation. The residue of deference also plays a part, and it becomes too easy to repeat the past rather than map out some better future.

In all this, one has to be honest about the present and future. The coronation presented Britain's head of state as serving God rather than the British people. The Church of England secretly asperging (i.e., sprinkling) the monarch with holy oil is more appropriate for some Crusader king than a modern monarch. The coronation cannot present a monarch as the embodiment of democracy when the crown is inherited, and endorsed by an unaccountable episcopal hierarchy. If the present or any future

Prince of Wales wishes to be legitimised by public consent and acclamation, the pledges to the people could more usefully be set within a more neutral space belonging to the democratic state, such as the Westminster parliament.[8]

What was witnessed in the 2023 coronation amounted to a few modern ingredients sprinkled into a very old recipe. In so doing, vested interests and establishment power were curated through a submission to precedent, tradition, nostalgia, pageantry and ritual—and all executed with military precision. In all this, the subjects and objects were misplaced, and an opportunity lost.

The truth is that new rituals would better encapsulate the hopes of a nation with words and symbols that offer a narrative for the monarch and people moving forward together in the 21st century. Instead, the 2023 coronation chose to look backwards, and with some rather wistful longing. May it be remembered as the last one to do so.

7

TO BE OR NOT TO BE?

It came as a surprise and shock to most British people in June 2020 when the large bronze statue of Edward Colston (1636–1721) was unceremoniously dumped in Bristol harbour by a group of protesters. Colston was a prominent transatlantic slave trader and with his wealth was a major civic benefactor of the city of Bristol. The statue had become the focus of agitation during the protests relating to the death of George Floyd in the United States at the hands of the police, and the subsequent mobilisation of the Black Lives Matter movement. Colston's statue was toppled, defaced, and pushed into Bristol harbour. The incident constituted a minor civil riot—a protest at whitewashed history that fails to take account of the past. In refusing to engage with the past, the wrongs of the present cannot be addressed.

It would have escaped most people's notice—the English—that the Colston protest fell on the centenary of Britain's first major race riots. In 1919–21 seaports such as Liverpool, Manchester and Cardiff saw white union dockworkers strike out violently against the black, Chinese and Arab dockworkers gathered from across the British Empire during the First World War. The riots lasted around eight months and, though sporadic, saw one lynching in Liverpool (Charles Wootton, an African-Caribbean worker) and numerous instances of migrant workers being knifed and their homes firebombed. The post-war white dockworkers feared that migrant workers were undercutting their labour, and the government was forced to intervene during further rioting in 1920 and 1921. The British government offered foreign workers modest resettlement allowances if they agreed to repatriate. Few who lost homes, property or livelihood were compensated.

In some respects, there is a very peculiar problem with English racism. It is mostly unconscious. To some extent that trait is shared with other European nations active in the slave trade too. And the root of this lies in the fact that crimes against humanity were committed well away from home; the systemic brutality of enslavement and enforced transportation was not witnessed on British shores. The only people from home to witness the cruelty and barbarity of the slave trade had to travel thousands of miles to do so. For many English people, slavery was out of sight, out of mind.

Perhaps this explains why, even today, outbreaks of racial discontent and even riots puzzle and perplex the English but seem not to invite deeper questions of the past. As Torsten Bell has noted, one simply 'cannot be patriotic these days without being moderately socially liberal, because Britain increasingly is'.[1] It is the same puzzle that confounds Anglican conservative evangelicals. Mortified at the prospect of prayers of blessing for same-sex couples, a breakaway group commissioned a few dozen 'overseers' to provide spiritual support for disaffected clergy and their congregations.[2] The new group was overwhelmingly white and upper middle class by background, and historically unaware of the historical racism embedded in their adopted term 'overseer', once widely used in slave-trading.

Beyond the church, nationally, the lack of investment in communities, infrastructure and opportunity over the past fifty years has led to profound and increasing fragmentation throughout the most deprived parts of Britain. The fault lines in urban conurbations tend to follow demarcations that trace ethnic inequality. The social, legal and economic disparities will be apparent in the present—one need only consider the markedly different statistics for police arrests across the racial groups, continued issues in the armed forces, or preferment for senior posts in the Church of England—to see that this an issue for institutions that are part of the British establishment. But the reluctance to link the present to the past is a kind of learned amnesia.[3] Britain is a nation in decline, and is led in this by the English. The past is lionised and glorified, while the present and future continue to be neglected.[4]

Months after Colston's statue had been thrown into Bristol harbour, Mary Wills and Madge Dresser produced an audited (accountability) report for Historic England listing in detail the stately homes, churches, concert halls, museums and other monuments to philanthropy that were funded by the proceeds of slave trading, and by men like Colston. It makes for uncomfortable reading for those who might be fond of churches and chapels built in the Hanoverian period. But as Wills and Dresser point out, following the money is hard:

> Further investigations are needed into [stately] house owners who made their monies in earlier centuries and then sold off their holdings or who made their monies without being plantation owners, for example, aristocratic families embedded in the military and administrative life of the slave colonies. The impact of the business of slavery was felt across all English regions, so more research would be welcome on tracing this impact on other urban centres. Identifying the money trail in local development is key: how the wealth of a family with

> connections to the transatlantic slavery economy was invested in the built environment of the local area in housing, civic society organisations, churches, village halls, farms, shooting lodges.[5]

As implied above, British racism is primarily an English vice. The history of exploitation, violence and enforced servitude inflicted on Scotland and Ireland does not need rehearsing here. We need only note that the religious and civil wars from the 16th century onwards, fought on Scottish and Irish soil, wreaked colossal economic and demographic devastation. Famines, forced migration and penal servitude, in turn, affected America and Australia alike in how they were settled. As a body, the Church of England was conspicuously silent in such actions yet happy enough with the free ride they afforded to make a global Communion on the back of an ever-expansive empire.

British or English?

We are now peering over the verge of a rather perilous precipice. This is one that asks us to cast a more discerning and critical eye over the terms 'British' and 'English'. The custom for the English to use the terms interchangeably has been noted by many, and while that may be changing in the 21st century, the presumption and assumptions of previous centuries remain embedded in the legacy. There are reasons for this.

For example, the Bank of England was created in 1694 in the wake of the English suffering catastrophic losses against the French in naval battles. In order to modernise the navy, it needed to be refinanced, and the Bank was created, in part, to facilitate this. The Bank was therefore instrumental in financing and ensuring the safety of the colonies and the sea lanes that connected them. But note, this was the Bank of England—not of Britain. Despite there being one monarch for England, Wales,

Scotland and Ireland, there was no Act of Union, and no political, military or economic union, nor a common market.

Scottish entrepreneurs and civic leaders, fearing that England would gain an empire while Scotland lost out, briefly embarked on their own venture. Between 1698 and 1700, key Scottish investors backed the establishment of a new colony (called New Caledonia) on the Isthmus of Panama. The financial reasoning was that an overland route could connect the Pacific and Atlantic Oceans, and the trade route would yield substantial gains to the Scottish economy. However, around 80% of the settlers died within a year of landing, and the colony was plagued with disease and harassment from Spanish and Dutch colonies, and beset by other problems. Predictably, nearby English colonies declined to come to the aid of their Scottish compatriots.

The economic consequences for Scotland of this ill-fated exercise in colonisation were disastrous. The Panama experiment had attracted huge Scottish investment, with estimates varying from 20% to 40% of all Scotland's liquid wealth committed to the venture. The failure decimated the Scottish economy, which was hardly helped by the closing years of the 17th century being some of the coldest on record, leading to food shortages, crop failures and inflation. Climate crises leave long legacies. There is a well-known maxim that, while the English led the British Empire and its colonial expansion, the Scottish did much of the management of colonies thereafter. There is some truth in this, and that is in no small part due to the organisational graft rooted in local expressions of Presbyterianism.

It is small wonder that by the mid-18th century, many English-owned slave plantations were run by Scottish and Irish managers. These plantations were fortified, too, against the natives and contained small arsenals and supplies to withstand food shortages, sieges and other challenges the settlers might face. What was being done in Virginia was, at the same time, being repeated in Ulster and other English-owned (but British-staffed) colonies much closer to home.

The Scots–Irish supervisors of these fortified agricultural businesses had first-hand experience of being on the outside of the English plantations in Ulster or the new mega-estates in Scotland. Now it was the turn of the Scots–Irish managers, who had been forced to become economic migrants in the wake of the fiscal collapses, to inflict on others what had afflicted them. The onset of the industrial revolution, and the clearing by newly moneyed English landlords of great swathes of Scottish and Irish rural acreage to create large estates and farms, also led to a steady migration of the Scots–Irish populations to the Americas. The English, it seems, have a lot to answer for here.

It takes a particular kind of mental gymnastics to presume that the economics of slavery can be divorced from systemic racism. But if one looks at how Captain James Cook's expeditions to Australia and New Zealand treated the indigenous populations, the exploitation, subjugation and racism are just as apparent—albeit taking different forms. Likewise, the colonisation of Africa and India, and China, too, saw the English blurring the lines between slavery, indenture or servanthood, on the one hand, and racism, on the other. Historically, the English, between 1600 and 1900, enslaved and exploited more ethnic groups than any other nation in the whole of history.

Back home in England, all most people ever saw of this was an accrual of wealth and power, economic benefits, a greater range of consumer goods, and the philanthropy of those who profited from the proceeds of slave-trading. English expansionism—often confusingly camouflaged as the British Empire—was built on such foundations, and the growth and influence of the Anglican Communion followed in its wake. But we should not be in any doubt that the Church of England always functioned as the spiritual wing of English empire-building and expansionism, with all the commercial, political, social and fiscal gains that would come with these new territories.

The Church of England may wish to claim that it cannot be held responsible for the actions and attitudes of the past. Perhaps. Yet while it may not be responsible, it is accountable. King's College London, a specifically Anglican foundation established in 1828, included slave owners like John Gladstone, John Bolton and John Atkins MP as major benefactors. Christopher Codrington endowed a library at All Souls Oxford from the proceeds of slave-trading. From the 16th century to the present, the Church of England has been a direct and indirect beneficiary of the trading that made the empire: it increased the wealth, status and power of the church, transforming it from a national ecclesial body into a global church. Tempting as it may be for some to regard the post-Second World War and post-colonial period in the consciousness of the Church of England as a kind of awakening or enlightenment, I am less sanguine.

Indeed, one detects a kind of dissonance and disease at the heart of English Anglicanism precisely because it lacks self-consciousness in relation to its own role and identity during these centuries. Rather like the English Conservative Party, bishops find themselves caught between being a bulwark of traditional values and culture, on the one hand, and an instrument of progressive or even radical values, on the other. The oscillation between liberalism and conservatism is constant. English Anglicans seem to be obsessed with global status and pedigree but highly resentful of international obligations or interference from overseas. Bishops are rhetorically committed to justice, fairness, transparency and truth in public life, but they are ideologically allergic to those standards operating within the church, or to any attempt by the secular state or courts to intervene in church matters. The Church of England is a law unto itself.

English Mythology

For Anglicans, especially the Church of England, there is a deep reluctance to accept the part that they played in their role as the spiritual wing of the British Empire, with its imperialism and conquests. In the ill-fated 1798 Irish Revolution—the British refer to this as a 'rebellion', which is quite different—Anglican clergy were driven out from their livings in the south and west of Ireland, where they lived comfortably well-off if not wealthy lives, owing to the tithes they drew from the locals.

As demands grew for parliamentary representation for Irish citizens and constituencies that did not require adherence to the doctrines of the Church of England, United Irish militias formed across the island, which brought together Presbyterians, Catholics and others, all seeking to overthrow a class-based hierarchy that was a compact of Anglican landowners and their clergy. The Society of United Irishmen was formed by a trans-denominational alliance of liberal Protestants and Catholics in Belfast in 1791. It quickly spread, as the Society sought reform of the Irish Parliament, the repeal of punitive penal laws, and Catholic emancipation. In the violence that followed, Protestant gentry were even known to contribute funds towards the repairing of Catholic churches that had been burnt in the riots.

The newly formed United Irish militia that emerged all over Ireland called upon the French for support to establish an Irish Republic. In Belfast, Protestants and Catholics stood together and fought together for freedom. Indeed, the first Orange Order to be established through the Society of United Irishmen was a revolutionary group advocating an independent Irish republic that would unite Catholics, Protestants, liberals, radicals and dissenters.

Many Anglican clergy responded to the threat by deliberately unsettling and destabilising the unity and common cause that

Protestants and Catholics had found in their attempt to rid themselves of English rule. This was mostly done through propaganda that stressed alleged Catholic atrocities against Protestants, and by stoking fears of foreign conquest. With the suicide of Wolfe Tone in November 1798, the revolt fizzled out, and the British Act of Union (1800) was hurriedly pushed through Parliament to ensure Ireland remained subordinate. However, this was achieved at huge cost. The 1798 Irish Revolution and its aftermath lasted for a few more years, resulting in brutalities and slaughter not seen since the time of Oliver Cromwell. The British executed Presbyterian and Catholic clergy who had led the fight for a united Ireland. One Anglican clergyman declared with some satisfaction that reprisals meted out in the wake of the failure of the revolution had also destroyed 'the brotherhood of affection' between Catholic and Protestant.

In Hans Kundnani's recent study, *Eurowhiteness*,[6] we are presented with a different take on the post-colonial legacy. Just as European nations mythologised their expansion of capitalism alongside Christian mission—both would bring the benefits of civilisation to the rest of the world—the post-colonial era has needed a new myth to narrate the post-war era. Here, Europe has developed its own entirely new myths of multiculturalism. In fact, Europe—or at least its centres of power—remains very white. Europe, regionally, is more like a kind of nationalism on a continental scale. So, while those who are pro-European Union will invariably demonise nationalism, the EU remains a union of states engaged in self-protection since 1945.

The European Union was meant to make it impossible to have a war between France and Germany ever again—or, for that matter, Britain and Spain. But the devil is in the detail here. The EU makes it hard—economically, legally and politically—to do combat in Europe, but not outside its borders. When the European Economic Community (EEC) Treaty of Rome was signed in 1957, the Belgian and French colonies in Africa were still subject to brutal suppression and economic exploitation. Britain's record was no better. The post-war, post-colonial era created a kind of 'Eurafrica', again under the guise of civilisation that would eventually lead to the once-exploited nations' independence.[7] Provided, of course, that all forms of communism were excluded, and vital raw materials remained under the largely monopolised control of the original colonisers.

In many respects, 'one faith, two worlds' describes three centuries of denial and obfuscation regarding the Church of England's legacy in relation to the Anglican Communion. The Anglican expansiveness that followed in the wake of the growing British Empire was primarily driven by the English. Irish, Welsh and Scottish Anglicans had little part to play in this. The phenomenal growth of the British empire in the 19th century simply masked a fracture that has remained unhealed; a gradual bifurcation between the Old World and the New, between a monarchical and a democratic mindset.

For the British, or rather English, the investment in an ecclesial polity that embodied temperate, mild-mannered reserve, and practised social distancing in pews (long before Covid-19) has more recently been buffeted by the winds of revivalism, charismatic renewal and Pentecostalism. The chill winds of Western secularisation that have blown through congregations have forced conversations—and even the occasional decision—on gender, sexuality and the like. Bishops speak of the church suffering from an 'integrity and trust deficit' over historical cases of child sexual abuse. The perceived lack of integrity in the church, and the truth decay among the bishops that has precipitated the collapse of trust, may be irreversible.[8] As Jeremiah 31:29 famously notes, 'the fathers have eaten sour grapes, and the children's teeth are set on edge'. But this time there is no obvious way back from the pervasive truth rot.

Added to which, the four new horses of the apocalypse are not those of Revelation 6, carrying Death, Famine, War and Conquest. The new horses carry different threats: rising maintenance costs; shrinking and ageing congregations; public mistrust and indifference; and unholy rows about money, sex and power that tear through the church like some plague, to which there is no end or antidote. The Ecclesia-pocalypse has arrived.

In the New World, which takes its relatively new democratic forums as the primary means for debate and resolution, discussion is essential. Anglican Episcopal culture, like the English language, finds that what was shared has also split. So, when it comes to contentious issues like racism or the legacy of slavery, Americans cannot avoid discussing them, while the English, on the whole, just don't like to talk about them. Monarchy silences us before the ruler: democracy requires us to speak.

Crisis? What Crisis?

Democracy is under threat as never before. Autocracy can reign in democratic states, as several modern states can bear witness. The potential for tyranny never entirely vanishes, and when democracy finds itself under the heel of autocracy, the only defence of freedom that is left lies with the law. Autocrats know that too, and will turn on the judiciary, prorogue parliament, change the laws, suspend the constitution, and seize hold of 'emergency powers'.

Crises of any kind can be the occasion for mounting a coup against the citizenry. The church is no different. Many ordinary members of the Church of England have now given up counting the number of suspended livings and front-line parish jobs, or established committees sidelined or made redundant. At the same time, the members decline to sign up to the new agenda for numerical growth—'essential for survival' is the language—that has displaced or overturned the basic character of the church. Here, the New World being ushered in starts to look like a more sinister version of the Old World. This time it will not be Charles I reigning by some 'divine right'. It will be an executive committee with more power and authority than any Stuart king could have dreamed of.

In some respects, this might also help us understand why Americans insist on the separation of church and state (unlike Europe) but are at the same time much keener on religion mixing in politics (unlike Europe). Once you understand what the state represents (e.g., monarchy, unaccountable power, etc.), and what politics can be (e.g., democratic, not autocratic, etc.), then faith in public life evolves differently. But to be clear, this is still one faith, albeit in two different worlds.

In the present age, the Church of England is hopelessly caught between models of governance and oversight that blend plutocracy, autocracy and despotism with monarchical and democratic ideals. It has ontologised quasi-managerialism into a new ecclesiocracy, and has christened it as leadership. The result leaves the episcopacy stranded as resented rulers who no longer represent the will of the people in pews. Furthermore, the continued extension of democratisation through the information revolution means that the clergy, laity, people and nation are not required to take the word of their respective religious leaders as gospel. The first information revolution was writing, namely the Axial Age of the 8th–3rd centuries BCE, referring to the transition from oral cultures and languages to written, and thereby creating an independent bank of social and communal memory. The second age was that of mass printing, which in the 16th century enabled the Reformation.[9] Religion thrived, diversified and expanded across these two eras.

The third age is the present, namely, one of instant, ubiquitous, universal information overload, such that even 'alternative facts' can flourish in a post-truth aeon. Faith communities, and their leaders and religious identity, are struggling with this third age. The constant flow and overload of information increases choice and empowers democracy but also increases the possibilities for individualism. The third age, like the first two, questions the need for intermediaries to hold or interpret knowledge. People can decide for themselves. Anxiety and even anger tend to increase, and authority only becomes more flustered as it loses the trust and confidence of its former adherents.

Church leaders, typically, tend to double down at this point and seek to reassert old patterns of power and authority on a new order. Rather like trying to travel back through time, and govern the church as though there was no printing, the challenges of the third information revolution have yet to be computed by those leading (or revolting within) the Anglican Communion. This third age cannot be countered by charismatic, executive or bureaucratic expressions of quasi-regal power lodged in the episcopacy. It requires a more evolutionary approach to democratic empowerment that can be delivered through devolved channels of information. All the signs at present point to an episcopacy and ecclesiocracy that would rather invest in the kind of opacity that enabled the proverbial Wizard of Oz to preside and rule over the Emerald City. Yet all it takes is for the curtains to be parted to see that there was just an ordinary man pulling the levers of power. Nothing more.

So, to be, or not to be? That is the question for the Anglican Communion. I suspect that we cannot know the answer just yet. An ecclesial polity takes its justification and roots from the ordinary, secular polity. Our age is still one of liberal democracy, so we assume that winning elections that are fair and open is the beginning of a process, not an end. A good government is one that can appreciate and work for all. For most, that is also a start, not an end. For democracy to mature and flower, it must also reify additional qualities and character. It must be fair, tolerant, decent, inclusive, correctable, reformable and capable of receiving criticism. It must be honest and restrained.

In many respects, the vision for a state is like Paul's vision of love and charity, expressed in 1 Corinthians 13. States that are liberal democracies won't be the same everywhere. They will be as different as your neighbours in the street: generous to others, not simply pursuing their own interests; there to help when needed. Majority rule is an act of service to minorities. We are judged on how we treat the weakest, not by how we choose to reward the strongest; the right to vote, and to do so with a clear, free and unfettered conscience; and to have that vote counted fairly. We work against deliberate discrimination; but we also work against inadvertent discrimination.

Yet the English continue to believe in and invest in their national myth: that the empire was basically good and noble, offering Christianity, civilisation, commerce and conquest—the last because British military rule was plainly preferable to anything that preceded it. Apparently, this British empire was a service to the world, and a gift. All the problems that former colonies have experienced in the post-war era demonstrate just how much 'stability' British military rule brought to foreign countries. Even today, many in Britain will opine that such nations were doing just fine until the British left or were forced to leave. Similar sentiments can still be heard regarding the forced enslavement and transportation of Africans to the Americas. It is amazing how such abuses of power and exploitation of peoples can still be justified in the 21st century.[10]

It is only by paying attention to the connections between money, power, labour and ownership, that we begin to get near to the story of Victorian expansion in Christian mission. The industrial revolution enabled the British Empire to expand further. The Church of England simply hitched a ride, with the result that the Anglican Communion came into existence by the last third of the 19th century. The Church of England has never processed this as part of its history. Likewise, the problem for church–state relations in England today is not the close relationship between the Church of England and the government or parliament (which is a common feature of European nations), but rather the 'hidden wiring' of the constitution that binds the Church of England to a different ordering of power—the monarchy and its supporting cadre of elitism, entitlement and unaccountable authority.

8

ANGLICANISM

A MORAL RECKONING

In 1944, the remarkable Trinidadian scholar Eric Williams published his landmark study of *Capitalism and Slavery* (now a Penguin Classic). No historian of colonialism or slavery can ignore Williams's work. The book endures as a seminal moment in the historiography of the British Empire, and shows how slavery directly financed Britain's industrial infrastructure. The trade in cotton, rice, sugar, tobacco, cocoa, coffee, mahogany, rum and many other raw materials helped fund major British ports such as Liverpool and Glasgow and, earlier, Bristol. The huge profits in slavery provided the financial foundations for driving Britain's wealth and economic growth. Beneficiaries ranged from Lloyd's of London (insurance) to Greene King (brewers).

On the eve of the American War of Independence (1775–83), plantation income accounted for 64% of British-American wealth. That same year, Jamaica generated 10% of the net wealth of England and Wales. Jamaica was intensively developed through its plantations and had over 300,000 slaves, while the number of

English settlers numbered under 20,000. The financial returns for slave-owners and for those invested in shipping, insurance, banking, trading and commerce were colossal. Yet the English remain curiously blind to their role in driving the slave trade and continuing to profit from it. The Church of England, likewise, has failed to come to terms with its roles in and rewards from the trade, which resulted in substantial endowment and wealth, and laid the foundation for expansive mission and influence across the British Empire, in what only later became sacralised and saccharine under the banner of the 'worldwide Anglican Communion'. As Maxine Berg and Pat Hudson note:

> the place of African enslaved labour in British … and west European history contrasts with its role in the US. Slavery in the US has an immediate presence because it occurred on domestic soil and left a demographic, racial and social legacy in plain sight. By contrast … British enslavement of Africans remained largely out of sight … The distorting effect of geographical distance on approaches to slavery has been compounded by the foregrounding of Britain's role in abolition … [diverting] historical attention away from Britain's leading part in the operation of the slave trade and in the development of the plantation system.[1]

It is hard to come to terms with the brutality of the slave economy. There were several Berbice slave uprisings in Guyana before the slaughter that took place in 1762–3. British reprisals were brutal, as we noted in the previous chapter. In the adjacent Dutch Guyana (now called Suriname) the methods of reprisal in the 18th century were especially evil and vindictive. One sentence handed out in 1790 stipulated:

> The Negro Joosje shall be hanged from the gibbet by an iron hook through his ribs until dead; his head shall then be severed and displayed on a stake by the riverbank, remaining to be

> picked over by birds of prey. As for the Negroes Wierai and Manbote, they shall be bound to a stake and roasted alive over a slow fire while being tortured with glowing tongs. The Negro girls, Lucretia, Ambia, Aga, Gomba, Marie and Victoria, will be tied to a cross to be broken alive, and their heads severed to be exposed by the riverbank on stakes.[2]

The Dutch, like the British, punished civil disorder against the King ('the sovereign lord'), colony and country with death. Decapitations were normal, with heads speared on poles to warn others. Questioning authority and asserting freedom was a death sentence. The Dutch abolition of slavery did not come until 1863, and even then, much as for those emancipated by the British, the legal resolution to grant freedom required slaves to work on plantations for a further 'decade of transition', which was considered a 'partial compensation for their owners'.

Reparations Reconsidered

Upon the accession of Charles III, the Grenada National Reparations Commission issued a direct appeal for compensation and a proper apology for the role of the British monarchy in slavery. The request was cast in the language of reparative justice—not restorative justice. Grenada, in common with many other exploited Caribbean states, is not looking to reboot its relationship with Great Britain. It is signalling severance. It wants to have its share of a divorce settlement. The theological case for reparation is considerable and deeply rooted in the Old Testament ethics of jubilee. Despite this, the Church of England has stopped well short of using the language of 'reparation' since the church won't be compensating individuals. It is hard to fathom how any remorse or repentance can be genuine if the reparation is to be so hypothetical and aloof.

Unsurprisingly, perhaps, of the twelve countries in the Caribbean Reparation Commission (CARICOM), set up a decade ago, all have expressed their expectation to establish 'the moral, ethical and legal case for the payment of reparations by the Governments of all the former colonial powers and the relevant institutions of those countries, to the nations and people of the Caribbean community for the crimes against humanity of native genocide, the transatlantic slave trade and a racialized system of chattel slavery'.

A recent (2022) trip to Jamaica by the Prince and Princess of Wales (William and Kate) included the staging of several events that were highly reminiscent of the visit of Queen Elizabeth II and Prince Philip many decades previously. This backfired, however, with a notably cool reception from the Jamaican prime minister at the state banquet, and a chiding speech to the royal couple on the legacy of slavery and the socio-economic problems it has bequeathed Jamaica to this day.

When the members of the Church Reparation Action Forum (CRAF) in Jamaica met representatives of the Church of England, to discuss how to repair relations with the people of Jamaica and other countries whose people were enslaved, the rhetorical chasms and cognitive dissonance between the parties surfaced. The Church of England expressed the hope that there could be 'healing' and greater understanding, in order to rebuild relations. In some respects, the privilege and patrimony of progressive dominion theology (and ecclesiology) is most apparent at such junctures—English church leaders still call the shots.

In contrast and in contradiction, the Jamaican churches observed that the funds set aside by the Church of England—£100 million—were 'quite small in terms of the dislocation and damage' perpetrated. The Jamaican churches expressly stated that they would 'not want to be too quick to accept the funds' and thereby miss the deeper problems and greater cause. Jamaican churches suggested that a full apology from the Church of England might be a start. They are still waiting.

The Export of English Morals

The other hidden aspect of what the Church of England has exported to the colonies and cultures across the British Empire is traceable to elitism and class. As we have seen, this has found expression in concerns about 'breeding', fecundity and civilisation and in eliding English values with alleged Christian moral imperatives. In the 19th century, this was apparent in teachings on marriage and family life, ethnicity (and superiority), and views on sexuality.

The homophobic teachings of the Church of England are among its most prolific exports. In 41 of the 53 countries within the British Commonwealth, homosexual conduct is still regarded as a serious crime. This categorisation and legal stigmatisation of homosexuality was largely 'made in England' in the 19th century, and imposed on cultures and emerging countries that hitherto had not been homophobic. This is one of England's less wholesome exports. The Archbishop of Canterbury should accept responsibility for the part the Church of England has played in perpetrating this discrimination and the subsequent injustices—and then publicly repent of them.

Interestingly, the legal regulation of sexual behaviour was exclusively a matter for ecclesiastical law until the 16th century. The involvement and interest of the state—civil law—had to wait until Henry VIII initiated an *Acte for the Punishment of the Vice of Buggerie* (punishable by death) in 1533. This was the same year that Henry VIII declared in another Act of Parliament that

> this realm of England is an Empire, and so hath been accepted in the world, governed by one Supreme Head and King having

> the dignity and royal estate of the Imperial Crown of the same, unto whom a body politic compact of all sorts and degrees of people divided in terms and by names of Spirituality and Temporality, be bounden and owe to bear next to God a natural and humble obedience.[3]

The 1533 'Buggerie Law' was the first civil sodomy law in the world. While anyone could technically be convicted under the Act (e.g., men in sexual congress with women), it was same-sex convictions that were the most common. It wasn't until 1828 that the Act was repealed and replaced by the Offences Against the Person Act of 1828, which focused solely on male same-sex activity. But it is the 1533 Act and its legacy that provided the foundation for sodomy laws exported around the world under British colonial rule over the course of the following centuries.[4]

The last two men to be executed for same-sex acts in England, James Pratt and John Smith, were executed by hanging on 27 November 1835. In 2023, when Uganda—supported by Ugandan Anglican bishops—passed new laws criminalising homosexuality, the ensuing silence from Lambeth Palace was striking. When censure came, it was weak and tepid, falling well short of condemnation. It is hard not to see this abhorrence of homosexuality as an extension of the middle- and upper-class fear and loathing of its very existence and modern explicitness. In contrast, the Lambeth Palace censure of American Episcopal affirmation of same-sex relations has been unmistakable.

Interestingly, republican and non-monarchical polities took a different view from the outset. Just as the French abolished the category of slave in the immediate aftermath of the Revolution, and freed the slaves of French Guiana, so it was that France introduced a new penal code stating that private acts by private individuals were not a matter for state intervention. This made France, with its Penal Code of 1791, the first modern nation to explicitly decriminalise same-sex sexual activity since classical antiquity. The global mapping of human sexuality, the law and churches becomes an interesting exercise in cartography at this point. In virtually every country colonised or conquered by the British Empire, same-sex activity has been named, shamed and criminalised. It has left a particularly punitive legacy in parts of Asia, most of Africa, Australia, and across the Caribbean. By extension, some of the Australian law, derived from Britain, has been handed on to Polynesian countries.

It might just be a coincidence that punitive regulative laws on sexuality find a home in former colonies that still have a constitutional monarchy. Democratic republics, in contrast, have usually been at the forefront of promoting the legal equality of individuals, extending to sexuality and religious freedom. Perhaps the differences between American Episcopalians and English Anglicans on sexuality may, after all, be less about morality and scripture, and much more to do with classism, monarchy and democracy. The mutual incomprehension of both parties in such debates suggests that what divides them is not the visible, but rather that which lies below the surface.

The critiques are hardly in short supply, and are probing. Feminists, those engaging in queer studies or those in the proper pursuit of black history can all testify to how challenging it is to revise a syllabus. Whether it is lobbying for women writers to be placed on faculty readings lists, or reminding students that texts and authors may carry pointed implicit or explicit insights on gender and sexuality, the continual necessity in our critical reforming of curriculum cannot be neglected. There is also a direct correlation between congregational and denominational powers and politics, and the God called upon to legitimate the structuring and exercise of ecclesial authority.[5]

The history of sexuality and gender in the Anglican Communion is inherently bound up with power and vested interests. The 'don't ask, don't tell' protocol that infects and affects all aspects of Anglicanism was learned through the class system of the English and its public schools. The gynophobia and homophobia spring from these sources. The wealth and power that protect and enshrine discretion, complicity and duplicity are cultural and class-based behaviours that have acquired thick ecclesial camouflage and theological veneer. Explicitness, existential honesty and identity integrity in respect of gender and sexuality must, therefore, be subjugated to the interests of the ruling elite, who do not wish to see such matters surface, let alone resolved. This is a peculiarly English problem. The very things the English (middle and upper class) don't want to talk about in public are the same things that cripple the Anglican Communion.[6]

Liberationist approaches to religious history, institutional identity and organisational analysis are therefore crucial. In choosing this liberationist approach, we are placed in a far better position to deal with the difficulties of the past that continue to shape and determine the present. It also allows us to reimagine Anglican disputes and divisions in ways that are more illuminating and potentially more liberating.

Creeping Sectarianism and Centralised Control

If I am right, and intra-Anglican-Episcopalian splits are more the result of Old World and New World divisions, there is greater potential for a new freedom in how we might think about ecclesial life. Critics of this thesis may want to argue that the Church of England has democracy, and point to General Synod, diocesan synods and local parochial church councils (PCCs). Were the democracy functioning at all, one might have some sympathy for this counter-argument. But in truth, General Synod functions more like a party-political conference in a one-party state. There is no opposition to speak of and, except for intra-party divisions on sexuality and gender, no real division. General Synod creates the visual impression of being a parliamentary democracy, but it functions like a one-party political body in a self-reinforcing relationship with the ruling elite.

Thus, motions will 'urge Synod' to improve safeguarding, do more to reach out to young people, act now on climate change, and condemn the invasion of Ukraine. Quite why Synod thinks its views on these issues matter at all to anyone outside the echo chamber is a mystery to most. But sound travels slowly in the General Synod echo chamber, as does light. The Church of England continues to discriminate on grounds of sexuality and gender. Those debates—unresolved in the Church of England—progress at the pace of a partly fossilised snail. But the snail is crowded out by the volume of mammoths. Such elephantine issues will not be on the agenda.

For example, as an organisation, the Church of England has a poor record on accountability, transparency, fairness and integrity. But it would rather you did not know that, let alone discuss it. Clergy complain of low morale, of being bullied by bishops, and poor process. They are joining unions like Unite in record numbers. Others are quietly leaving. The bishops worry about how this all might appear in the media and would rather not look in the mirror. Cue motions on climate change, Ukraine and [fill in the blank]. Meanwhile the people in the pews worry about where their next vicar will come from, and how to afford the roof repairs for a Grade 1 listed medieval church.

The Church of England has retreated—ever so slowly—into its own bunker, equipped with a special echo chamber. It was once a support-based institution but has collapsed into a members-only organisation. Local clergy and chaplains heroically resist this trend and do what they can to continue serving their constituencies and communities, despite the demand to focus on membership drives. Here, the leadership of the Church of England has been seduced by faddish managerialism and brand strategising.

With a sharp decline in affiliation (of any kind) to the Church of England, and a rising tide of cultural disenchantment with its leaders, a serious crisis is emerging. In recent decades, the Church of England has invested significant time, energy and money in branding, marketing, mission and reorganisation. Every initiative has resulted in greater public distancing from the Church of England, and a steeper decline in attendance.

The Church of England leadership now functions like some unaccountable executive in a political party (communist, pre-Berlin Wall) that cannot step outside its own bubble. Speeches at conferences get longer, the agenda less relevant, and the procedural motions riddled with minor points of minutiae. Party loyalists are rewarded, and dissenters quickly distanced or, if they persist, denounced and denigrated. There is a faint whiff of dictatorship in the wind. The informal protocol and practice perpetrated by the leadership is a kind of 'lidism'—a word coined by Professor Paul Rogers in his studies of democracy, peace and reconciliation. 'Lidism', as the word suggests, is the term for a leadership trying to close the lid on scandal, shut down alternative viewpoints, and otherwise contain dissent.[7]

The archbishops have been pulled into an occasional long-distance commuting relationship with reality. The only way they can control reality is to retreat or try to keep it in some airtight jar. Debates on sexuality, gender and equality, to say nothing of those on reparation for victims of abuse, are just 'canned'. The archbishops will simply set up another review group to consider the work of the previous review group that was taking forward the ideas that the original review group considered. That way, the issues are contained. But the public (rather like voters at elections) no longer support or trust a body that does not seem credible or relevant to their daily lives. Operating within a culture that is shaped by privilege and patrimony, and that is non-transparent and unaccountable even to loyal members, will not win new converts to the cause.

That said, aspects of the Church of England continue to be an important English collective national treasure. Few want a relationship with their remote delivery depot. Likewise for the Church of England at local levels, parish ministry and chaplaincy continue to be cherished and valued, making appreciable differences to community and civic life. Few want to know anything about the diocesan headquarters. Yet as centralisation increases, this is translating less and less into church attendance. The more the central governance of the church tries to invent new initiatives to address its own numerical anxieties and other neuroses, the more the public back away.

To recover public trust, the Church of England would need to submit to external scrutiny, and demonstrate transparency and genuine accountability, and a fully engaged integrity. The trouble is, like other institutions that lose authority, power, respect and trust, it is afraid of what else might be found if external and independent scrutineers are allowed to probe further. Yet this deadlock can be broken, as institutional crises in countries such as Australia demonstrate. With scandals in Australian policing, government, school, churches and the military, there was the political and intellectual will to develop 'integrity frameworks' to oversee institutions, regulate them, and take account of public concerns.

An integrity framework would be a wholly new concept to most English people, but, like the Nolan Principles, the Australian National Audit Office has developed an overarching structure for supporting and managing the integrity of institutions. The Australian National Integrity Framework arose out of scandals in policing, military service, government—and was latterly applied to the churches in the light of their opacity on sexual abuse cases. The Integrity Framework serves to assist in ethical decision-making and risk, fraud and misconduct management.[8] It handles conflicts of interest, vested interests, whistleblowing and corruption, as well as the covering up of incompetence and misconduct. Its enduring focus is on promoting integrity as a value that is embedded in our work and culture.

The lack of an integrity framework for the Church of England means that it will continue to engage in bullying behaviours, obfuscate and evade scrutiny, avoid transparency and accountability, and seek to remain outside normative standards and codes of conduct for public life. The consequences of this will fall upon a never-ending supply of victims seeking justice and reparation. The nature of monarchical power that lives in English Anglican episcopacy is such that bishops don't have any real accountability. They need never explain their action or inaction, are aloof from scrutiny, and never truly apologise for their sins of omission, culpability or liability. The result is the erosion of trust and confidence in the person and the roles they inhabit. Like a monarch, they need never respond to an immediate issue unless they choose to, and the response will in any case be carefully crafted by a communications courtier. The ultimate end, however, will be the dismantling and death of an institution that was once loved and admired by the public, but that can no longer command the faith and respect of its employees and people who once gave their lives to work for it.

The present state of the Church of England would pose an enormous challenge for the very best estate agent to elicit serious interest in, let alone a sincere offer. True, the Church of England is not for sale. But it is constantly on the lookout for long-term and loyal tenants who will take care of the store front as though they were the owners. Upkeep, appearance, productivity, regional brand compliance and purpose are devolved to the local occupiers, who mostly do an extremely good job on very tight budgets.

For all their labour, laity and clergy will receive little thanks from their somewhat distant landlords, who are only interested in the productivity and turnover—and compliance, too, unless diversification delivers growth. We now have a situation in which the Church of England's senior leadership are remortgaging the church on a regular basis. In this, they are banking on the past and borrowing from the future to try to resolve the present issues and crises. As many will know with their own homes, it is risky—and only makes sense if the value of your property goes up. But as the social, moral, spiritual and intellectual capital of the Church of England is all in negative equity, there may be a default at any point.

However, remortgaging the Church of England is a risky business. And bridging loans are unlikely to be extended. Local branches may want to start asking some quite basic questions. Who really owns this business? Who does it serve, and for what purposes? Who are these people in regional and national headquarters, telling others how to run things locally and cutting local support while increasing their own?

To be sure, obedience is a valuable gift and charism for any church or denomination. But it depends on trust, not force or presumption. A trusting person rightly assumes that a trustee will respond to the trust invested in them. A trusting person will assume the trustee is bound in relation to those beholden to such trust. Most of us assume the trustee has moral obligations to help the person who has placed their trust in an organisation or institution. We would all assume that a trustee should be inherently trustworthy, competent, fair, truthful, honest and committed to integrity.

Yet bishops still rule and reign within their monarchical versions of Anglicanland, albeit with greatly diminished authority and recognition. Here, we reflect that the fashion of a bishop signing their name with a cross to precede their Christian name—for example, +Peter or +Susan, or +Dunelm or +Oxon—is a late development in Anglicanism and has increased in direct proportion to clergy and bishops having less 'rank status' in the public domain. For centuries, bishops signed with their first name, and possibly the name of their see afterwards—but only if writing formally to those beyond their diocese. It is a measure of how remote and 'other' they regard themselves that all correspondence has now been subjected to hierarchical formality. Lest we forget who they are.

Anglican bishops proceed, moreover, as though they are somehow protecting the vulnerable, and that without their intervention, society will unravel. The late-19th- and early-20th-century statements on women reflected concerns the (male) bishops have *for* women. Debates on birth control are concerns *for* the family and society. Later debates on sexuality were, likewise, narrated as concerns *for* natural order, stable family life and Christian 'tradition'.

Suffice it to say, the moral reasoning of the Church of England ignores basic principles of jurisprudence, legal accountability, oversight and governance. The small cadre of lawyers working in the discreet field of ecclesiastical law maintain the separatism of the church from wider accountability and regulation. The bishops still presume to lecture the wider world on what is good for it, and what it should avoid. But any talk of regulating unaccountable bishops, introducing equality into personnel problems within the church, and otherwise acting fairly, as a public body should—well, the silence from the bishops will be deathly. Within the Church of England, the primary 'tradition' is to prioritise expediency over principle, in the hope of maintaining a calmness and keeping some peace.[9]

What ultimately comes to pass is quite sobering. Bishops resisting normative progressive cultural currents are destined to become footnotes in history. They may eventually feature in obscure journals and expensive monographs—exemplars of eccentric quirks, pastoral insensitivity and intellectual backwardness. Thereafter, they are otherwise quietly forgotten.

The English Revolution came about because people no longer trusted the monarch to put the interests of the people first. Charles I was executed because those prosecuting sensed that no matter what guarantees the monarch might give, no king could be trusted to keep their word. The power of the autocrat lies in the capacity to confuse the audience as to what is real and what is an act. The whole principle of ruling by 'divine right' was, under Charles I, another form of progressive dominion theology. The same problems pertain to English Anglican episcopacy. With the role of judge, ruler, prosecutor, defender and pastor held in one office, bishops are able to implement or ignore ecclesiastical law, and are also free to disregard or interpret secular law without any consistency or accountability. That is, ultimately, a pale reflection of the caprice found in many small-state medieval monarchies. But as a model for a modern democratic polity—in the church or the world—it is undeserving of trust and unworthy of assent. As church leaders are discovering, obedience and compliance are increasingly hard to obtain.

9

COMMUNION AND COMMONWEALTH

In the mind's eye of those who speak fondly of the Anglican Communion, the debt to the coherences narrated of the British Empire and the unity provided by the service of imperialism is obvious in shaping conceptualisations of a trans-continental ecclesial community. I can recall, even recently, bishops speaking with wistful nostalgia of a denomination that stretches from Malagasy to Mongolia, from Sweden to South Africa, from India to Tasmania, and from the United Kingdom across the whole of the Americas. Such nostalgia paints a rose-tinted picture of global coverage, as though the extensity of the Church of England (or Anglican Communion) were akin to every community having a post office and a postal service.

The reality is different, however. Coverage is patchy, and it is increasingly difficult to understand how in terms of compatibility, coherence and commonality the various components constituting this church are able to claim the name 'Communion'. Even if the term is used, it is plain that many who use such language no longer mean the same thing. Furthermore, others regard the term as problematic—either a dangerous fiction or a disingenuous description. 'Anglicanism', it seems, is increasingly a term of ascription that is contested and divisive.

Honesty and clarity about the past can only help, otherwise amnesia and myth-making memory will reign. The roots of the Anglican Communion and the Commonwealth arise from the Empire, which was driven by trade, consumerism, military action and imperial expansionism. This was, primarily, an English project, in which the Church of England served as the legitimating spiritual arm and capitalised on the territorial expansion, which afforded it an aura of catholicity.

But how involved was the Church of England in the competition and scramble for imperial power and pre-eminence across the globe? Daniel O'Connor[1] notes that all British ships of a certain size—navy and merchant navy—were required by English law to have Church of England chaplains on board. While it is undeniable that the Scots played a significant role in the administration and expansion of the East India Company—especially in parts of India and Hong Kong—overall economic control by the English was normative. The Church of England benefited directly and indirectly from this control, in a way that the (Presbyterian) Church of Scotland was seldom able to access or profit from.

O'Connor notes that the Church of England clergy in cahoots with the East India Company were often called preachers, ministers, padres and chaplains. Over 665 of them served in the East India Company alone, and with the Royal Navy chaplains factored in on top, the figure for the English expansion of the Empire, dating from 1601 to the winding up of the East India Company, easily amounts to well over 1,100. For the Church of England clergy, this was all valorised as 'missionary venture', and those prepared to undertake it were celebrated back home in the shires as much as they were in their postings abroad. The East India Company's merchants were called adventurers precisely because they ventured their money in the risky markets of the Spice Islands and the fabulously wealthy Mughal Empire.

In one sense, the Company's entire 250 years constituted an exciting and dangerous adventure, and created over time, by violence and corruption, an empire that largely served the interests of the English. Contrary to the common view, the Company always claimed a Christian identity, and that was overwhelmingly gifted courtesy of the Church of England. The role of the chaplains on their voyages and in their trading 'factories' and garrisons was to guard the moral welfare and morale of their operations. This the chaplains did with varying conviction and success.

In all this, we should note that the Irish only ever secured a net deficit in any English-sponsored military empire-building endeavours. The legacy for the Irish continues to this day. At Mass, men will still tend to kneel on one knee only—a culturally learned defensive posture in the event of their church being raided. Mass is less than half an hour and has no singing, lest the congregation worshipping in secret be overheard and discovered. To this day, many Irish only sing in bars, but never in churches. Fear of English oppression leaves strange legacies.

Weather Forecasts

In terms of climatology, we might say that the single unbroken 'continent' of belief imagined by those using the term 'Communion' has been subjected to substantial social, political, moral, cultural, theological and ecclesial 'global warming'. The hot waters of disputation have cut through soft earth and entirely overwhelmed low-lying land. The continent of the Communion is now a series of islets, lochs and territories that were once one but are now many. The union has been consumed by forces it could not control, and has evolved into a federation of islands that don't necessarily relate to or communicate well with one another.

To those who still incline towards 'Communion-speak', it does not matter much if this former unbroken continent is now a federation of semi-submerged islands. Many kinds of collective belonging can be christened as a company, communion or corporation. But the term 'Communion' can no longer carry the original weight and same freight that an imperial empire, or even a United Kingdom, lent by way of affinity. Recent turbulence in the history of the Union—British—amplifies more differences than what unites. North–South divisions, economic disparity, Brexit, Scottish independence and more besides suggest that this national church—the Church of England—is only the church of the English. It is not British. Nor is it especially European. Its place in the Commonwealth is ambivalent, too, and is unable to confidently own any clear identity.

Meanwhile, as the union of the United Kingdom creaks ever more loudly under the weight of its own English-originated mythology, it becomes harder to deny that the forces that propelled the Church of England Abroad into becoming the leader of the worldwide Anglican Communion now lack currency and legitimacy. Monarchical power and rule, the culture of which still dominates the Church of England, are largely rejected by modern republics and democracies. The identity of an anti-Catholic Protestant nation, where the religion established is, by law, Protestant, looks increasingly precarious in an age in which few subscribe to such beliefs. In a secular age, few will be convinced that the national security of its people, and the independence of the nation as a free entity, are protected by privileging Protestantism and explicitly excluding Catholicism.

Furthermore, the underlying statistical trends for church membership suggest that the powers and privileges of the established church no longer reflect popular support. There is no serious public mandate for one denomination to enjoy automatic rights to sit in the House of Lords and legislate for the union of nations as a whole, when the vast majority of the English population have no say or stake in such representation.

The imperial expansionism of the British Empire in the 18th and 19th centuries brought Anglicanism along with it. To begin with, all of the colonial churches were under the jurisdiction of the Bishop of London. Only after the American Revolution do we start to encounter parishes, priests and bishops who owed nothing in fealty to the Old World. The New World that began to develop in the late 18th century was pragmatic, democratic, enlightened and post-colonial. In many respects, the history of the Church of England thereafter can be seen as a national church searching for global legitimacy. The Anglican Communion was still, even in 1850, non-existent. Overseas Anglican provinces, except for America, were essentially the Church of England Abroad.

The modern Anglican Communion, unsurprisingly, needed modernity in order to exist at all. The invention of the telegraph, steam-powered shipping and the railways made an enormous difference to the development of 'high imperialism' in the later 19th century as well as to that of the Anglican Communion. It was in this context that the Lambeth Conferences emerged. Obviously, the first Lambeth Conference preceded the concept of the Anglican Communion. But what caused the first Lambeth Conference? The factors in play were variable. Modern communication, including relatively rapid transportation, had led to several startling epiphanies in the Church of England. As the 'Church of England Abroad' gradually morphed into a set of loosely connected provinces that were bound by a common culture and common liturgies but not universal legal ties, this meant that the implicit bonds of unity would need to be made more explicit. For the English, of course, who have no written constitution, any emergent structural framework was almost bound to be configured through collegiality. For the Church of England Abroad, the differences and potential areas of disunity needed to be addressed. But without a common legal framework, how could this be?

The initial impetus for a Lambeth Conference—gathering all the Anglican bishops from across the world—was first suggested in a letter to the Archbishop of Canterbury by John Henry Hopkins in 1851. Hopkins was the Bishop of Vermont, and his seedling proposal fell on fertile ground, as the Anglican missionary agencies were also meeting that same year in an attempt to coordinate their mission activity in the colonial world. In 1865 the Canadian Anglican Synod dispatched a letter to the Archbishop of Canterbury, Charles Thomas Longley, urging him to convene a gathering. Longley assented, and the first gathering took place in 1867, with all 144 Anglican bishops from around the world invited. In the event, 76—about half the number of invitees—attended. Some were wary of any centralising control that might emerge, while others stayed away from a gathering that would merely discern the mind of the bishops regarding the issues of the day.

Such was the scepticism about the gathering within the Church of England that the Dean of Westminster Abbey declined to allow the closing service to be held there, as he was unsure about the status and presence of prelates 'not belonging to our Church'. From the outset, the Lambeth Conference determined that it was not a governing body; that any resolutions it carried had no legislative authority but would have moral and spiritual weight; and that the gatherings were to discuss matters of practical interest in order to set guidelines for future action. The first conference met in Lambeth for just four days, with the sessions all in private.

It is not our purpose here to describe or list the business of the first Lambeth Conference. Suffice it to say, the pulse of controversy and disagreement was present from the outset. The Archbishop of York and several other English bishops boycotted the event, as they felt it would increase confusion about 'controversial issues', thereby implying that the fact that there was any discussion at all on some matters signalled compromise. The boycotting bishops would have had in mind the controversial John William Colenso, first Bishop of Natal. Colenso had been deposed and excommunicated for heresy because of his allegedly unorthodox views on the Old Testament.

Colenso was a Cornish cleric who had studied mathematics at St John's College Cambridge. He'd also served as rector of a Norfolk parish, and been influenced by the theology of F.D. Maurice and Samuel Taylor Coleridge. Colenso dedicated a book of sermons and reflections to Maurice. But it was Colenso's views as a theologian and biblical scholar that established a paradigm for future Lambeth Conferences. In 1853 Robert Gray, Bishop of Cape Town, had invited Colenso to become the first Bishop of Natal. Colenso learnt Zulu, published the first Zulu grammar, and translated the New Testament into Zulu too. He took his ministry seriously and meant his mission to be appropriately enculturated.

But in 1855 Colenso published his *Remarks on the Proper Treatment of Polygamy*, in which, using his Old Testament scholarship and theological mind, he presented a cogent Christian-based case for the tolerance of polygamy. In his published commentary on Romans (1861), Colenso also questioned the doctrine of eternal damnation for non-believers. He pointedly refused to preach to the Zulu that their ancestors—who were not Christian—were to be unavoidably damned to hell. Colenso's radical biblical scholarship, together with his no less radical conviction that Africans were not inferior to the white settlers and that all were equal, caused consternation and controversy in his day. Critics of Colenso refused to countenance the possibility of biblical fallibility or that some parts of scripture should be read as analogy, not history.

In 1863, Bishop Robert Gray sought to depose Colenso. Colenso refused to appear at the local trial and instead appealed directly to the Privy Council in London, which determined that Gray had no power to coerce Colenso. The Privy Council declined to rule on the allegations of heresy. But despite Gray limiting Colenso's preaching thereafter, consecrating a rival bishop and establishing a rival diocese and cathedral, the effect of the Privy Council ruling was to leave Colenso in place. Colenso continued to champion local African causes, thereby further estranging him from colonial society.

Several of the bishops attending the first Lambeth Conference wanted Colenso's views to be condemned. But others, including Archbishop Longley, declined to issue any condemnation on the grounds that this would cause hurt to others and rupture the emergent Anglican Communion. Colenso's advocacy on behalf of several falsely imprisoned African chiefs on Robben Island made it awkward for the Lambeth Conference to move against a bishop who, to this day, is known as 'Sobantu' (Father of the People).

Polygamy never really did get resolved across a century or more of Lambeth Conferences, and as a divisive issue it has quietly dropped off the agenda. To some extent, as we can see even from the first Lambeth Conference, the hidden agenda being addressed was to minimise and address the chaos, complexity and complications in being a global church. The Church of England Abroad opted for applying the rhetoric of 'Communion' to the ever-increasing bandwidths of belief and practice that were taking shape across the world. Could it have evolved differently? Perhaps. But to consider that, we need to explore the concepts of chaos, complexity and complications in more depth.

Complexity and Complication

There is no neat way of distinguishing between complexity and complication. Dictionaries link the two terms and root both in being concerned with the interconnectedness of parts. However, most of us would agree that the human body is a complex organism—but that we are not at risk of dying from complexity. The risks come from complications—a malfunction of a part, disease or some other kind of harm. To express this in corporate terms—social bodies, communities and associations, for example—complexity can be built in, and may be essential. It does not follow, however, that something complex is inimically affected by complications. The latter require attention; the former is simply the product of organic evolutionary development.

In general terms, we can say that complexity is an emergent structure. The heart is a complex organ, and such organs have evolved over millions of years. What your heart doesn't need is additional complications. When we encounter these, the complexity reduces the organ's function, and the parts become greater than the sum. Likewise, the tipping point for a functioning healthy society is when the whole complex is undermined by the complications of its constituent parts.

From earliest times, the church has been the development of a complex system from a simple system. Households of faith became more organised, and, with that, over time, hierarchical, routinised and bureaucratised. A global church is a complex body that develops over time. The complexity is tested by the challenges, chaos and complications that the body is required to absorb and address. But how does this demarcation help us address the complexity (and complications) of the worldwide Anglican Communion?

To partly answer this, we can turn to David Hume's *Treatise on Human Nature* (1738), which was concerned with moral reasoning, sentiment and sense. Hume was a leading light in the Scottish Enlightenment, and in his *Treatise* he wrote with great prescience on the relationship between passions, desires and rational-moral reasoning. On this relationship, he notes:

> Nothing is more usual in philosophy, and even in common life, than to talk of the combat of passion and reason, to give the preference to reason, and assert that men are only so far virtuous as they conform themselves to its dictates. Every rational creature, it is said, is obliged to regulate his actions by reason; and if any other motive or principle challenge the direction of his conduct, he ought to oppose it, till it be entirely subdued, or at least brought to a conformity with that ... Reason [however] is, and ought only to be, the slave of the passions, and can never pretend to any other office than to serve and obey them.[2]

Hume is helpful at this point, because we already know that we can find any number of moral, theological, ecclesial, historical or otherwise rational accounts for the existence and persistence of the Anglican Communion. There will always be, and always have been, legitimating narratives for a pan-global church. However, Hume's quibble is not with such reasoning. He sees it merely as the slave of passions and desires. The question therefore arises: what were the *sentiments* that caused the Anglican Communion to exist and have driven its rationale ever since?

Here, we enter a much more fertile inquiry. If, as seems obvious, the theological justification for the Anglican Communion is not its progenitor but rather the progeny of such union, then what were the sentiments, desires and passions that led to the reasoning for the Anglican Communion? The debacle over Colenso casts some light onto this, namely the slippage between unity and uniformity, and the desire for control. But, going much further back, we can also deduce that the driver for the expansion of the Empire—English imperialism, no less—was a vehicle that carried religious freight.

The Church of England Abroad is an evolving iteration of the bulwark that seeks to temper the influence and power of continental Catholicism. An English Protestant monarch (whether king, queen, emperor or empress) and the supporting national church are the guarantor of the ascendant hierarchy, at home and abroad. In many respects, this is what the rhetoric of 'Commonwealth' came to mean even though, plainly, not much of the wealth was ever going to be common. The sentiment of 'commonwealth' serves the power interests that promote the polity and the language.

As Luis Bermejo SJ has noted,[3] passions play an integral part in the formation of complex systems such as the church. All creeds were formed through fractious meetings that were rooted in controversy. Christians—and perhaps especially Anglicans—sometimes forget that the Holy Spirit works through meetings (often taking a long time, and over many years); it is how Episcopalians arrive at truth. Bermejo argues that there were always four stages in the evolution of complex ecclesial life: communication, conflict, consensus and communion. All disputes within the Anglican Communion are refracted through this fourfold process. That, argues Bermejo, was how the Holy Spirit moved through the church.

Bermejo asserts that it was never the case that only the last of these four stages—communion—was the 'spiritual' stage, and the three previous stages were merely preliminary. The work of the Holy Spirit was also manifest in conflict—helping the church to be pruned and refined. Thus, Anglicans agree on what the Bible says—but not always on what it means. The polity is invariably more relational than propositional. For that reason, and to concur with Hume's observations on sentiment, Anglicans can sometimes be characterised as more interested in *how* they disagree, and a little less in *what* they actually disagree on. Style may matter more than substance.

Catching Up with Culture

There is a maxim that declares the Church of England is lagging about 25 years behind the times. Some think it may be more like 50 years. Either way, one can be sure that the tried, tested and discarded practices of yesteryear will eventually be utilised as 'cutting edge' for the Church of England. It is hard to find any recent review of leadership, strategy or management written by the church that was not a couple of decades out of date at the point of publication. Anglicans like to talk about relating to contemporary culture but are poor at telling the time. The problems they address and the solutions they propose are invariably out of date.

For Anglicans across the world, the reality of a global church shaped by a post-Enlightenment and post-colonial culture has eventually caught up with ecclesial practice. There is another fourfold distinction to note at this point.[4] Jim Davis and Michael Graham, drawing on the work of Tim Keller, assert that Christian faith is a 'four-chapter gospel' (or perhaps four-square?):

1. Creation—God made it, and it was good.
2. Fall—humanity sinned, and Creation was cursed.
3. Redemption—Jesus saves sinners and inaugurates the new Kingdom of God.
4. Consummation—Jesus' kingdom is ultimately realised and Creation is redeemed.

Granted, this is a characterisation of the Christian story. But as characterisations go, it is not unreasonable to suggest that the story of Anglican imperial missionary preaching and endeavour from 1700 to the end of the 20th century focused exclusively on Fall and Redemption, to the exclusion of Creation and

Consummation. The message preached was one of personal salvation. This is the Old World gospel.

The New World gospel, which requires new wineskins, is one in which Creation and Consummation—with emphases on ecology, environment, decolonisation, equality, justice, peace, fairness and social responsibility—are to the fore. It is not that Fall and Redemption are relegated or excluded. Rather, the New World apologetics requires Creation and Consummation to be treated as equal entities within the four-chapter gospel paradigm. The one faith, two world paradigm is most clearly in focus at this point, and the lines of demarcation are not North–South or conservative–liberal. All corners or stages of the paradigm are committed to the same Jesus Christ, the same creeds and gospel, and the same Christian faith. In many cases, the same liturgy, styles of clerical apparel, customs and cultures are virtually identical. This is manifestly one faith.[5] But it is the worlds they imagine, inhabit and seek to reify that are different—though this is hardly an easy gestation.[6]

The Old World is of the hoary conversionist culture, and is subject to decay. Indeed, it is degenerating, slowly but surely. The New World is of an innovative culture that seeks the salvation of Creation itself. The democratising forces at work in the New World cannot ignore the disenfranchised, marginalised and disinherited. The New World no longer asks or demands to be lectured on the old gospel story. It wants the gospel to be demonstrated. This is the 'tell me' versus 'show me' approach to the gospel proclamation. The Old World will keep telling, talking and lecturing: the New World wants to see change and know transformation.

Perhaps the turn the Church of England now needs to take at this point is to the left, not the right. It also needs a thorough audited account of Englishness in the past and what it now constitutes in the present. Instead of being the Conservative Party at prayer, it can recover its roots as a local agency that cares for others, serves the community, and faithfully worships, yet does not seek to justify itself by being clothed in the rhetoric of success and growth. To take this turn would only require looking to the radical nature of its founder, Jesus. To be the body of Christ today means the church—especially a national church—should operate more like a field hospital than a customs house: there to tend and care, not to tax and control.

To be sure, the present age is not for the faint-hearted. Local churches and congregations, for the most part, remain remarkably resilient communities of grace in these demanding times. It is not easy to plan for tomorrow, never mind outline a strategy or vision that might inspire believers (and even work?) for the next ten years. Too often, such talk in the recent past has turned out to be a mere chimera. Anglicans need new purpose and direction, not based on survival, but on service; not rooted in preserving social status or hierarchy, but in spiritual wisdom to enrich the world.

It is tempting to anticipate the future, and many leaders try to 'get ahead of the curve' (or use other clichés that imply they can see around the corner, or over the horizon, or read a 'dashboard'). The 21st century demands action where words and assurances once sufficed. The Church of England Abroad has not perceived that the desires of countries and communities have changed forever. Only when the Church of England's leadership ceases to imagine that the Anglican Communion can be managed and changed by how it thinks and speaks, and instead embraces the (obvious) epiphany that it is only by how it acts and loves that the commonwealth of belief can survive, will there be a revolution. But at present, the episcopal custodians of the Church of England—largely white, male and cerebral—hope that their words can be spun into new webs of meaning. This is Old World thinking. In the New World, it is the fruits of love and faith that count.

10

THE ENGLISH ENIGMA

Does the unity of the Anglican Communion lie in some liturgical agreement or in methods of theological reasoning, ecclesial governance and shared resources? Plainly not. It is a fact that both the Church of England and the Church of Scotland, as national Protestant churches, owe their very existence to the rejection of supranationalism. Both churches set out to represent and cater for their specific constituency, with Scotland as Presbyterian and England as Anglican. Neither of these ecclesial polities planned or imagined they would become international. It is perhaps especially odd for Presbyterianism to be a 'national' church at all, since its theology hardly lends weight to such claims. Anglicanism in the 17th century came to a different mind on nationhood, but that was very much bound up with English defensiveness against Catholicism.

For sure, unity between the bishops and their flocks cannot be presumed. Consistent polling data shows that English Anglicans are by majority Conservative voters, and this is increasing as the population ages and churchgoers continue to become more elderly. On the Brexit vote of 2016, both the

Archbishops of Canterbury and York nailed their colours to the mast of pro-European Remainers. But they were out of step with their congregations on this, who had gradually become disenchanted with the supranationalism of the European Union and also started to show signs of moving towards more right-wing economic politics.[1]

There is no 'Christian vote' in the UK of the kind one may identify in the United States. However, we can note that, historically, Labour has tended until recently to perform strongly in Catholic heartlands. This has of late led to a pronounced disparity between English concerns with the union of Great Britain and the wider shifts towards devolution. In both Scotland and England, the church and nation were virtually contiguous until the last quarter of the 20th century. But as both churches have suffered significant collapses in morale, numerical strength and cultural purchase in the 21st century, the elision of Englishness and Anglicanism can no longer be assumed, any more than Scottishness and Presbyterianism.

An Untied Kingdom

If national unity is no longer held together by a common, default denomination, then what does the unity inside these churches look like? With cultural or ethnic normativity now pluralised and diverse, what does hold a denomination together? Here it is worth briefly reflecting on the issue of liturgical unity. Samuel Seabury was consecrated as the first bishop of the US Episcopal Church on the condition that he adopted the Scottish Prayer Book. That was done, formally, in 1789. Yet the Scottish Episcopal Prayer Book had a chequered history. The version taken back to Connecticut was the 1764 Scottish Liturgy.

Previous to this, the Scottish Reformation under John Knox had taken a more Calvinistic turn. With the accession of James

VI of Scotland to the English throne (as James I), an attempt was made to align the English and Scottish Prayerbooks, but without securing agreement. Charles I also attempted this, and here the intervention of the Archbishop of Canterbury William Laud was more successful in 1637. In fact, Laud's Scottish liturgy was closer to his more Catholic theology than it was to the predecessor to the English Book of Common Prayer of 1662. The differences between the Scottish and English Prayerbooks were largely matters of theological emphasis in respect of the Eucharist. Naturally, the adoption of the Scottish rite did not require worshippers to pray for the monarch.

The past is a foreign country with a complex state of affairs. Worldwide global Anglicanism is complicated and fluid; so is the Church of England; and so is the history of England and of Englishness itself. Those on the inside of these bubbles often lack self-awareness and even self-consciousness. The English are past and present masters of assuming they are the planet Earth's default normative people, to whom every race, tribe and nation naturally looks for guidance and leadership. The English heavily over-invest in their history, presuming that others envy the glories of empire and its legacies, including Christianity and civilisation. But that is not the view that travellers outside England necessarily encounter.[2]

Nor is it the view across the rest of the United Kingdom and Ireland. It took just over a century from the much-promoted unity of the monarchy between England and Scotland under James I (or VI if you are Scottish) in 1603 to develop into a political union (1707). And it took another century for Ireland to be incorporated into what became Great Britain (1801). However, the formation of this united kingdom into *the* United Kingdom was hardly a smooth journey for the churches. With the fires of spiritual strife still smouldering well into the 17th century, religious divisions continued to cause internecine civil war.

The 16th century also left Britain with an odd religious geography and legacy. The majority of the Scots were Presbyterian—yet Charles I had still sought to impose bishops and the Book of Common Prayer on a dissenting majority. England's Puritans and Presbyterians were undoubtedly supportive of Oliver Cromwell's government, but they were a religious minority—the majority being quite content with the Book of Common Prayer and bishops. The Irish, meanwhile, remained Roman Catholic and resentful of the Presbyterian and Church of England settlers in Northern Ireland, who established plantations and estates and subjugated the local population.

Going to war over the legitimacy and power of bishops and whether to use a prescribed Prayerbook would seem inconceivable to modern readers. However, the Bishops' Wars – two brief conflicts—were fought between Charles I and the Scottish from 1639 to 1640. The wars were prompted by Scottish resistance to Charles's endeavour to enforce Anglican observances in the Scottish Church, and the determination of the Scottish to abolish episcopacy. The Bishops' Wars were the first of the conflagrations known collectively as the Wars of the Three Kingdoms (1639–52) in Scotland, England and Ireland.

The purpose here is not to detail the course of these wars, but rather to highlight the enigmatic nature of the countries and culture in which they took place. For it is such complexity that helps us to understand the tensions that subsequently emerged in global Anglicanism long before the worldwide Anglican Communion was even conceived of as an entity. The historical approaches taken by Diarmaid MacCulloch and Eamon Duffy, while not aligned in their methods or conclusions, have nonetheless both shown how patchy and variegated English religious reform was at local and regional levels, irrespective of any national resolutions.

Scotland was no different, of course. And since Scotland holds one of the most important keys to understanding the emergence of independent American Episcopalianism in the 18th century, some brief observations are worth noting, if the enigma of Englishness and British identity is ever to be unpacked and decoded. Like all coding, it is not straightforward.

First, the welcome reception of Presbyterianism and the rejection of Anglicanism was variable. Aberdeenshire and other parts of north-east Scotland remained relatively well-disposed to Anglicanism throughout the 17th and 18th centuries. This was partly a matter of class, with large estates and landowners sympathetic to the Royalist cause. But it was also a part of Scotland that had kept strong connections with both Protestants and Roman Catholics through education, commerce and even military action in north-western Europe. In the same way that both sides in the Spanish Civil War drew some brigades from Britain, the Thirty Years War (1618–48) saw Scottish mercenaries and regiments fighting mainly for the Protestant powers, although some were to be found fighting for the Catholic alliance. This reflected the tensions that persisted in Scotland and were to continue until the end of the Stuart claim to the throne.

Second, the palette of regional differences in Scotland in respect of aspects of religious reform is worth noting. Resistance to episcopacy was strong in Glasgow, probably due to the perception or misperception that bishops represented English classist domination and would enforce baronial rule and taxes to add to *their* wealth. The same was less true in Edinburgh, where the stigmatisation of English episcopacy was relatively weak, and bishops were regarded as a potential indication of good social order.

Third, just as there were divisions between east and west Scotland, so were there highland and lowland divisions, which in turn reflected landed and financial interests. Some clans were Jacobite and Royalist sympathisers or supporters. Others had never abandoned Roman Catholicism despite having made accommodations because of the new state-imposed faith. Others had embraced the order and simplicity of the Presbyterian Kirk and would have resisted a model of English baronial episcopal power operating north of the border. The rejection of Charles I's attempted imposition of the English Book of Common Prayer was therefore bound up with resistance to English monarchical forms of power, authority and control mediated through the episcopacy.

Fourth, national culture and religious geography have a complex and dynamic relationship. Scottish Episcopalians, by the end of 18th century, were still under suspicion of being Jacobite, non-juror and sympathetic to Roman Catholic (and so foreign) persuasion. Bishops for the Episcopal Church of Scotland had returned, but part of the price of restoration in the social contract was that they remained low profile and low church. However, the Revolutionary and Napoleonic Wars with France meant that wealthy Scottish landowners and merchants began sending their sons to English rather than French boarding schools. Eventually, this would result in exposing the sons of wealthier Scottish families to the influences of the Oxford Movement. And so it was in the 19th century that ritualism returned to the Episcopal Church in a manner that might have been illegal fifty years previously in the Church of England. But in Scotland, the Episcopal Church was not subject to fears of nascent subversive Catholicism, and so the liturgical changes were matters of style and not of doctrinal or political substance.

Yet the picture that emerges from the past still casts a shadow over the present. One of the very first pronouncements required by law of Charles III is that he will uphold Scotland as a definitively Presbyterian country. In 2023 that came as news to many Scots, who had no memory of the last time the pledge was made by Queen Elizabeth II. Is Scotland really a 'Presbyterian country'? Many inside the church would dissent on that claim, and many outside the Kirk resent it. Peculiarly, the reigning monarch may worship in any church or place of worship—just as long as it is not Scottish Episcopal, which is specifically excluded, since the Jacobite legacy of suspicion still holds.

In fairness, similar kinds of exclusions and snubs were exercised for centuries should Presbyterians be minded to wander south of the border. There is no escaping that unholy trinity of narrow nationalism, hegemonic establishment and ecclesial entitlement. But such patterns can no longer be exported abroad, be deployed and operate in other nations in a post-colonial era. The entire global cultural grid system is different. Your national church does not work overseas in the same way that your electric plugs and appliances won't. Everything needs conversion or translation.

A Church in a United Kingdom?

The unity of global Anglicanism rests on the creeds, scriptures, traditions and culture of a federated network of churches that are simultaneously Catholic and Reformed (i.e., Protestant). This bold ecclesial expression is incredibly broad and diverse, since it includes viewpoints more at home with Calvinists, Lutherans, English Roman Catholicism, evangelicalism, Pentecostal inklings, liberalism and those who are militantly passionate for a *via media* (middle way). In effect, this is like a single English political party that is the merger of Conservatives, Unionists, Labour, Liberal Democrats, Greens and latter-day nationalists. With compromise always adopted as the key charism for the Church of England, it is no wonder that it is frequently rendered ungovernable on any divisive matter.

There is a sense in which national unity on either side of the Pond can cope with this wide range of viewpoints. But can a church or denomination manage such a broad bandwidth? Yes and no. Any congregation in almost any denominational tradition will contain most of the range described above. Very few clergy or pastors will encounter political, social, cultural or ideological homogeneity among their faithful, let alone the parish or community they serve. But the social contract in most churches is not to make prominent such divisions in a way that alienates others.

The issue becomes trickier at the meta-level of a denomination or party assembly (e.g., evangelicals). On climate change, for example, there will be those advocating progressive stances and policies, which will be the 'official' position of that denomination. But the denomination will still carry within it climate sceptics and climate crisis deniers. Similar dynamics will be evident on gender, sexuality and other matters of equality. In turn, many of these issues will have a different calibration across countries and cultures. Any denomination seeking global unity will face substantial challenges in arriving at consensus and communion on contested issues that play out differently in countries and cultures across the world. We can say here that Anglican difficulties are, therefore, essentially a by-product of globalisation and modernity.[3]

But perhaps the central question that remains in all of this relates to what the desires of the Church of England were. As the conceptual *via media* that emerged out of decades of bloodletting and violence in the cause of religious reform and the eventual Counter-Reformation, the most obvious passions and desires that arose as early Anglicanism took hold under Elizabeth I were to bring an end to oscillating religious retribution. Anglicanism sought to establish—and enforce—peace as the modus operandi and modus vivendi for English life. The Church of England was therefore prepared, from the outset, to accept compromise.[4]

At a local level, the clergy presumably want to serve and (hopefully) be loved, cherished and respected for the ministry that they sacrificially offer their communities and parishes. Pastoral theology was therefore one of the earliest forms of distinctive wisdom developed in Anglicanism. Aesthetics—music, hymns, decor and architecture—also combined beauty with simplicity, and one can plainly see that, from the 17th century onwards, one of key drivers in Anglican aesthetics was that they were *inoffensive*. Keeping the peace between competing convictions is therefore a fundamental element of Anglicanism.

While we can admire and praise such a polity, challenging issues arise for episcopal and ecclesial leadership when peaceable coexistence within the Church of England is stretched or actually broken. Compromise will only work to the point where those who hold competing convictions remain committed to those they do not agree with. Liturgical reform, debates on gender and sexuality, governance and finance will all be subjected to theological reasoning at this point. But as David Hume said, 'reason is the slave of passion'. Desires will drive any apparent theological debate.[5]

Crucially, for the English, the polity of the Church of England finds this to be its Achilles heel. A culture rooted in elite white male class-based manneredness becomes sacralised in ecclesial settings. Mild, slightly aloof and distant forms of engagement are developed as normative, in order to avoid the difficulty of dealing with competing convictions and the underlying passions, emotions and desires that are part of them. The English, perhaps until recently, had a broad appreciation for an ecclesial polity that dovetailed with the normative 'national mood', viz., mildness.

However, the post-colonial era cannot operate with such presumption in England, let alone globally across the Anglican Communion. Even something as normal as tears, weeping and crying in public—overt displays of grief—has evolved considerably in the national consciousness and repertoire in the post-war era. As Thomas Dixon notes,[6] the English are now less reserved about their passions and desires, and more prone to expressing their emotions. Anglican polity is a suppressant to that, and far from being a comfortable enabler.

Since denominations do evolve—slowly and over time—the structural changes in the polity are worth noting. As the Church of England slowly loses its status as some national treasure, and instead becomes an agent in need of membership, support and sustenance, the identity of the polity shifts from being that of public service to one of community surcharge. The episcopal and ecclesial leadership find themselves unable to resist the temptations of centralised and bureaucratic oversight, including financial control. In turn, that slowly evolving stance depends on demonstrating competence, trust, accountability, transparency and fairness. It is at precisely at this juncture that monarchical models of leadership are at their most exposed and weakest. They have few skills for such work.

Trying to overcome this with new strategies for growth will not compensate for the sense—the feeling—that the Church of England is in the hands of the few, and not necessarily on behalf of the many. Furthermore, public pronouncements on a narrow range of ethical issues, combined with an aversion to internal moral decision-making on issues such as gender and sexuality, and the leadership's desire to be all things to all people, only lead to indecision and silence. In a post-war era, moral silence will mostly be interpreted and experienced as immoral.

The post-war and post-colonial reality for the Church of England requires a different kind of emotional intelligence to lead an international Communion. One can simply observe that the British Commonwealth has faced similar challenges since its foundation almost a century ago. That has required a significant audit of all the problematic baggage that comes with being a former empire along with its imperialism, including expectations of pre-eminent self-importance. Unless the Church of England can own its ambivalent and problematic role in the British

Empire, the sheer weight of its history will render it powerless. The 21st century is an era in which the Church of England badly needs new leadership, theological wisdom, and structural and fiscal overhauls if it is to serve both country and Commonwealth.[7]

When there is no moral or theological leadership, expedient political compromise will always fill the vacuum, in the forlorn hope that splitting the difference will somehow keep everyone happy. Despite this being a provenly flawed approach to ethics, the Church of England leadership still believe that compromise will win out over competing convictions. The English Anglican leadership—bishops and bureaucrats—strongly dislike voting and democracy. It robs the bishops and bureaucrats of their right to rule. So this axis of power has plenty of ways of getting around democratic decisions, or of just not being democratic at all. Anyone who attends General Synod or a diocesan synod will know that all the important decisions are determined before any debate even begins. If there was to be any uncertainty about the outcome of any debate, you can rest assured it won't be voted on at all, and the debate merely 'noted'. This is an illusion of participative democracy and a staged consultation process.

The Church of England's combat strategy has been to invest in organisational bureaucracy, intensify congregational identity, and then try to increase membership. There are the familiar PR exercises: a diocesan newspaper might offer a picture of a grinning bishop planting a tree to commemorate something or other, with a small group looking on, applauding. There might be a tweet of the bishop dropping in on a school or meeting young people at an event somewhere. The bishop might say something in the House of Lords about poverty, family or mental health. These sorts of activities feel like an easy win for the church, but they no longer cut the mustard with the public. As roles go, English Anglican episcopal ministry has become unmanageable.

Questions of Leadership

That said, the attempts made by Justin Welby as Archbishop of Canterbury to address the crises were largely half-baked, and yet were imposed with some degree of monarchical assertiveness. The creation of 'talent pipelines' in which church leaders can be incubated and delivered has largely produced compliant middle managers. Welby (a former oil executive) and his cadre of courtiers (usually given smart executive-type titles) had simply not understood the chasmic difference between leading an organisation and heading up an institution.[8] Thus, vacuous management-speak and bureaucracy—all geared to delivering growth—proliferated under his tenure, with spirituality, pastoral care, ordinary parish ministry and theological education all relegated and marginalised.[9]

With the advent of the post-colonial era, the Church of England has set out to imitate secular organisations and corporations. It has mostly failed to replicate the models of secular organisation and leadership, and ended up with extremely poor reproductions. At the same time, clinging to the privileges and powers of monarchical authority has led to a situation in which there is little public patience left with unaccountable and non-transparent corporate episcopal leadership. The lack of liability and responsibility in elitist models of control and governance has also rendered the Church of England's hierarchy morally and reputationally bankrupt.

As scholars of institutions and organisations know, the primary purpose of a system is what it does. One might expect Christian patterns of behaviour from the body of senior leadership within the Church of England. But it turns out that the purpose of the system is to look and sound good, manage reputational damage, remain independent, and stay in control. The bureaucracy resists external scrutiny, regulation and even English law, precisely because it disrupts corporate public relations. This leads to investment in reality avoidance, so that within the system there is deliberate dissonance that irons out the potential discrepancies between expectations and outcomes. The Church of England's hierarchy has evolved into one that mimics democratic accountability, organisational structure, professionalism and basic proficiency in fields such as safeguarding, employment law and governance. In reality, it has no investment in becoming effective in these spheres, as they would soon hold the senior leadership and their cadre of senior bureaucrats accountable to assessment and standards. The purpose of the system is to remain aloof, as monarchs might, and avoid being subject to external scrutiny.

For much of the late 20th and early 21st century the Church of England's senior leadership have been uncomprehending of the nature of the body they lead, and the contexts in which that body now operates. This partially accounts for the poor choices made for ecclesiastical preferment. The former CEO of the Post Office, Paula Vennells, was put forward as a candidate for Bishop of London—the third most senior bishopric in England. Vennells lacked the theological nous and pastoral experience needed for the role, yet somehow her role as a business leader was deemed to be a good fit.[10] Lord Stephen Green (ordained in Hong Kong, and a former chair of the international bank HSBC) was touted by Lambeth Palace as a possible Dean of Christ Church Oxford, though he lacked any of the relevant background in leading educational or ecclesiastical institutions.[11] Welby valorised both Green and Vennells, and recorded his debt to them in helping him shape and lead the Church of England.[12]

However, for those seeking to compensate for the declining lustre of the established church, the allure of a corporate leader also bearing a title of distinction or an honour is hard to resist. The occasional proposal or selection of such individuals for high ecclesiastical office reflects an anxious and fearful church that wants to send a signal that it can still attract people of the very highest calibre. It is signalling a capacity to deliver modern corporate step-change management, and yet also wants that candidate recognised through monarchical validation.[13] That said, monarchical polities only tinker with cosmetic reform, which is designed to signal modernisation and relevance. The underlying culture of deference and courtiers remains intact, and in turn this will always resist external scrutiny, independent regulatory accountability and even transparency.[14]

11

CHURCH, COMMUNION AND CLASSISM

The Church of England is one of the few major British institutions remaining that tick the box of 'establishment'. So looking for signs of change, or trying to chart its slow inexorable decline, can be like watching paint dry. It is happening, but it hardly makes for compelling viewing. The Church of England is hardly unique here, since all denominations tend to motor in the slow-change lane. The difficulty for a Protestant national church, however, is that this slowness may alienate the constituency it primarily serves—the nation. Herein lies the conundrum for English Anglicanism. Is it 'tracking' and trying to minister to the social and cultural changes taking place in England, or not changing lest it lose some softly defined role in the global ecclesial polity? The lack of self-understanding in the Church of England leadership accounts for many of the muddles about what to reform and, if so, at what speed.

Furthermore, cognitive dissonance now plays a significant part in the institutional dynamics of the Church of England. Yet these dynamics are hardly unique to English Anglicans. Derek Scally's *The Best Catholics in the World*[1] is the remarkable result of a three-year odyssey. He takes us on a quest to unravel the tight hold that the Roman Catholic Church once had on the Irish. Scally travelled the length and breadth of Ireland and across Europe, going to masses, novenas, shrines and seminaries, talking to those who have abandoned the Church and those who have just about held on; to survivors and campaigners; to writers, historians, psychologists and others. Rather like our study, Scally's book is about one faith but two different worlds. He is dealing with those murky, difficult questions that face any society coming to terms with its troubling past.[2]

Scally, a journalist and a Dubliner, spent decades reporting on the changes in Germany before, during and after the collapse of the Berlin Wall. He often returned home to Dublin from Berlin, and one Christmas Eve went to mass. He was puzzled and troubled by what he found. On visits home he found more memories than congregants in the church where he had once been an altar boy. Not for the first time, the collapse of the Catholic Church in Ireland brought to mind the fall of another powerful ideology—East German communism.

Journalism, like good research, is essentially organised curiosity: poking and prying with purpose. Journalists and researchers know the least-questioned assumptions are often the most questionable. Journalists, like researchers, understand the open-mindedness with which one must look and listen, and record in astonishment (or sometimes dismay and despair) that which could not be guessed. Journalists, like researchers, ask awkward questions and take little at face value. Some are locked up for this; others are quietly done away with.

As Scally pointed out, the fundamental ingredient at the heart of late-20th- and early-21st-century German transformation lies in truthfulness. Having faced their degeneration into pogroms and war crimes, fuelled by racist hatred, they had collapsed as a moral society. Lest we forget, Nazism was invested in a

Thousand Year Reich: it sought to be an empire that none could match. Crucially, degeneration cannot be subject to denial; only when faced can it be overcome.[3]

Engaging with the three traumas—the Treaty of Versailles, the Holocaust and Communist oppression—is on every single German school curriculum. No education is complete without the obligatory trip to the Holocaust museum or seminars about Stasi-led 'purges' that flouted natural law and justice. As the Old Testament proverb has it, 'our fathers have eaten sour grapes, and the children's teeth are set on edge' (Ezekiel 18:2). The answer to the proverb is education. As for children's teeth then, so now: you teach; you educate; you set an example now—if you want to change the future. Alternatively, deny and keep silent ... and continue to slowly degenerate.

While Germans have been engaging truthfully and earnestly with their past, and regenerating their moral purpose, Scally saw nothing comparable going on in his native land. As he remarked, if you raise the question of child abuse in the Irish Catholic Church, the subject is quickly changed or the discussion shut down. There is no regeneration, only denial. Bishops, clergy and laity all collude. No one wants to talk about it. And as the church won't deal with its past, it cannot escape it. The shadow of abuse lives like a cancer in the church—and cannot be contemplated.

The Church of England is in the same position as the Irish Catholic Church. With so much to face up to and repent of, the leadership would prefer the slow death of degeneration to the purifying pain of regeneration. So the shame festers and grows. The German lesson is this: a society or group that cannot truthfully take responsibility for its sins and failings is destined to atrophy and doomed to die. This may take a long time, but gradually it will wither and eventually perish. Denial is not a cure; partial treatment and triage is not an option. True, we are not yet at the stage of writing an obituary or eulogy, let alone organising a requiem, for a once-ascendant Church of England. The trajectory of decline is, however, unavoidable. Only the truth would set the Church of England free (John 8:31–2). But its bishops and leaders just don't want to go there.

Race and Oppression

The racism and oppression with which we have been concerned in this exploration of church and empire remain with us, even today. The film *Spartacus*[4] needs little introduction. It is based on a historical novel by Howard Fast[5]—inspired by the real life of a Thracian slave who led the revolt in the Third Servile War of 73–71 BC. A small band of former gladiators and slaves, perhaps no more than eighty in number, led by Spartacus, grew to an army of around 125,000, to challenge the might of the Roman Empire. Kubrick's film, which starred Kirk Douglas, Laurence Olivier, Peter Ustinov, Jean Simmons and Tony Curtis, won four Oscars.

Less well known is the film's own story of rebellion. The screenwriter Dalton Trumbo, along with other Hollywood writers, had been blacklisted for his political beliefs and his association with movements seeking equality for coloured and black people, as well as with members of the American Communist Party. Even though the age of McCarthyism was crumbling, it still took a young aspirational Senator—John F. Kennedy—crossing the picket lines to see the film, to help end Trumbo's blacklisting.

We can guess why Trumbo's script should have caused audiences to ponder some potential for subversive political messages. Much of the United States was still colour-segregated in 1960. But we are introduced to Draba, a heroic black slave, first overpowering the white Spartacus in gladiatorial combat, and then sacrificing his own life in protest at the oppression of slaves. On the silver screen, the thought of large armies of oppressed black slaves revolting filled audiences with the same fears as English newspaper readers will have had reading of the Demerara Uprisings of 1823 in the Caribbean. (It would be another fifteen years before slaves in British colonies were freed.)

Slavery was the foundation—perhaps the mainspring—of the British Empire and of English colonial expansionism. It is surprising, therefore, that so few studies have emerged within theology or ecclesiology to challenge the notion that the Anglican Communion, as a theological construction of reality, has a highly problematic identity and legacy. Indeed, the Communion piggy-backs on the British Empire, and the money, resources and power that returned to Britain through such imperial expansion inevitably produced benefits for the Church of England. The role of the Church of England in supporting the expansion of the empire—for the most part uncritically, and without conscience—must be reckoned with.

The scale of entanglement is undeniable, and includes endowments for foreign mission (and clergy serving in such), financial support for churches and chapels throughout the Communion, divisions between racial groups either endorsed or perpetrated, and financial gains through investment. This is to say nothing of the systemic injustice of racism and classism that combined to maintain structures of subjugation.[6]

British complicity and ongoing entanglement with slavery continued through its colonies, the colonies it traded with, and the industries, commerce and civic amenities whose financial security drew on the proceeds of slavery. The Church of England was one of many beneficiaries, as were its newly established colonial churches and the subsequent Anglican Communion. Even when slave-trading and then slave-ownership were formally ended in 1807 and 1833, the Church of England with its foreign missions was able to create and articulate a new ecclesial and evangelistic rhetoric around 'civilisation', which involved taking the gospel to the heathen, and therefore more justification for imperial expansion and the repression of any who resisted that.

The Church of England may well argue that it was not responsible for the exploitation of nations and peoples that came about through the British Empire. But as a church, it is certainly accountable, and the articulation of the global Communion, and even anti-slavery appeals, only served to supply the British Empire with a moral sheen that justified further impositions of 'civilisation'.[7] While some may blanch at this, it is hard to see how systemic and structural inequalities—especially racism—can ever be addressed without high degrees of audited accountability taking place within institutions. Where this is denied, the response to ongoing injustice will always be 'But you can't blame us for the present, as that is all in the past'. A weak apology might be added after a lot of pressure, but this is light years away from repentance and reparation.[8]

The Society for the Propagation of the Gospel (SPG) was overseen by Church of England leaders, and the incumbent Archbishop of Canterbury would typically serve as its president. In November 1758, Thomas Secker, then archbishop, chaired a meeting of the SPG and agreed to reimburse funds to the Society accounts for buying enslaved people after being told that 'fine crops' on sugar plantations owned by the church's missionary arm primarily relied on 'yearly purchases of new Negroes'. In 1710 Christopher Codrington, colonial administrator and plantation owner, left on his death a bequest to the SPG of two plantations in Barbados. His will stipulated they should be maintained and 'continued entire with three hundred negros at least kept always thereon' and that the estate should be used for education, with 'a convenient number of professors and scholars ... all of them to be under the vows of poverty and chastity and obedience'.

The slaves had 'Society' branded on their chests, lest they forget who owned them. Death rates among enslaved people were high. From 1710 to 1838, it is estimated that between 600 and 1,200 lived and died on the plantations. From 1712 to 1761, the SPG purchased at least 450 enslaved Africans.

In Africa, the SPG cooperated with English slave traders in establishing a mission at Cape Coast Castle, at the heart of the transatlantic slave trade. The SPG helped lay the foundation for black Protestantism. However, pessimism about the project grew internally, and black people's frequent scepticism about Anglicanism was construed as evidence of the inherent inferiority of African people. Through its texts and practices, the SPG provided necessary intellectual, political and moral support for slaveholding around the British Empire. The rise of anti-slavery sentiment challenged the principles that had long underpinned missionary Anglicanism's programme. What is interesting is that abolitionists viewed the SPG as a significant institutional opponent to their agenda.[9]

Interrogating Imperialism

Some British and American readers might register a note of concern at the term 'imperial' here. Was Britain imperialist? Obviously it was, and the title was often owned with pride. That said, for many in the 20th and 21st centuries, the only major imperial force in the world has been America. Here, we simply note that imperialism is a national attitude towards other nations, and will cause military, economic, legal and other actions to be taken on smaller or weaker nations in the name of global order. Imperialism can stem from republican democracies (e.g., ancient Rome) as well as monarchies (e.g., Japan).[10]

One of the many reasons that stories like Tolkien's *The Hobbit* works or, for that matter, the *Star Wars* movies is that they pitch the Shire against the Empire, or the community and federation against the totalitarian conglomerate. What is idealised in such genres is the integrity and self-sufficiency of the small free state, and the evil of a dominating regime that depends on force in order to rule and reign. To be sure, one should not compare the Archbishop of Canterbury to Darth Vader or Sauron. However, it is worth noting that 'the force' in *Star Wars* and the underlying Spirit of integrity, virtue, fortitude and resistance one encounters in *The Lord of the Rings* and *The Hobbit*—one thinks of the trees of Middle Earth, for example—function as symbols for the progeny of natural goodness and virtues. When innate goodness is threatened with annihilation by the forces of darkness, a saga of steely resistance and virtuous revolution is born.

Such tropes are no less present in American self-understandings in relation to their own revolution from 1775–83. David and Goliath offer us a similar saga. It is hard for a nation or people to imagine itself as a Goliath or an invading agent of imperialist expansion. Yet historically, in ecclesial terms, denominational command-and-control is always at risk of being narrated as the dominant reigning power over and against the congregation.

Readers will, by now, already be clear that the proper work of history must also involve serious attention to the alienation and subjugation that the silenced voices of the masses have had to endure, if there is to be any hope of freedom and the possibility of truth and justice. One of my concerns in this book is to frame an agenda that disrupts the conventional ways in which Anglican history and Episcopalian identity are normally received and understood. Here, I draw on thinkers such as Rosa Luxemburg who argued that radical change could not come through reform, but instead needed an explosion of consciousness that would unmask and unseat the prevailing powers. Reform maintains prevalent power structures and sustains the lines of authority that permit the status quo to remain intact. Without revolution, history continues to be written by the winners. And the winners, usually, are those with inherited or residual power and privilege. They are invariably reluctant to relinquish that power or cede to any revisionist histories that might re-narrate their past.

That said, the English and the Church of England are not about to vault into some new era of revolution. Despite the repeated deployment of tropes promising renewal or reform, the current age is largely characterised by turbulence, enormous fluctuations, a lack of public composure and little in the way of a leadership rooted in calm, courageous wisdom. The swings in politics breed short-termism, bolstered by charismatic leaders promising change and success. The Church of England's leadership over the past fifty years has shown the same propensities, and the only steady state that congregations now experience is one of top-down badgering for constant change. Initially exciting (potentially) and arguably necessary, it has now imploded into becoming dull, exhausting and a source of widespread mistrust and festering resentment.

English Anglican Amnesia

The English, for the most part, suffer from a kind of collective learned amnesia with regard to their past empire. As the nation is not able to audit its own historical accounts, important and telling details get lost in the valorisation of its past, values and legacy. Few will recall the 1911 Festival of Empire to celebrate the coronation of George V (a king and an emperor, no less). Held on a specially constructed site at Crystal Palace, the Festival would be regarded as a PR disaster by today's standards. But the English media were warm and appreciative at the time.

The Festival included a tramway to take visitors across representations of peoples and countries within the empire. The tramcars transported the five million visitors who attended the Festival past a mocked-up Indian tea estate, a South African diamond mine, a Jamaican sugar plantation, an Australian sheep farm, a jungle 'well stocked with wild beasts', a farm with 'natives at work', some specimen Māori, and some Malays building houses. There was a 'typical' Irish cottage to visit, too, and various nods to the exoticism of India. There were also large-scale pageants dramatising British history.

The event was, in effect, a human safari park created for several months of entertainment and education. Unsurprisingly, the organisers (drawn from the elite of English society) regarded the Festival as a kind of snapshot of the gathered British family. It sought to strengthen bonds between 'the greatest empire the world has ever known' and its dominions. It was also a showcase for the colonies, encouraging visitors to consider emigration as a further means of introducing the wider world to the benefits of English culture, civilisation and Christianity.

Lest one hope the Great War reduced the capacity for celebrations of colonialism, the infamous launch of 'Empire Pudding' in 1924 was created to complement Empire Day, which Britain and her colonies had first celebrated on 24 May 1902. It wasn't until 1916 that Empire Day became officially recognised, and, with it, schoolchildren across the globe were encouraged to look at maps of the world which showed one-third of the Earth shaded in red. Empire Pudding was a media-led PR campaign to rebrand the normal Christmas pudding, but with all the ingredients drawn from across the imperial domains, with every nation contributing something. To add the necessary English Anglican approval, the Collect for the Sunday before Advent was invoked—the traditional prayer for 'Stir-Up Sunday' in the 1662 Book of Common Prayer.[11]

However, this being an English initiative, there were the inevitable unintended omissions. The recipe failed to include anything from Wales, Ireland or Scotland. Canada was dismayed to be merely cited as the source of minced apple. Cyprus was so upset that the official recipe lacked a Cypriot ingredient that the colony complained the recipe could only be published if the brandy sauce for the pudding included Cypriot liquor. Others were far from happy. New Zealand was omitted entirely, presumed to be included within Australasia.[12]

The revised recipe that was eventually published with royal assent included beer and eggs from Ireland. Cyprus had to be content with sharing the brandy honours provision with South Africa, Palestine and Australia. This might have been a celebratory Empire Pudding, but as an English invention, with the architects of the public relations campaign all coming from elite families, public schools and the like, the stunt effectively degenerated into an Eton mess.[13] Empire Day, incidentally, was eventually rebranded Commonwealth Day in 1966—some forty years after the Commonwealth had been inaugurated in 1926.

Assuming we accept that the foundational iteration of the Anglican Communion is what we have termed 'the Church of England Abroad', and that it clung to the coat-tails of imperialism and an expansive empire from 1700 to 1945, we are inevitably faced with awkward questions relating to its ecclesial identity. It is our contention that every form of ecclesiology is a form of sacralised social behaviour and patterning. All ecclesiology amounts to being the social consequences of any group's theological commitments. Churches reflect the God they worship, the vision of Christ they uphold, and what it is they believe the Holy Spirit has set before them. This is not some supine reductive claim. It simply recognises that churches and denominations will reflect the forms of gathering, governance and gospel they believe to be revealed by God.

David Hume was surely right when he claimed that reason is the slave of passion, and perhaps this is especially true in ecclesial contexts. If one considers the most successful 'exports' from the Church of England, one would quickly find opinion fondly coalescing round the annual Festival of Nine Lessons and Carols, Evensong, and perhaps Harvest festivals and Christingle. Nine Lessons and Carols was an innovation that largely postdates the end of the Great War, being inaugurated at King's College Cambridge, and was an attempt to address the religious illiteracy of the working class and returning war veterans, by telling the whole Christian story from Genesis to Revelation in an hour. Eric Milner White, the Dean of King's College, chose scripture readings, and mixed these with anthems and carols that evoked the nostalgia of old English folk melodies. To this day, the Festival of Nine Lessons and Carols remains one of the most revered 'exports' across the Anglican world and beyond, though few will be aware of its origins in apologetics and social class.[14]

Ordinary Rites

One can experience the class divide in today's civic religion. I recently attended a Remembrance Day service at a Church of Scotland kirk. Civic leaders were well represented, as were the ancient city guilds, along with the Orange Order. It was striking that the military on parade were all Scottish veterans and current cadets, with no obvious sign of any senior officers. (They would be English.) No veteran had more than two medals. The set prayers were moving—remembering women deprived of security through loss, mothers left to struggle with children, those disabled, maimed and left traumatised by service. This was a Remembrance Service for the unranked Scottish soldiers of our conflicts, and the 'kirking of the trades' within the ceremonies reflected the interests of labourers in manufacturing industries.

Two hours later, I found myself at a different Remembrance Service, replete with officers (none had less than three medals), and a considerably smarter range of military uniform was on display. The officers were largely English. The prayers here were more distant and cerebral. For all the beauty of the choreographed liturgy, these prayers did not dwell on the women and children who were victims of loss. This liturgy was created for and by an entirely different social class.

Witnessing the two services so close together, one could hardly fail to sense how the impact of war was experienced in different class-based social communities. In the second, smarter Remembrance Service, the economic consequence of loss for the bereaved was not even mentioned. In the earlier service, it was the first petition to be prayed.

Liturgies arise out of social, class-based and civic needs and also crises. In the case of Harvest and Christingle, there is no monopoly on their origin. Christingle can be traced back to Germany in 1747, and the innovation of Moravian Bishop Johannes de Watteville. The ritual was intended to provide an elementary aid for children, using a red ribbon wrapped around a candle to teach about Jesus. The ritual evolved further under Protestant missionaries, and the custom was adapted by the Church of England in 1968.

The roots of Harvest festivals lie in ancient religious, Jewish and Christian traditions, ranging from the extravagant celebration of Mehregan recorded in ancient Persia to the week-long autumnal festival of Sukkot for observant Jews. Lammas Day was popularised across the medieval world, with the mass and the festival marking the successful gathering of the harvest. More contemporary encounters with the Harvest festival in the Church of England are rooted in Victorian nostalgia.

Although there is a sense in which harvest has always been celebrated (Lammas and Rogationtide come to mind), the modern fondness for harvest is traceable to the Revd Robert Hawker, a Cornish priest, who began the new services we now recognise as 'Harvest festival' in 1843, at his parish in Morwenstow. It was Hawker who, building on earlier Saxon and Celtic customs, began to decorate his church with home-grown produce, a practice that has now become widespread for nearly two centuries. Throughout the Victorian era, the festival was steadily embellished and romanticised, probably to act as a counterweight to the growing influence of the industrial revolution and secularisation.

Hawker was an enterprising clergyman. While an undergraduate at Pembroke College Oxford, his father informed him by letter that the family could no longer afford the tuition fees. Hawker's solution was to immediately return to Cornwall, where he proposed marriage to his very wealthy godmother—a woman some 21 years his senior called Charlotte Eliza Rawleigh. She rode back with Hawker to Oxford 'pillion style', where he remained as a kept man for the rest of his time as an undergraduate. She died at 81 years of age, and at her funeral Hawker wore a bright pink brimless hat, for which he claimed Eastern Orthodox churches offered warrant (suffice it to say, a tricky liturgical precedent to trace). Hawker continued as vicar of Morwenstow, and married again the following year—to continue as a kept man.

12

CULTURAL WEATHER FORECASTS

The weather is inevitable. The only question left to address is: how do you weather it, especially when preparation depends on accurate forecasting as well as hindsight? When all is said and done, what can we change? Not the past, for sure. The present is tricky enough. But what of the future? Especially if we know what is coming, can we alter course and so avert situations that might otherwise lead to disaster? The story of the *Titanic* and the iceberg from 1912 is, after all, a modern parable on a par with the wise and foolish builders, and the houses built on the sand and the rock (Matthew 7). Hindsight is a luxury afforded only to survivors. Predicting cultural weather is a science and an art to which few are wise.

As noted earlier, it is something of an irony that the Anglican Communion—Church of England churches outside the British Isles—began by accident with shipwrecked sailors on Bermuda in 1609. Just as with St Paul's detour to Malta (Acts 28), it was stormy seas and a shipwreck that led to Christianity reaching the island so early. The irony is that if we were to include Bermuda in the Caribbean (as most would), then how the Anglican

Communion started off is how it eventually ended up becoming: that is to say, multiple islands and territories of various sizes, which may or may not relate to one another. Some are aligned to the British crown; others are republics; others still relate to their nearest continent—North or South America. Some churches fall under the US Episcopal Church, others in a regional federation, and others still relate directly to the Church of England. Different currencies, legal systems and cultures are the accepted norm. The Caribbean, in other words, is a blueprint for what the Anglican Communion is rapidly evolving towards. By that, we imply that any Anglican federalism of the future will be far looser and less interconnected. As the cultural seas warm, Anglican dioceses and provinces, just like Caribbean islands, anticipate the erosion of their mass and increasing challenges to their ecclesial ecosystems.

For Anglicans seeking a cooler, more Eurocentric analogy, one need look no further than Switzerland—a federal republic comprising 26 cantons. The Swiss Federation gained its independence from the Holy Roman Empire in 1648. The Swiss Protestant Church is a federal communion of 24 member churches, all of whom are in the Reformed tradition. They have different histories in terms of the ordination of women and the blessing and marriage of same-sex couples. The French churches tend to be more Calvinist in theology; the German are usually more Zwinglian. Organisationally, the churches are entirely separate cantonal bodies with their own synods. Some regional churches collaborate closely with others, while a few prefer to remain independent of their neighbours.

As with the Church of England, Swiss Reformed Church collaborations are at their closest where theological, cultural and historical proclivities are aligned. Arguably, the federal model of ecclesial communion worked once the Swiss realised, in the 19th century, that creeds could not be prescribed in order to forcibly unite cantons and their churches. Like Swiss Emmental, the holes inside the wheel of cheese are part of its charm. The holes don't seem to diminish the whole—a lesson some denominations only learn once cut apart.

No church, denomination or ecclesial tradition is immune from the cultural weather. All are affected by the cultural climate changes. Both the Old and New World church communities will have to face the political, social and environmental challenges of the 21st century. If the climate events of the 18th and 19th centuries produced religious revivals, the opposite seems to be the case in the 21st century. We are witnessing a larger and faster decline in worshippers across Europe, North America and Australasia than in any other time in history. According to some estimates, 40 million Americans who used to go to church no longer do so. That is 16% of the adult population.

Church, Culture and Climatology

In the First Great Awakening (c.1730–40) and the Second Great Awakening (1870 onwards), church attendance jumped from 10% to almost 20% of the American population. In context, therefore, the dechurching of America in the early 21st century represents a truly vast haemorrhage. As Jim Davis and Michael Graham note,[1] the numbers who have left easily exceed the new adherents in the First and Second Great Awakening and in all Billy Graham crusades combined. Davis and Graham suggest three reasons why this is so.

First, with the Cold War a distant memory, the terms 'Christian' and 'American' are no longer synonymous. With no threat to the American way of life (save perhaps religious extremism), one can handle being American and non-Christian. Second, the rise of the religious right has proved to be both polarising and alienating. What was formerly the middle ground is now positioned as the liberal-left, and many Americans (not unlike the English) simply opt out of choosing. Third, the performance of believers has been substantially altered by social media and the internet. To coin a phrase, 'the truth is out there', and it does not require adherence to a church if truthful information is a mere mouse-click away.

As Davis and Graham observe, this is not a steady-state trajectory, as 'the dechurched will give way to the unchurched—those who never attended church to begin with'. As the infamous trope has it, when people stop believing in something, they don't then believe in nothing: they will believe in anything. Correspondingly, those under the age of 40 are far more inclined to have an assemblage of personal moral, spiritual and value-led proclivities. Atheism and, indeed, agnosticism are so last-century. The emerging generation are spiritual but not religious. They believe but do not belong.

In terms of future weather patterns, it has been a general assumption among conservatives, some other parts of the church, and even secular analysts and commentators that the future of churchgoing lies with the informality, orthodoxy and certainty proffered by evangelicalism, which in turn will flush away a weak and dwindling liberal remnant. Church of England and wider global Anglican approaches to mission seem to have such assumptions within this world-view. But again, the 21st-century religious and spiritual weather is rather unexpected.

The dechurched rate of marriage is higher than that of evangelicals. The dechurched also have a lower rate of divorce than evangelicals. Churchgoing is becoming a minority activity, not normative. Evangelical denominations such as the Southern Baptists are experiencing sharp declines in membership. Episcopalians, in contrast, have shown very modest increases in membership in recent years. Fractures in evangelicalism no longer run along ethnic lines or narrow doctrinal distinctions. The divisions are likely to be over sexuality, gender, climate crisis and movements such as Black Lives Matter. There is a profound generational shift at work in these divisions too.

Within the extensive network and range of global interconnected evangelical cultures, the prevailing internal assumption is that the Old World is giving way to the New World. For most evangelicals over the age of 40, the Old World is characterised as being largely populated with what have become ossified denominational structures and a kind of fossilised liberalism. The same group characterises the New World as informal and relaxed in worship style, and 'biblical' and theologically orthodox in its proclamations. Its apologetics are reasoned, its teaching didactic, and it possesses convictions of certainty. But is this really of the New World?[2]

In a word, no, precisely because this belief system was created to combat Enlightenment rationality, the advances in sciences, and the preconceived threats to the pre-eminence of revelation. Just as the Roman Catholic Church had resisted the insights of Copernicus, so it was in the 18th and 19th centuries that evangelicals felt obliged to resist and out-narrate geology, early evolutionary theory, and modernity in general. The differentiation that eventually emerged between competing convictions within English Anglicanism can only be read as evolved reactions to environmental changes that the Church of England could not control. Evangelicalism and Anglo-Catholicism, and the ecclesial distinctives that emerged, were attempts to create identities that somehow connected to pre-modern worlds. The 21st century is post-modern, post-colonial and, in the developed world, increasingly post-evangelical.[3]

With evangelical coherence breaking up along new fault lines such as inclusion and exclusion, abortion rights, LGBTQ+, and debates that are polarised to the political left and right, it becomes harder to assert orthodoxy as the barometer of true believing and belonging. In its place, orthopraxis assumes a new pre-eminence, which makes denominational identity harder to define and even harder to police and enforce. The emergent generation are powerfully aware that they, and the planet, are living on borrowed time. The year I am writing this happens to be 2024—the warmest year on the planet since the last Ice Age. The oceans are warming and rising. The polar ice caps are melting. If another 7% of the Amazon rainforest is lost, the change to future weather patterns will be irreversible. The Amazon was once a carbon-reducing rainforest and within the next decade is likely to become a carbon-producing ecosphere.

For those who are 40 and under, our era is the Anthropocene epoch—that unofficial unit of geological time which is used to describe the most recent period in Earth's history when human activity started to have a significant impact on the planet's climate and ecosystems. The Anthropocene epoch began in the early 18th century, when the story of religious, social and political change also began. The industrial revolution and the expansiveness of 18th-century imperialism—perhaps especially that of the British Empire—triggered the Anthropocene epoch. That era cannot last forever. The epoch is temporal, and it may only give way to even more challenging times.

The threat is nothing less than the extermination of the fundamental conditions for collective human existence, with shortages of water and food and climate crises all playing their part. Unless humanity can learn to live within the means of planetary boundaries, the projected nine-billion global population will place demands on natural resources that cannot be met. The conditions for revolution are to be found within such an equation, since the survival of societies, nations and humanity will become an increasingly competitive matter. That, of course, was how the exploitation by empires for slaves, commodities, territory and natural resources triggered earlier revolutions.

The emerging generation within the developed world is unlikely to be persuaded to follow Christian faith by denouncing Charles Darwin or Richard Dawkins. Godless atheism is not on the front line of challenge for most Americans or Europeans. Even if it were, one encounters very few evangelicals these days who have any particular grasp of (or interest in) specific distinctive doctrines within evangelicalism. Evangelical theories of scriptural origin and authorship are largely post-Enlightenment notions. Emerging evangelicals are concerned with agendas to do with justice, equality, peace, AI, nuclear proliferation, heat and meat, the actual climate crisis, and social flourishing. The current leadership of evangelicalism has more in common with the 18th than the 21st century. They are still fighting battles that ceased to matter in current culture wars long, long ago.

Analogically, religious global warming catches up with everyone in the end. The increasingly heated arguments over orthodoxy and orthopraxis, coupled to the rising tides of individualism and consumerism, and the growing chasm between believing and belonging, affect every denomination. Evangelicals are not immune from this weather, nor are they any better prepared for it than other denominational or ecclesial traditions. Indeed, the very informality of evangelicalism, and its dependence on rational apologetics, will come to be seen as a serious deficiency in facing the longer-term challenges posed by 21st-century cultural change.

Weather Protection?

The emerging British Empire—not formed until the second half of the 19th century—is partly what enabled the Church of England to move from being a national church to projecting itself as a global Communion. The expansion of Anglicanism was both an ordered and untidy affair; simultaneously systematic and unsystematic. After the Roman Catholic Church, it regards itself as the most widespread denomination in the world (if one discounts the Eastern Orthodox as a single family).[4] However, unlike its rivals (which probably include Presbyterian, Methodist, Lutheran and Baptist), Anglicanism is mostly confined to the Anglosphere of its former colonies.

The serious fiction of global Anglicanism tends to be shy and squeamish about important details. The end of the Napoleonic Wars saw an Anglican presence established in Rome for the first time in 1816, and a chaplaincy ten years later. Anglicans generally regard their presence in Rome and with the Vatican as a significant indicator of their 'top table' ecclesial status. However, there is no reciprocity from Rome to Canterbury—a fact that might indicate significant inequity in valuation. When the Vatican started to evolve into a land-locked miniature independent state from 1871 (in the wake of Garibaldi's unification of Italy), Papal diplomatic representation in Great Britain did not come about until 1914. The Vatican did not formally acquire independent status as a micro-state until 1929—less than a century ago. It is the only state that makes a claim that its ruler can pronounce infallibly on certain matters.

Of course, the doctrine of infallibility was itself a way of asserting power and authority at a time when the Holy Roman Empire had been dissolved by the emergence of modern democratic nationhood. From the mid-19th century, Europe endured a spate of revolutions (known as the 'Springtime of the Peoples', dating from 1848) that gave rise to a proliferation of constitutional democratic nation-states, which were often locked in tense conflict with the Roman Catholic Church. Conflicts ranged over control of institutions—schools, universities, publications, censorship and the like. Conflicts also extended to marriage and family life, social practices, politics, gender relations, medicine and the public sphere.

The Papal doctrine of infallibility was a kind of sacred nuclear deterrent: unlikely to be ever deployed, but the threat was there so that future 'culture wars' would never ultimately be lost. Infallibility is a trump card. But it can seldom be played. As a doctrine, it also stands as an act of symbolic plagiarism. Just as Jesus had stood before the Roman ruler Pontius Pilate and stated, 'My kingdom is not of this world' (John 18:36), so now the Pope could claim to be the ruler of a far greater kingdom than any monarch on earth could claim.

In many respects, the infallibility deterrent worked its magic until the early 1960s. Secularisation and the sexual revolution changed that. Were the doctrine of infallibility to be deployed now, it would likely provoke widespread derision and outbreaks of anti-clericalism.[5] Interestingly, for all of the anti-modernism of late-19th-century Papal power, this was the same time that all Catholics were now expected to have a portrait of the Pope in their own homes. With cheap printing readily available to all and sundry, the faithful duly complied. Thankfully, no Archbishop of Canterbury has ever issued such an edict.

The Church of England does not have a Pope, diplomats, embassies or any standing as a state. But in its ecclesial, political and spiritual narration, it imagines something very similar to embassy status in European capitals through its chaplaincies. But the post-colonial legacy has bequeathed a rather larger compass of oversight, and it is fixated on its global status and 'top-table' position among other denominations. True, the Archbishop of Canterbury is the spiritual leader of all Anglicans worldwide. But nonetheless there can be no escaping that the office of the Archbishop of Canterbury has undergone significant transformations over the last 150 years. Since the more formalised establishment of the Anglican Communion—which arguably dates from the first Lambeth Conference in 1867—the office of Archbishop has essentially moved progressively from being one of straightforward primatial ecclesial authority within England to that of *primus inter pares*, globally. Yet again, Anglicanism is imprisoned by its own projections, and a captive of its own narrative.

The reality is rather more sobering. In the East–West schism of 1054, the worlds of the Roman Catholic and Orthodox Churches divided. For almost a millennium since then, the Orthodox churches have evolved into a loose federal family of distinctive national expressions of Eastern-rite Christianity, united by common ancestry and familial bonds. Unlike Roman Catholicism, Orthodox churches do not have a common figurehead to lead them.

Just over 500 years ago, the Roman Catholic Church began to part company with protesters—later known as Protestants—in Germany, Switzerland, England, Scotland and across Scandinavia. The Protestant churches quickly developed into national churches with increasingly varied liturgies and practices that set them apart from one another. They too are a loose federal family, share a common ancestry but have gone on to become estranged from one another. All of these churches have, at some time or other, claimed to be universal or even catholic. The truth is that there is only one universal church, and that is the Roman Catholic Church. No other denomination is global, universal and catholic. No other church is held together by faith, order and authority as Roman Catholics are.

Thus, Anglican claims to universality, catholicity and comprehensiveness rest on a spiritual simulacrum that owes more to the expansionism of the English and their empire than it does to ecclesial and theological catholicity. It is therefore very unsurprising that the Anglican Communion struggles to maintain its coherence and unity in a post-colonial age. The foundations that gave credence to the appearance of such a character have largely been dissolved. So, is the Anglican Communion an inefficient, tangled and complex body that needs to be reshaped organisationally? Or is it an institution whose tangled and complex structures are, in fact, part of its very identity and value? Indeed, something like a family, perhaps, or even a 'household of faith' if one wanted to be more biblical about this—and so not easy to organise, and not always obvious where membership begins and ends, and who belongs?

It is neither fully one nor the other, of course. But on balance, a church—even one single local one, let alone a complex Communion of 65,000 congregations in 164 countries—is far more akin to an institution than it is to an organisation. The Anglican Communion is only 'universal' in the spatial sense that the imperial empire made possible.

Meanwhile, the Church of England is a national Protestant denomination that has retained certain Catholic accents and affectations, and a presumptive episcopal polity that mostly enables bishops to evade questioning, accountability, transparency or democracy. Subjects may have to put up with such hegemonic rule and authoritarianism, but citizens do not, and increasingly bishops find themselves operating with an ancient model of leadership that simply does not command respect, trust and confidence, and is resisted or just ignored.

The emergence of the information society in late modernity has meant that episcopacy has lost its mystique, in much the way that monarchies lost theirs in 18th–19th-century revolutions. Once episcopacy is made to justify its reasoning and account for its legitimacy—which is entirely proper—then the caprice of monarchical-episcopal oversight no longer holds. Fragmentation quickly follows, with the formerly whole polity collapsing into miniature fiefdoms configured through 'opt-in' theological assertions. Legitimacy becomes local, not universal. On the whole, provisions for such dissenting—to conservative evangelicals and Anglo-Catholics—have become normative, and alternative episcopal oversight has inevitably undermined the entirety of episcopacy across the Anglican Communion.[6]

The Caribbean typifies the complexity. Politically, it consists, as a region (identifiable, though with contested boundaries), of an area that stretches from Grand Bahama Island in the north to Curaçao in the south, and from French Guyana in the east to Belize in the west. Even ignoring the many Central and South American nations that border the Caribbean Sea (whose cultural and linguistic heritage sets their history out of the scope of the region), there are a total of sixteen independent or sovereign states and nine island groupings that remain dependencies (in one form or another), of the United Kingdom, France, the United States and the Netherlands. There are at least eight currencies in circulation. If one includes the South and Central American Caribbean countries, the total number of nation-states and dependencies is thirty-five.

In Anglican terms, some of these countries are part of groupings of dioceses in the Episcopal Church of the United States: Haiti or the Dominican Republic, for example. Others are part of the Province of the West Indies, which includes Barbados, Belize, Guyana, Jamaica, the Bahamas, and Trinidad and Tobago. Yet even the name of the Anglican province is potentially awkward for colonial and post-colonial identities. From 1958 to 1962, there was a short-lived country called the Federation of the West Indies composed of ten English-speaking Caribbean territories, all of which were (then) British dependencies. The West Indies cricket team continues to represent many of those nations. The very name of the Anglican province reflects this experiment in post-colonial organisation. But it did not last long politically or economically.

But as noted, reason is the slave of passion, and the existential desire for self-preservation is hardly contestable. But if the reasoning for the entire narrative of the Anglican Communion is a subordinate of passions and desires, we might ask what it is that this body desires. As an international body, it craves unity—but not all agree on that, or on the terms and conditions for such homogeneity. Is the unity an agreement on the Fall–Salvation paradigm we previously outlined? Many Sydney Anglicans and conservative evangelicals would say so. Or does the unity require agreement on matters of Creation, justice, equality and the Kingdom of God? Many would say so. But Sydney Anglicans and conservative evangelicals are suspicious of such emphases, regarding them as a Trojan horse and likely to contain problematic political and liberal ideologies.

In the meantime, the seas warm and the weather becomes ever more extreme. Flooding, famines, degraded soil and the rapid parching of earth go hand in hand. The land cries out for justice and peace. It is, ironically, at this point that the Church of England could recover its sense of purpose in global mission. It was John Jewel's *Apologia Ecclesiae Anglicanae* (Apology for the Anglican Church) written in 1562 that sought to argue for a national church free of the 'tyranny' of (Roman) bishops. I doubt if Jewel would have approved of English bishops acting just like their Roman counterparts, ruling and reigning without accountability. Richard Hooker, likewise, would have been unimpressed with an episcopal leadership more wired-up to monarchical domination than democratic deliberation.

Even at the apex of imperialism and empire, there were wise Anglican theological dissenters such as F.D. Maurice (1805–72), who argued that the primary identity of the Church of England was bound to incarnational theology and social inclusivity. The current episcopal leadership, in contrast, are unable to affirm the Human Rights Act (1998), equality legislation on sexuality and gender, or basic employment rights for their clergy. As C.S. Lewis opined, 'We all want progress. But progress means getting nearer to the place where you want to be. And if you have (already) taken the wrong turning, then going forward does not get you any nearer.'[7]

More Bad Weather to Come

Current wrong turns in the Church of England include the inflated importance of diocesan headquarters, which cost millions of pounds to staff and run, while parishes receive less and less. Less investment in theological education but more investment in futile evangelistic initiatives would be another. Failing to give a clear moral lead, likewise, produces further fragmentation. Some evangelicals even argue that the church *should* be left to die, so that Christian faith can finally be free of the cumbersome migraine of institutional organisation, as though the true elect would then be relieved of all that prevents the nation from responding to another wave of evangelism. Trying to reassert models of governance that failed centuries ago is also unlikely to win new converts.

There is also an alarming depletion in theological education. The use of the word 'education' here is quite deliberate, and I distinguish it from 'training'. One of the slow, wrong turns taken by the Church of England and other Anglican parts of the Old World has been to withdraw from a pedagogy of education and invest in programmatic training. The latter appeals to groups who wish to produce consistency and uniformity in belief and practice. But as Paulo Freire, the great South American liberation theologian, pointed out, the training model risks the 'castration of curiosity', and is also unable to engage in the radical quests for wisdom that might challenge the status quo. Many Old World Anglican provinces have pulled out of the theological education courses offered by universities and opted for training—with an emphasis on outcomes, techniques and stipulations.

The future of the Anglican Communion, and of the Church of England, lies in being honest about its origins. It is a 16th-century

Presbyterian and Protestant church that retained Catholic accents and aesthetics. It is a *church*—one of people, fabric, aesthetics, pastoral care, memory, and generous and inclusive social mission. It is not some empty vessel encumbered with red tape and history, longing to be set free to serve some post-church agenda. The intent lies in knowing and nourishing the rich organic relationship that is envisaged with its people—the body of Christ for the body of the people—often connected through buildings and festivals.

It is a national church that did not intentionally set out to become an extension of imperialism and the British empire. It was English and monarchical for a couple of centuries, until democratic governance began, ever so slowly, to become the normative expectation for oversight. Time only moves forward, and in the post-colonial era, it is the New World model that will continue to eclipse the Old World paradigm. The Old World model will implode of its own accord, as more post-colonial dissenting churches emerge. In the meantime, the Church of England's support for a monarchical culture and ecclesial polity means it can only continue to operate as an anti-democratic body.[8]

Underneath this are the English themselves, struggling with their issues and identities, which inevitably spill over into the Church of England. Here, church and nation see themselves as major global players and power-brokers, yet are increasingly strapped for cash and resources. Church and nation have largely divested themselves of full-blown monarchical power, yet democratic processes can be flawed, which often leads to institutions being run by figureheads. As for the monarchy itself in church and nation, the very vagueness of monarchical authority functions as a kind of political and social glue which looks increasingly unable to mend the cracks in society and hold the whole together.

English identity is a peculiarity on many levels. England has no national song, though 'Jerusalem' (1804), 'I Vow to Thee,

My Country (1921) and 'Land of Hope and Glory' (1902) serve as surrogates. The actual national anthem for Great Britain, 'God Save the King', was first sung in 1745 in the wake of the Jacobite uprising. Cultural commentary can often slip-slide into value-related statements. For example, any achievement can be 'another triumph for Great Britain'. Any failure, by the same token, can be 'England loses again'. But as with slavery and other moral matters, the English are quick to transfer responsibility to the British. In terms of national mood and humour, the days of stereotyping jokes at the expense of the Irish, Scottish and Welsh are rightly long gone, although the lines from Michael Flanders and Donald Swann's self-parodying 'Song of Patriotic Prejudice' (1963) bear testimony to this.

The English language can also be a vehicle for a kind of snide elitism. 'Leggism' is an archaic jibe, but it comes from James Legge, a Scottish sinologist and missionary, and first professor of Chinese at Oxford. The term 'derogatory' was coined to demean people who were adjudged to be too respectful towards the Chinese. Having 'the Mother of Parliaments' is an oft-repeated English claim, irrespective of the ways in which democratic process might be abused in England (it does happen), or despite the fact that one comes up against monarchical power and the lack of a written constitution. The legacy of empire and imperialism, it seems, makes up for this. The established church, likewise, seems unable to see itself as anything less than the pre-eminent paternal broker of unity, power and authority across the world—the *via media*; the perfect synthesis of Protestant–Catholic theology and ecclesiology. Here, the Church of England has not even begun to engage with its post-colonial identity. In the rhetoric of 'Communion', the Church of England imagines itself as the central hub of the multiple spokes of some giant wheel. Suffice it to say, very few share that construction of reality.

13

THINGS FALL APART

The relatively recent adoption of four instruments of unity to enable the Anglican Communion to cohere—the Archbishop of Canterbury (recognised as *primus inter pares*), the Lambeth Conference (which first met in 1867), the Anglican Consultative Council (which first met in 1971) and the Meeting of the Primates (i.e., archbishops of other provinces, which first met in 1979)—are very late additions to the Anglican polity. Globally, there is no international judicial oversight, no shared canon law,[1] and even the Thirty-Nine Articles of Faith (dating from 1571) are not adopted by all of the 46 member churches. A number do not even refer to 'Anglican' as their denominational name.

The attempts by global Anglicanism to express its purpose, unity and identity reach back to the strains and stresses the early Communion experienced from birth. An American priest-scholar, William Reed Huntington, wrote an essay in 1870 entitled *The Church-Idea: An Essay toward Unity.* Huntington sought to establish some basis for either reunion with the Roman Catholic and Orthodox churches or mutual recognition. He proposed a framework (often referred to as the Lambeth

Quadrilateral, although it originated from the American House of Bishops meeting in Chicago) that articulated Anglican identity and theological reasoning. As a frame of reference, the Quadrilateral is simple and holds that all decision-making in the church is held by the Holy Scriptures; the Nicene and Apostles' Creeds as 'sufficient statements of Christian faith' (to attain salvation); the sacraments of baptism and Holy Communion; and the historical episcopate ('locally adapted'). Huntington's framework was adopted by the American bishops in 1886 and at the Lambeth Conference of 1888.

It does not take much nous to figure out that the framework is generous to a fault. The Scriptures and Creeds are common fare across the Anglican Communion, as are sacramental life and the role of bishops. In that sense, there is one faith. It is hard to find any Episcopalians who reject any part of the Quadrilateral. Yet, as students of Anglicanism know, the framework merely sets out the scope of the battlefield on divisive issues that require further interpretation and implementation.

Because of the Roman Catholic Church's excommunication of Elizabeth I in 1570, and in response to the Act of Supremacy (1559), the Church of England has consistently claimed it is not a new ecclesial foundation but rather a reformed continuation of the ancient 'English Church' (*Ecclesia Anglicana*). While this is an attractive theological construction of reality, the very existence of the Anglican Communion, and the claims laid upon it, rather undermine this. The Church of England is a distinctly national phenomenon, and its international extension not comparable to the ecclesial reach of Roman Catholicism.

The assertion that the Church of England is somehow a 'continuation' of the pre-Reformation Catholic Church is open to question. Certainly, the selection of the term 'continuation' has to do an awful lot of heavy lifting. Continuous ought to imply 'unbroken', but that cannot be so. There are, to the best of my knowledge, no Americans that still claim to be British. Their revolution, like those of Europe, was a severance of ties with the political state. True, there may well be families that trace their distant ancestry and heritage to Great Britain but that does not confer British citizenship.

In this respect, the Church of England is closer in relationship to the Church of Scotland. Both are Reformed Protestant churches that broke away from Rome—the English from 1529–36 and the Scottish in 1560. Both countries acquired national churches governed by Parliament and monarchical authority, with Papal authority abolished. It is peculiar to claim a church is a continuation of its predecessors. The breaks with Rome were clear and decisive.

From Presumption to Consumption

Once upon a time, an English person who was unable to say with any precision what denomination they belonged to would automatically be allocated to the Church of England. Presumption or assumption was normative. Unconscious Englishness had a spiritual home—almost as though everyone belonged to this quasi-spiritual National Health Service. You were in, unless you'd opted out. The Church of Scotland (Presbyterian) functioned in the same way for the Scottish. You were in, unless you knew you were without. However, the post-war era is one of religious consumption—choosing and opting in, rather than being counted in unless counted out.

Neither the Scottish nor the English require a national church to consolidate their national identity anymore. Being a Christian is not even essential these days, as former prime minister Rishi Sunak (Hindu) and former first minister for Scotland Humza Yousaf (Muslim) testify. Faith and public life have been living apart for some while. They are not yet divorced, but they are estranged. A marriage that was once solid and firm is now on the rocks (and not in a good way). This is the heart of the issue for the Church of England and its global expansion.

In the post-colonial era, successive Archbishops of Canterbury have fought a desperate rearguard action to maintain a semblance of a global Anglican Communion, yet one that cannot be enabled by either Empire or Commonwealth. A gradual loosening of ties, however, has hardly helped to keep this ecclesial family together. Relations are painful, strained and broken. Anglicanism is now something more like a widely dispersed archipelago spread across hundreds of thousands of square miles. It has become a connection of provincial islands that still share one faith. But it lacks unity and agreement on sources of power and authority, and on cultural and moral reasoning. Global Anglicanism is no longer one vast, seamless catholic continent. It is more akin to the Caribbean and Atlantic seaboard of North America—which is where the story of the Communion essentially began.

The Archbishop of Canterbury's eventual abdication of the primacy ('Primate of Primates'—first among equals) within the Communion will merely represent a timely recognition that, in a post-colonial era, he cannot stake a claim to be the head of a national church and an international denomination. Popes do not have to be Italian in order to be the Bishop of Rome. Recent history has served up German, Polish and Argentinian pontiffs. None of them is required to head the Italian Roman Catholic Church at the same time. That business belongs to the Italians.

It is therefore quite odd for the former Archbishop of Canterbury to opine that the leadership of the national Church of England can be led by someone who does not share in national identity or interests. Were the role of Archbishop of Canterbury to be split between heading the national church and heading the global Communion, it is plainly easier to retain identity in respect of the Church of England than it is to assert extensive international authority. One option is to affirm the Archbishop of York as Primate of All England, and leave the Archbishop of Canterbury to be from any other province. But that could be a province that was politically republican in character, and therefore would produce a candidate who might not feel able to assent to an oath of loyalty to the monarch. That may be fine, but the candidate could not then serve on the Privy Council, and there would be a host of other clashes between the English state and the Church of England, with an archbishop heading it who was effectively a non-juror bishop.

I suspect that matters will be taken out of the hands of the Church of England in the near future. The consequential renouncing of primatial power or authority over the provinces of the Communion is more descriptive of the present than prescriptive for the future. That said, abrogation of an international primatial role would bring an end to the Catholic fiction that Anglican-Episcopalian identity and polity are more akin to Roman Catholicism (especially in the ontology or ordination) than to Protestantism. The Church of England has tried, for centuries, to play a pivotal international role by claiming to be a *via media* between Catholic and Protestant ecclesiology. Up to a point, that constituted a worthy goal. But the goal has proved to be unattainable, and the game is plainly now over. The provinces perceive themselves to be addressing different risks that express their divergent values.[2] As a marital motif, they now want different things out of this historical relationship. The parties have drifted apart and are mostly content to live separate lives.

Post-Colonial Prospects

Since the ordination of Samuel Seabury as bishop of the US Episcopal Church in 1784 signalled an end before there was even a beginning—that one can be an Anglican bishop without referring to or drawing upon the Church of England, or acting in deference to the Archbishop of Canterbury—post-colonial Anglicanism and its fragmentation have been unstoppable. It may not be what was intended, but the Protestant Episcopal Church of the thirteen original colonies led the way, a century before the Anglican Communion was established on the back of the expansiveness of the British Empire. Even before that empire, there was a post-colonial province doing things differently. As the empire has gradually dissolved, so has the Anglican Communion. The Commonwealth (founded in 1926) was a stopgap in the dissolution of an empire, and a mere prelude to its eventual termination.

In the meantime, the legacy of the British Empire ripples on. In Britain, through public outrage at the Windrush scandal, for instance—a political debacle in 2018 concerning at least 83 people who were wrongly detained, denied legal rights, and threatened with deportation—the empire has been striking back at Britain. The *Empire Windrush* ship carried just over a thousand migrants from the Caribbean to the UK in 1948. It became a symbol of a wider mass-migration movement. Many of the Windrush generation, as the migrants became known, experienced a remarkably cool reception from Church of England congregations. That many of the migrants had nascent or active membership of the Anglican Church through the earlier centuries of enslavement and colonisation appeared to count for little in Britain. But perhaps this should not surprise us.[3]

As noted earlier, part of the English blindness towards its role in the slave trade was that nobody could, legally, be a slave in England. Plantation owners who might bring a slave home with them while on furlough consistently discovered that English law did not protect their ownership and power in respect of human 'property', if on English soil. (The colonies were a different matter, however.) The English, as a nation, have generally lacked self-awareness in respect of their slave-trading legacy. Indeed, some of the incomprehension could be said to be rooted in the fact that the experience of first-generation Africans and African-Caribbeans in Great Britain was primarily through immigration. In contrast, the first-generation Africans in America were primarily slaves. There is a world of difference between economic or political motives for immigration and enforced enslavement.

All that remains is post-colonial independence and self-determination. As the Nigerian author Chinua Achebe prophesied in his 1958 novel, *Things Fall Apart* (the book's title was borrowed from W.B. Yeats's gloomy poem-prophecy,[4] 'The Second Coming'), context is all. Yeats wrote his words in 1921, just a few years after the collapse of empires in the wake of the First World War—and of the Russian and German revolutions—and as the British began to lose Ireland. Yeats saw that the centre could no longer hold. Passionate intensity would drown out and overwhelm any hesitancy in conviction.

Yeats's words apply to the Church of England and the Anglican Communion. Canterbury and Lambeth Palace once constituted some kind of centre. It has not held. It matters no more to Anglicans in Uganda or Guyana than the location and function of the Commonwealth Secretariat. Sydney has only followed an older path that was first trodden by 18th-century American Episcopalians, with Scotland providing the means. With the recent emergence of the Global Anglican Future Conference (GAFCON), the Diocese of the Southern Cross (another Sydney initiative) and the ACNA network, the empire has struck back at the progenitor of the Anglican empire.

Truth Decay

One of the defining characteristics of the 21st century—so far, at least—has been the corrosion of trust in facts. The condition of post-modernity is more of a description of such erosion than it is a driver of distrust. While suspicion of comprehensive accounts of events (to borrow from the French philosopher and literary theorist Jean-François Lyotard—'incredulity at metanarratives' is how he terms it)[5] may signpost the deterioration in our certainties, societies that jettison truth and objectivity quickly disintegrate into dangerous forms of subjectivity. The impact on law and order, civic and political life, and justice and truth, has already been discerned.

If opinion and personal experience are valued more than facts, and the lines between attitudes and beliefs are blurred with actual reality, then words themselves lose their power. Language, truth and logic begin to lose their currency. With that, the capacity to genuinely communicate is compromised, leading to less trust in political discourse and civic institutions. Disengagement, cynicism and alienation quickly set in.

The erosion of trust in facts—'truth decay'—is a serious social and cultural problem.[6] It ought to be one that churches and denominations are at the forefront of addressing. Yet with rare exceptions, most church leaders are accomplished practitioners in contemporary 'newspeak' and fluent in the dialects of marketing and public relations. While this is often justified as apologetics, the result is that denominations and their leaders end up being labelled as disingenuous and even given to deception. A recent poll conducted by University College London's Policy Laboratory showed public trust in the Church of England was at 38%, fourth from bottom of the league, above the two main political parties and 'big business'. This is a catastrophic fall from grace (so to speak), as only fifty years ago the level of trust in the Church of England was more than double this, at over 80%.[7]

The instinct for institutional self-preservation is invariably strong, and doubtless this accounts for survival strategies and tactics over decades of despondency. Desperate times call for desperate measures. Yet desolation, and even death, are integral to the Christian ecology. Mortality is the lot of humanity, and the fatality of institutions—even churches and denominations—ought to be less troubling to a religion that places its faith in resurrection. Our decay, downfall and eventual demise is a given. When this is embraced, truthful realism can begin to resume its place and value in the ecology of Christian comprehension. It becomes possible to face the past, and not evade it; to own uncomfortable facts and truths, even if they hurt and fatally damage the church, because evasion will only stave off the inevitable. As the Gospel of John (8:32) notes, quoting Jesus, 'And ye shall know the truth, and the truth shall make you free' (KJV). Denial and truth-avoiding tactics and strategies will only deepen the decay already at work.

Organisational Failure

The present state of affairs sees the Church of England ailing under growing bureaucracies, hierarchies and around 12,000 medieval buildings out of its 16,000 churches. There have been recent attempts by archbishops to compare local churches and their parishes to the National Health Service (the Church of England likened to a spiritual NHS: there for all, even those who have opted to go private).[8] Many churches cannot stay open during the week, and in rural areas services may take place once a month or less. Yet the Church of England is beholden to its autonomy and will do all it can to remain aloof from external scrutiny. Its leadership cannot abide the prospect of those who reign supreme ever becoming accountable subjects. Several other European countries have handed their historic buildings to local authorities for care and upkeep, and some have been helpfully repurposed to share sacred and secular functions.

Yet letting go of power is the sticking point for Church of England bishops. That is why principles for conduct in public life (e.g., the Nolan Principles) are avoided, and law on equality, employment and accountability evaded where possible.[9] At the same time, the Church of England wants to look like a modern corporate organisation—yet retain all of its residual monarchical power and authority in the hands of its episcopal leadership and senior executives. But even that pact is breaking apart, as the bureaucratic mechanisms of the church seem to acquire some God-given ontological status.[10]

The current turn toward ecclesial organisation and management focuses particular attention on how people become part of the church.[11] Specifically, it presses the question whether the global expressions of the Anglican polity are distinctive, bounded and overtly member-based organisations in character, seeking clarity of identity, or whether they are broader social and sacramental institutions to which a much wider public relates in a variety of ways. Mindful that most ecclesial ecologies will contain both of these elements, we note that denominations will often be a blend of those who feel a sense of strong attachment (often expressed as 'membership') and those whose basically affirmative relationship to the church involves a more variegated form of commitment.

All institutions need some level of organisation. The family unit is the oldest institution in the world, and each and every family will often be bound together by some shared stories, common origins, values, mutual respect, kindred spirit, and the commitment to cherish, care for and love one another despite differences. Institutions, like families, quickly unravel when such qualities are absent, as the Church of England knows to its cost. However, the relationships in such bodies are rarely contractual and instead depend on soft forms of power such as goodwill, voluntary support, trust, careful attention and mindful service. But the concern here is with the concept of membership in the Anglican polity as a whole.[12] If the church is consumed with its own managerial and organisational goals, including that of increasing its own numerical growth and disciplining its members, it will have lost its soul.

Sometimes it takes a much older set of myths to cast light on the present ones that English Anglicans toil under. In his prescient book *Gods of Management*, Charles Handy playfully pitches the managerial and organisational culture in the context of four ancient deities: Zeus (dominant, monarchical), Apollo (contractual, communication and order), Athena (cooperative and practical) and Dionysus (creative and individualistic).[13] While these paradigms are nicely poised (two male deities, two female), Handy uses them to suggest that the endgame rests on the tension between organisational imperatives (Zeus directing, Apollo managing) and individual imperatives (Athena and Dionysus) which cannot be resolved.

Treating people as individuals rather than as human resources in a system is the direction of travel. One encounters the Athena–Dionysus culture in ordinary parish and pastoral ministry, but in the diocesan hierarchy Zeus and Apollo reign. The result, increasingly, is one of dissonance. This emerges when those who style themselves as leaders, and the body they purport to lead as some kind of compliant subject, simply cease to engage. Bishops find themselves in office but not in power. They continue to act as a modern-day Zeus or Apollo might, yet are increasingly ignored.[14]

This tongue-in-cheek cultural reading of modern episcopal power owes more than a small debt to the social psychologist

Murray Bowen and his family systems theory.[15] As the Church of England seems to lurch from one crisis to another, one may surmise that the chaos is providing some cover or distraction for issues and problems that the 'family'—the Anglican one in this case—would like to evade and avoid. Thus, instead of the Church of England's leadership facing the actual problems that need to be resolved, the leadership becomes frantically occupied in fire-fighting crises and managing disasters of their own making. As long as there are crises, there can be no change.

All of this keeps the leadership in control—like some government declaring a constant state of emergency and so seizing emergency powers—and allows the cadre of leaders to decide on priorities, bypass democracy, and make arbitrary decisions that are no longer subject to scrutiny. With the Church of England 'family' headed by a Zeus-type figure, the demigods and mere mortals inevitably squabble over power. That Zeus can be angry, capricious and moody and harbour grudges, as well as dole out personal favours and rewards to loyal servants and those who are valorised as heroes, only increases the anxieties of the family system and its ultimate unpredictability. The body lives in a permanent bipolar state while also being on the edge of a collective nervous breakdown. To that end, the crises that have been created by the monarchical gods ensure they will always remain in control of such worlds.[16]

In all this, the cult of Zeus will be served by the courtiers—acolytes attending to the cosmetic of the temple. The courtiers will subvert democracy to maintain the tensions. Resolving them would render many courtiers redundant or reduce their power. As a consequence, under the fictions of 'balance' and 'unity', the courtiers will undermine democratic decisions on women priests and bishops or, more recently, on sexuality. By making perpetual concessions on moral issues, the courtiers ensure that their role as functionary-diplomats and ecclesiastical civil servants remains protected and privileged.[17] Murray Bowen's family systems theory would undoubtedly conclude that with a Zeus-type leader in charge, the only way to keep the Greek tragedy running for another season is to ensure that defeat is always snatched from the jaws of victory.[18]

In her no less prescient book, *The Precarious Organisation*,[19] the Dutch sociologist and ecclesiologist Mady Thung suggests that national churches in Northern Europe have come under increasing pressure in the post-war years to become self-consciously 'organisations', marked by 'nervous activity and hectic programmes ... constantly try[ing] to engage' their members in an attempt to reach 'non-members'. She contrasts the 'organisational' model and its frenetic activism with the 'institutional' model of the church—the latter offering, instead, contemplative, aesthetic and liturgical models that take longer to grow and are often latent for significant periods of time, but may be more culturally resilient and conducive than those of the activist-organisational model. Thung suggests that the model being adopted by many national churches—a kind of missional 'organisation-activist' approach—is what drives the population away. It leads, logically and inexorably, to sectarianism.[20]

Thung concludes her work with something of a prophetic warning to churches—and here I include global Anglicanism. She notes the inevitability of churches needing to become more organised, and more like organisations, replete with plans for numerical growth and measurable impact. But she also sounds a note of caution, namely, that every step churches take *towards* the tighter and clearer forms of organisation, coupled to overt mission and evangelism, is one further step *away* from the public at large, who, she claims, are looking for more open forms of institutional life, which offer more by way of obliquity than clarity. Ultimately, Anglicanism's pastoral practice, mission and ministry are not rooted in the identity of an eclectic and selective member-based organisation, requiring prescribed and detailed confessional subscription from believers.

Yet Anglicanism in its later 17th-century guise was intended to be far broader: an institutional body that had many kinds of support and supporters, including very haphazardly occasional ones alongside those who wanted to regard themselves as insider-subscribers. Perhaps the future for the global Anglican polity requires an incorporative model of church: a non-member-based institution that seeks to serve society as a whole, rather than a member-based organisation that primarily exists for its committed subscribers. It is undoubtedly hard to face up to the reality of a dominating 'transnational Anglo-culture' that was advanced by a combination of military, imperialist and capitalist ambitions.[21] It is also a dominion of a certain kind of elitism, classism, manneredness and deference towards the mystique of monarchical power. Hereditary monarchy together with devolved dominion (to hereditary peers) is a dubious concept in its own right and does not need the endorsement of a Christian denomination. If the right to rule and reign is passed through a bloodline, then other older examples of hierarchical racism, sexism and ethnicity can presumably look forward to rehabilitation in due course.

14

BEYOND CONTROL

As noted in the Introduction, this book has something of the character of a 'forward-looking obituary' in its composition. Yet if we look forward to 14 November 2034, that date will not immediately present as an especially auspicious anniversary to anticipate. Yet this date (Samuel Seabury's consecration, 1784) will mark the 250th anniversary of the decisive split in the worldwide Anglican Communion. Moreover, the date also marks the beginning of a rather different future for Anglicanism. If we are right, and the Old World order of monarchical power is giving way to a New World of democratic consensus (albeit with challenges from authoritarianism and autocracies), then this is a timely moment for organising some reasoned and peaceable revolutions.

In an age when nationhood itself is breaking down, denominations across the world have a particular responsibility to model forms of commonwealth and communion that do not depend on protecting some national narrowness or sectarian interests. We do well to remember that there are around 200 countries in the world but more than 5,000 ethnic groups. Our planet probably does not need more fragmentation into ethnic enclaves. Instead, we need to work harder at peace-building across ideological, class, ethnic and religious divisions—and increasingly across borders that separate oppressed from oppressor, rich from poor, those who are free to move from those who are restricted and lack liberty.

Soft vs Hard Power

This may seem like a thankless task or vocation (and frankly, rather a liberal one too, I confess). Yet thankless though it may be, there are plentiful alternatives to top-down monarchical control or some restrictive iron cage of imperialism and empire. Unity and federalism are not mutually exclusive. In the classic dictum of the political philosopher Joseph Nye,[1] the choice may seem to be between hard power and soft power, but the use of force and coercion (i.e., hard power) is rarely an option and, even if it is so, should only be a last resort.

Most denominations outside the Roman Catholic and Orthodox Churches only have forms of soft power available for their formation, organisation and leadership. They cannot direct members as subjects. Their polity depends on consensus, negotiation, persuasion, patience and developing communion, even where there is no consensus. Democracies depend on such conditions. The Church of England and the Anglican polity need to do much, much more to find a new theological rationale in such charisms, and find life in conversations, accommodations and negotiations—not weakly applied subjugations.

One of the key tests for church leadership in the future must rest with restoring the concept of faithfulness and fruitfulness, which are quite different from the concepts of success and results that the world around us may value. What is needed now is prophetic action, but also strategic patience; resolve and renewal, but also reflection and substantial overhauling and restructuring.

One key element in this is humility, the development of a humble church that understands its core duties and obligations are first and foremost to God and to society, not to loyal paid-up members of some religious supporters' club.[2] Christianity is a faith of conscription, not subscription. Believers do not elect to donate or contribute to the church in order to receive benefits and favours in return.

Degeneration is an entirely natural phenomenon. It can refer to the deterioration of cells, bodies, institutions and empires over time. Normal wear and tear and ageing take their toll. Sometimes degeneration is a social, cultural or personal lifestyle phenomenon. Sometimes it is disease, viruses, wars, famines and other crises that cause bodies to collapse and societies to crumble. Sometimes the seeds of degeneration have lain within the body from the outset, wired into a person's DNA or its social equivalent in wider society. Some degeneration can be predicted and resisted. But much cannot, and is part of the cycle of life and death.

Empires are not eternal; nor are nations.[3] Nor are denominations likely to be. Only God is, and God's kingdom is still to come. As the theologian Michael Jinkins points out, the churches would probably enjoy a better quality of life in the here and now if they could only learn to face death.[4] Denial is not an option. In a recent critique of the Church of England's safeguarding efforts at independent oversight led by Sarah Wilkinson KC, her report notes the essential conceptual confusion.[5] Namely, the now defunct body (Independent Safeguarding Board, or ISB) was misleadingly 'independent' while having no adequate terms of reference and no budgetary discretion. The church authorities seem to have been capable of holding two mutually exclusive ideas in their minds at once, without realising (or, more seriously perhaps, without caring) that these contradictions had real-life consequences for real people. As one legal critic noted,

> This fiasco [of the dissolution of the ISB] needn't have come to pass had the central bureaucracy not felt itself compelled to respond, in Pavlovian fashion, to a whim (even if that whim was invested with good intentions). Isn't it high time that the whole execrable notion of episcopal government and its ludicrous and risible pretensions to monarchical authority is, at long last, flushed down the pan where it belongs? Let bishops (who are too often manifestly wanting as managers) be pastors to the pastors, and let them be no more than that.[6]

There is very little that the Anglican Communion or the Church of England can do about the cultural weather that perpetually rains on its parades. Prayer won't alter the winds, storms, rain, floods and heat that lie ahead. The currents flow and the tides are coming in, no matter what Canute's courtiers may have hoped for. The weather cannot be altered or wished away. Yet there is arguably no such thing as bad weather—only the wrong selection of clothing and a lack of preparation. What churches must do now is avoid making heavy weather of the challenges that lie ahead.

There is a real contrast between the 'Old World' Church of England and that of the 'New World' democratic entity that quickly evolved in America. These represent two complementary but quite different forms of polity. These two worlds had entirely incongruent outlooks. The Old World believed in the pre-eminence of a God-willed monarchical authoritarianism. The New World believed in an inalienable right to democratic equality. The Old World offered monarchy. Even if benign, kind and good, its citizens were still '*subjects* of a realm'; there were those who were just born to rule over others. The New World is democratic, and governance and government can be changed by the will and consent of the people. All are equal. There are no subjects, only citizens.

Revolution and Change

The year 2023 marked the 175th anniversary of the 'Springtime of the Peoples' (or Nations)—the revolutions that spread across some fifty countries and states of Europe in 1848. To this day, it is still the most widespread wave of revolution to have occurred across Europe. The triggers for revolt were perhaps predictable. First, the revolutions were essentially democratic and liberal in character, seeking to remove Old World monarchical structures and oligarchies, and replace them with independent nation-states.[7] Second, growing urbanism, increased technology, economic developments and other social changes had led to widespread dissatisfaction with the prevailing political leadership. Third, demands for greater freedom of the press and wider participation in democracy stoked calls for universal suffrage, extending the power to vote beyond property owners. Fourth, rural-to-city migration was the result of food shortages, potato famines and an increase in the frequency of instances of mass starvation. Fifth, popular idealism sought to remove the power of the landed aristocracy and nobility, and replace these vested interests with meritocracy and democracy. Sixth, emerging liberal, socialist and romantic ideologies inspired the working class to rise up and challenge the prevalent social order, which was widely seen as elitist, self-serving and out of touch. Finally, the revolutions were initially empowered and effective as coalitions of radicals, liberals, reformers, the middle classes, workers, peasants and serfs.

However, as uncoordinated revolutions, they were comfortably suppressed by military force. Some suppressions were brutal, and tens of thousands were killed, forced into exile, or deported. By 1850, the revolutions had almost all been put down. The Holy Roman Empire had been dissolved under Napoleon's conquests of 1806, but the remnants of power and authority across small states continued to be exercised by the Catholic churches. For many Catholics, the failure of the revolutions was greeted with joyous relief.

But this was to be a pyrrhic victory for Catholicism over democratic republicanism. For failing as they did, the revolutions nonetheless marked an entirely new chapter of change for Europe. Many nations and states threw off the shackles of Old World monarchical power. The New World order that had been quickly maturing in the United States was now finally returning to its parental homelands. The Age of Empire was unravelling at home, even as it was being exported to the colonies. Liberal democracy was the future.[8]

Ultimately, the rejection of monarchical authority and power and the embracing of democratic accountability will be the fate of the Anglican Communion. Along the way, the majority of Protestant denominations will be unable to avoid internal civil war on sexuality and gender, and this will set off an unseemly fight over resources and naming rights. American Baptists and Scottish Presbyterians have already sampled such divisiveness in earlier centuries on other issues. Finally, this will mark the end of the Church of England as we know it. The civil war is already well under way. As a national and global church, it simply cannot be reformed any further, or find the pathways to hold together as one body. Only a decent revolution can save it.

Imperialism and the Anglican Theology of Niceness

Critics of Anglicanism have often mocked its Goldilocks or Laodicean preferences (see Revelation 3:14–22). So neither hot nor cold—just tepid; the classic *via media*—best served at 'room temperature'. And because Anglicanism is born of England, just like its climate, it often struggles to cope with extremities. Anglicanism is a remarkably temperate ecclesial polity: cloudy, with occasional sunny spells and the odd shower: the outlook, in a word, is mild. The English love mildness, and Anglicanism—at least in its English forms—has almost apotheosised 'mildness' as the ideal spiritual temperature to set the necessary tone and mood.

More seriously, one may surmise that the English proclivity for mildness goes further and invests niceness with sacred, moral value. Carrie Tirado Bramen's work[9] is alive to how the English export of niceness to the American colonies was eventually refracted and then diversified. The English proclivity tends towards expectations of civic order guaranteeing niceness in secular and ecclesiastical polity. For Americans, expectations of niceness are primarily located in individualism rather than corporate entities. The differences might look superficial, but they have a bearing on attitudes to empire and imperialism. The English have tended to see their expansive empire as one of benevolent assimilation and mild sway.

As a rule, the English do not like to think of their empire as being grounded in military force, coercion or exploitation. They mean to be nice, after all.[10] While one may wish to avoid national stereotypes, the notion of a national temperament has important consequences for the character and personality of institutions. So notions of niceness, niceties, politeness, manners and modesty will all play a significant role in forming the inchoate grammar of assent in a denomination, not to mention an empire. The obviousness of this can be seen in the export of pastoral, nice, kind, muscular-male images and ideals of Christ to the colonies in everything from stained glass images in colonial churches to selected hymns and liturgies, and sermons and teachings.

Unconsciously, the English exported their 'Christology of niceness', which of course they believed that they faithfully followed. Wholly unaware of the classism and inherent racism of this theology, the English are affronted by challenges to their preferred mode of conduct. With these theological constructions of reality in place, the English will struggle to ever see themselves as the aggressor in the empire, or comprehend the virtues and cause of the protester and rebel. Christ is no less present in such paradigms. But Jesus will not be portrayed as a disrupter of the status quo, whether civic or religious.

The English-made stained glass in the churches of the colonies upholds English virtues: manliness, strength, kindness—and the safety of a world that is improved by niceness.[11] The English are invested in niceness and mildness. This is only slightly offset by the total authoritarianism of a monarchical God (and his Church of England) that has the right and power to rule and reign, irrespective of the democratic will and consent of the people.[12] Here again, classism and those hierarchies inculcated through elitist education systems that institutionalise rationality and rules (and violence and punishment for their breaches) will all find their way into shaping theological horizons. The hidden rules of English behaviour have a lot to answer for.

This is a journey for the English as much as it is for the Church of England. The critical history we have told here—also a kind of critical ecclesiology—represents a critical excursion into the foundational myths that have told a story of a worldwide Communion. This is a post-colonial global denomination that is multilingual and multicultural. However, a lot more reflection, introspection and work would need to be done if such a body is to break free of its inherent classism, racism, homophobia, sexism and imperialism. That work would be very deep and far-reaching. Those occupying positions—with powers and privileges—will need to reckon with the past. It is still far too easy to call upon notions of sovereignty to deify ecclesial authority, and then rule through domination and subjugation.

Crossroads and Sacrifice

The choice before the leadership of the Church of England is now very stark. Does it hang on to the mystique of unaccountable and opaque monarchical power vested in episcopacy? Or does it embrace accountability and democracy? I would argue that any leadership harbouring imperialist outlooks and practices, and using quasi-monarchical patterns for oversight and governance, is destined for extinction. As a model of governance, it has lost the trust, confidence and respect of the nation, and the church members and clergy barely tolerate the tortured opacity of the episcopal modus operandi. Models of high-handed imperialism and quasi-monarchical leadership in the Church of England will eventually die.[13]

The context that requires this is England itself. It has entered an age of chaotic, unpredictable politics which are as much at home in the Church of England as they are in Westminster. The perceived betrayal of values and ideals—often screamed from both right and left—makes this a hard time to be a minister in government or a bishop. They seldom appease their own constituencies, let alone those who regard them as unsympathetic to their causes and beliefs. The labels and markers that used to serve as a reasonably reliable guide to the contours of disputes no longer work. British people can be both progressive and conservative. English churchgoers can be both orthodox and open-minded. Social class bubbles have long burst, and relationships across divides are arguably more complex and attenuated owing to social media and rapid increases in knowledge exchange.

Against this background, there is a global rise in gloom accompanied by chaotic world-views. Less social stability now means that individuals and groups can occupy 'contradictory class locations' (in the words of the social theorist Erik Olin

Wright). If there is to be progressive change in England and in the Church of England, there needs to be a new understanding of the chaotic complexity that shapes contemporary culture. Views are no longer fixed on a wide range of social and moral issues. Churches, political parties, institutions and organisations need to rediscover their charism for empathetic listening. They can no longer assume that believing and belonging are aligned, or that historical loyalties can be presumed upon. When we start to peer into the details of what we thought we saw, the picture that emerges can often be startling and unsettling.

A story from the Episcopal Church in the United States in its very earliest days is compelling at this point. The first Bishop of Minnesota, Henry Benjamin Whipple, tells of an incident in his autobiography, *Lights and Shadows of a Long Episcopate*, of the Sioux revolt (US–Dakota War) of 1862 under the presidency of Abraham Lincoln.[14] Whipple had been elected as bishop of the new Diocese of Minnesota in 1859. This was no doubt due to his faithful service to the poor immigrant population of Chicago, where he proved to be a consistent and caring advocate.

The culture of denigrating the indigenous population was long established. In 1859 the journalist Horace Greeley published an essay on the condition of the Native American:

> I have learned to appreciate ... and make more allowance for the dislike, aversion, contempt wherewith Indians are usually regarded by their white neighbours ... [To this] observer, the average Indian of the woods and prairies is a being who does little credit to human nature—a slave of appetite and sloth, never emancipated from the tyranny of one animal passion, save by the more ravenous demands of another ... I could not help saying: 'These people must die out—there is no help for them. God has given this earth to those who will subdue and cultivate it, and it is vain to struggle against His righteous decree.'[15]

The imperialist outlook here is unaccommodating. Yet while Minnesota was hardly fertile soil for Episcopalians, and despite Whipple working tirelessly to establish his denomination in a state only admitted to the Union in 1858, he found time to champion the cause of the Sioux and other Dakota tribes. The white settlers of Minnesota and his newly formed diocese were far from pleased with the pro-Native American stance taken by their bishop—not least as Whipple was known as 'Straight Tongue' by the Sioux for his scrupulously fair and honest dealings with the Native American tribes, and in speaking out against the deceitful and unjust Federal policies and practices. (It is hard to imagine a similar accolade being conferred on many Church of England bishops, though forked tongues are often mentioned.)

The attempted peace initiatives of 1862 were all to no avail, however. Having been driven from their land, the Dakota tribe revolted, and a large number of white settlers were killed in several days of massacre—mostly led by younger Indians, anxious to prove themselves. The Sioux were rounded up indiscriminately from their lands, and 303 condemned to death by hanging. Whipple pleaded to Lincoln for clemency, saying that most of the incarcerated men were innocent, and indeed many of them had risked their lives by hiding white settlers from the marauding bands of young braves. Whipple tried to intervene for the innocent men, and Lincoln duly commuted most of the death sentences: only 38 Indians would die. Lincoln's intervention was deeply unpopular, as was Whipple's. In what is still the largest mass execution in US history, the 38 were hanged for war crimes. The conflict resumed after the hangings.

But how were the 38 to be chosen from more than 300? It was a process of self-selection. The elders of the tribe—the very oldest men—stepped forward. They reasoned that they had seen their children and children's children. They maintained they had but a few winters left. So they volunteered to die in place of the young, who, even though they had committed the raids and massacres, still had children to raise.

The press reported the hangings in vengeful and macabre detail. One newspaper in Washington claimed the Indians had gone to their deaths 'singing their heathen death chants on the gallows'. But Bishop Whipple, who stood by the accused as they were hanged, records it differently. The ones executed were Christians, Sioux converts, and part of Whipple's flock. In his posthumously published autobiography, Whipple records that the Sioux went to their deaths chanting a Christian hymn written in the language of the Sioux, dating from 1842. The hymn's Dakota title is 'Wakantanka taku nitawa', and the text is based on Jeremiah 10:12–13: 'Many and great are your works, O God; Many and great are your works, O God; Many and great are your works.'

Legacy, Memory and Myth

At present, the post-colonial legacy of the Church of England and the British Empire has hardly been engaged with. The issues, failings, exploitation, felonies and violence present us with a tsunami of transgressions. Faced with this, those accountable (but not necessarily responsible) hardly know where to begin. They despair, and then prevaricate. However, this then leads to deeper and more extensive despair, as remorse, repentance and reparation are merely kicked further down the road. There must be a reckoning. We already know that most churches will seek to evade responsibility for their part in the collusion and cover-ups over sexual abuse perpetrated by clergy. It seems that only determined and lengthy campaigning for justice will win out. Empires, too, are reluctant to own their sins of the past.

And what of the monarchical modes of governance in the Church of England? A recent review of its church buildings—the publication of which was suppressed—noted failures in project management across the Church of England. In the somewhat oleaginous rhetoric of corporate-speak which is now normative in the church, the review noted that it was

> difficult to identify any planning and tracking of deliverables, metrics, timelines, milestones, risk management, resource allocation and prioritisation ... [There was a] lack of alignment around a single vision ... Church House [Westminster, the HQ of the Church of England] is not an integrated organisation: [it is an] atrophied bureaucracy which goes deeper than silos; more like turf wars ... with divided loyalties, [there are] political and negative discussions behind closed doors and personal attacks behind backs ... little [proper] check[s] on behaviours ... no meetings where tensions and worries could be discussed jointly, openly and safely ... [and leaders] accustomed to putting niceties of relationships above necessities of dealing with conflict.[16]

Precisely. Manneredness now matters more than morals, and expediency triumphs over ethics. This sounds more like the court of King Lear than an ecclesiastical headquarters. There are no conflict of interest policies in place, no register of interests, and no obvious means of bringing complaints against the hierarchy in cases of bullying, unlawful dismissal or other forms of harassment. The Church Commissioners, who preside over an endowment exceeding £12 billion, share the same building, but they have their own (higher) pay grades, a separate reception desk for their guests, their own lift and different expense policies, and otherwise operate a culture invested in monarchical superiority, able to set their own timescales and priorities.

The Commissioners act almost as though the East India Company had been reincarnated. Through investments in international financial markets, the Church Commissioners outguns the Church of England—the very body it was created to serve. As the historian Mark Harrison noted of the Soviet Union, when such leviathans evolve into becoming ever-more secretive, and any rules, checks and balances are removed from public scrutiny, everything that matters happens behind the scenes. Indecision becomes incentivised, and vested interests are never called out. The citizenry withdraw their trust, and a tiny elite just focus on making sure the entire system does not collapse. But collapse it will, largely, just as the bureaucratic imperialism within the Soviet Union did in the 1980s and 1990s. It will simply implode under the weight of its inefficiency, corruption and cover-ups.[17] Imperialism is a mode of governance, and can be found in capitalism and communism, monarchies and republics. It is also found in churches seeking to rule and reign without accountability, transparency or integrity, yet retaining all powers to themselves and their cadres of bureaucrats. Imperialism still thrives among many congregations and denominations.

An oft-repeated national myth is that no UK government will ever have the time or energy to reform the House of Lords, let alone disestablish the Church of England. Such counsel of despair assumes that this level of establishment will gradually wither on the vine, and the privilege and entitlement will eventually expire.

The Church of England, as part of the establishment, occupies a unique position as an institution with a protected privileged status. It operates under its own laws and courts and can even exempt itself from legislation that applies to the rest of the population. These exemptions extend to areas such as discrimination and employment rights. This distinct status is now evolving into a constitutional crisis. The case for change, however, is pressing hard. The maths is sobering. In 1970, the Church of England baptised 350,000 infants. By 2020, this had declined to 40,000. Of the 12,500 parishes in the Church of England, only 33 recorded 100 or more children (aged under 16) attending church on a Sunday. Of these, most are in London or the home counties, and just 7 north of Birmingham.

Marriages in the Church of England have seen a similar collapse. In 1970, there were 415,000 marriages in England and Wales; the Church of England presided at more than 170,000 of these. By 2022, it was a little over 35,000, with civil ceremonies accounting for 181,000. As for funerals, the Church of England conducted around 100,000 of 550,000 recorded deaths within England in 2022. Church of England attendance at Sunday services averaged 654,000 in 2022, down from over one million in 2010. That represents 1.15% of the population, with 40% of Church of England members now over the age of 70.[18]

This does not pass by unnoticed by the media. For example, a recent leader in *The Guardian* noted that there are more naturists in England than Anglican Easter communicants.[19] More than one million people watch a live football match at the weekend while the National Trust has 5.4 million members. For the Church of England, the virtual monopoly on the 'hatch, match, dispatch' religious provisions for the nation has evaporated. Meanwhile, financial demands imposed on parishes have increased well above the inflation rate. Central costs keep growing, while front-line pastoral ministry is subject to salami-slicing or enforced mergers.

The Church of England leadership also has old canards for dealing with grim statistics. It will selectively point to plump evangelical and charismatic congregations that are allegedly swollen with young people. They will argue that even more churches like this are needed and that huge sums of money are to be spent trying to clone their recipe. That isn't working either, however. A recently funded study from Durham University surveyed almost 5,000 students nationally, and found that moderate, middle-of-the-road Christians outnumbered their evangelical and charismatic counterparts by 10:1. The research found that the large, quiet majority simply disliked making much noise about their faith.[20]

Meanwhile, the leadership of the of the Church of England continues to centralise its bureaucratic oversight and fiscal control, ruling and reigning over parishes and clergy like some remote potentate. Yet all the signs now point to the imminent breakdown of such a polity. The hierarchy had little to say about the breakaway "ordinations" in London at St Helen's Bishopsgate or All Souls' Langham Place, announced in 2024. Or the designate-bishop of Wolverhampton presiding over an ill-advised consecration in Berlin.[21] The bankruptcy of quasi-regal models of leadership are now visibly at their most exposed and weakest. The Church of England's hierarchy finds itself fostering a culture of internal lawlessness, in which wealthy, powerful parishes and groups do as they please, irrespective of Canon Law or any demands made by a bishop. With congregations or bishops acting in an *ultra vires* manner, rather than *intra vires*, the relationship between leader and led is bound to become strained, and is close to collapse.

In some respects, these currents been observable for some time in the English Anglican polity. Henry VIII's self-proclamation as Head of the Church (Act of Supremacy, 1534, and the later incorporation of the Welsh churches in 1536) incidentally established English law as the mode of ecclesial governance. This was a legal and political break with Rome to effect Henry's change to the doctrine of marriage for the purposes of his succession. Only later in Henry's reign did the English Reformation acquire its theological rationale. English law is Common law – under which anything is permitted unless it is specifically legislated against. Roman Law – and this includes Roman Catholic Canon Law – is the opposite, and non-permissive in the absence of legislative directives that approve an action. Some English Anglicans may fondly fantasise about their reunion with Rome, or even claim to have some contiguous ecclesial character. But the Church of England's leadership will never submit to the fundamental principles of Roman law. The English prefer their Common law, and in the Church of England frequently finds that in the freedoms it affords to everyone, the leadership of the church is virtually bound to fail in maintaining unity, save by ever-thinner forms of quasi-regal assertion.

Thus, on issues such as contraception, divorce and remarriage, or the ordination of women, the principle of Common law is followed by the Church of England, which legitimates and regulates practices already taking place, or perceived to be expedient. The principle of Roman law takes the opposite view, and bars practices until they are specifically legislated for. Most English Anglicans who long for reunion with Rome simply do not understand that the structure of authority, law and regulation in Roman law would be, de facto, non-permissive of Anglican polity. Indeed, the Papal declaration – *Apostolicae Curae*, and issued by Pope Leo XIII in 1896 – stating that all Anglican ordinations to be "absolutely null and utterly void" was never really about the theological quality or pastoral validity of Anglican ministry. The Papal pronouncement was, rather, a legal document, that simply stated that the Church of England broke the law and split from Rome by doing so. The only route back to unification with Rome is for Anglicans to obey the (Roman) law and set aside all of its subsequent "unlawful" decisions and acts, which would cover such spheres as contraception, gender, divorce and remarriage, sexuality and the like. The Church of England, naturally, is not about to re-submit to the law of a foreign potentate, which is why the Church of England began in 1534. There is always a Quid Pro Quo involved in reunion. The Church of England will never pay that price.

What is the role of the Archbishop of Canterbury in what remains of the Anglican Communion? Little, it would seem.

The idea of the office and role of the Archbishop as a figure of global spiritual unity was a late invention, and the supporting acolytes of the Lambeth Conference, meeting of the Primates and Consultative Council later still. Precedent shows that that monarchs do not need the Archbishop in order to be crowned. The role has become largely redundant, despite trying to create the impression of all appearances to the contrary. So, the Anglican Communion is bound to its fate as a fragmenting global Protestant polity. And yet it remains in denial about its identity – a shrinking Presbyterian polity (except in England where it is established by law), albeit with quasi-regal bishops who can still throw their weight around without any accountability.

The Anglican denomination is an innocent hostage, captive to its own myth that it is somehow a universal catholic polity that rivals Roman Catholicism. This is a hopeless fiction and vanity, and an increasingly untenable narrative for members of the Anglican Communion across the world. Nobody really believes in it anymore, if indeed they ever did. The Anglican Communion was a consequence of an empire long-gone. It can no more rule and reign overseas as some presumptive ecclesial empire or spiritual commonwealth.

Yet to cover up all of this post-colonial and post-empire fragmentation, the Church of England leaders still invest heavily in their preferred path to spiritual and numerical recovery, championing what is favoured by the minority as the only option. The same minority favours doing far fewer baptisms and marriages (reserving them for believers only) and ruling out same-sex marriages. To keep the minority quiet(er), the Church of England secured statutory exemptions in solemnising such weddings.

There is no sign that the current favoured strategies backed by the leadership are performing better with the broader public. Various 'ecclesial brands'—such as conservative versus liberal, traditional versus progressive—often compete for attendees between themselves. But current statistics suggest this is more like business-to-business rivalry than an indication of revival leading to increased traction with the wider public. If these trends continue, the pressure to sever church and state can only grow.

15

GRAINS OF TRUTH

> Unless the husk of wheat falls to the ground and rots, the grain cannot bear fruit.
>
> John 12:24

The campaign to disestablish the Anglican Church in Wales took about seventy years, culminating in the Welsh Church Act of 1914. It was motivated by a desire for freedom of religious expression and legal and civil equality in the nation. In 1906, after a landslide Liberal election victory, a Royal Commission was set up to investigate the disestablishment of the Church in Wales. It eventually reported in 1910. Despite predictable opposition from peers, Conservatives and Unionists, the maths was hard to ignore. Statistics for 1910 recorded 550,000 Nonconformist communicants in Wales but only 193,000 Welsh Anglicans.

Because of political and ecclesiastical opposition, the Parliament Act had to be invoked to bypass the truculent defiance of the House of Lords. Although the Welsh Church Act was consequently passed in 1914, it was not implemented until after the Great War. Disestablishment for the Church in Wales eventually arrived on 31 March 1920.[1] The Act was 'to terminate the establishment' of the Church of England in Wales. This subtle nuance is overlooked by many. No longer would there be ecclesiastical royal supremacy in appointing church offices for Wales. Welsh bishops would no longer sit in the Lords, although, intriguingly, they elected to retain the customary title 'Lord Bishop' for themselves and their successors in perpetuity. In many respects, the Act did not disestablish the Church in Wales so much as remove the patrimony of the Church of England from within Wales. Arguably, the Church in Wales is not a disestablished church but rather a *non*-established one.

The potential lesson for the Church of England lies in the detail of the 1914 Act, with section 3(1) declaring: 'As from the date of disestablishment, ecclesiastical courts and persons in Wales and Monmouthshire shall cease to exercise any jurisdiction, and the ecclesiastical law of the Church in Wales shall cease to exist as law.'[2] At a stroke, the Act set aside purely ecclesiastical law. It was downgraded to the status of internal church rules, instead of forming part of the secular law of Wales. If a similar process were to be repeated now for the Church of England, it would likewise bring the church into line with statutory law on discrimination, employment, rights, representation and the like.

Furthermore, the Church of England would have to comply with the Nolan Principles of Public Life, and be open, transparent and fair in submitting to scrutiny on conflicts of interest, finances, auditing and governance. Currently, the Church of England has its own self-exemption certificate, deployed extensively within its courts in the hands of its lawyers who both draft and operate the myriad of labyrinth-like ecclesiastical law processes. However, as the disestablishment of the Church in Wales took about seventy years, the likelihood of a definitive severance between church and state in England remains in the distance.

Any UK government might consider statutory independent regulation to align the Church of England with the bare minimum standards expected of any institution functioning broadly in public life. But at present, all indications suggest that the Church of England hierarchy will fight a tenacious, bitter battle against any attempt to introduce external independent scrutiny. The Church of England says it is committed to serving the nation: it just doesn't want to follow its laws. This is increasingly untenable.

In theory, the Archbishops' Council—trustees of the largest Christian charity in England—ought to be able to take responsibility for governance and oversee areas such as expenditure, appointments, auditing and safeguarding. But this does not happen. Virtually all power lies in the hands of a few of the most senior ecclesiocrats, who tend to be recruited from the royal households. The ecclesiocrats specialise in a quasi-monarchical modus operandi. Little is committed to paper, with accountability, scrutiny and transparency degraded to inscrutable opacity. So polished are they at this that they've even managed to engineer exemptions from routine personnel or complaints procedures for themselves that apply to the rest of the Church of England. In the improbable event of any process being triggered, the ecclesiocrat who is the subject of the complaint would invariably commission and oversee the process.

Routine data and subject access requests are obfuscated, and members of the General Synod are not allowed to see complaints procedures, conflicts of interest policies, or inspect registers of interests relating to senior staff. The Audit Committee for scrutinising the operation of the Archbishops' Council is chaired by a trustee from that same council, and so lacks independence. Nor does the chair have the requisite professional qualifications to conduct audits. The Secretariat of the Archbishops' Council hand-picks the chair.

A Constitutional Crossroad

If the Church of England wants to serve the English nation, it now stands at a crossroads. Will its leadership take heed of widespread national indifference towards the misconceived attempts at revival? Or will it continue to sow the seeds of disquiet with a national church that refuses to follow the nation's laws? Perhaps revival might stand a better chance if the Church of England did not invest so much in being a 'law unto itself'. Until this is resolved, the appetite for service will continue to diminish, and the hunger for severance grow. Severance—transforming the Church of England into a non-established church—may now be the simplest way forward. Regulating the Church of England to bring it in line with ordinary statutory obligations would be an alternative, albeit hard to deliver.

For its own part, the Church of England needs to come to terms with its true identity in a post-colonial world. The other parts of the Anglican Communion no longer look to the Old World to run the New World. Back home, the Church of England now needs to positively embrace its position on the margins of society and focus on becoming a simpler, bolder and humbler church.[3] After all, its original vocation was to be a national church for the English, and hardly much more. That is quite enough of a challenge to be facing in the 21st century, and it will struggle to manage even that, let alone confront wider contests and global disputes.

The scale of the crisis is undeniable. Anglicanism could only have ever been conceived following the second information revolution brought about by the onset of printing, which also enabled the pan-European Reformations. If the Axial Age was able to alter the cognitive capacity of communities by moving them from oral cultures to written, the printing revolution gave citizens the Bible and liturgy in their vernacular language, and in a relatively inexpensive and mass-produced form that they could personally own. In the Church of England, printing delivered an Authorised Bible and the Book of Common Prayer in a matter of decades.

The present age is largely free of such authorised books. The Bible is available in multiple styles and formats, and any claim to be definitively authoritative would be hotly contested. Likewise, prescribed liturgies are subject to endless variables. The Church of England's recent volumes, *Common Worship*, offer a suite of options that allow every local church to adapt any provision offered in the text. The set liturgical menu of the 1662 Book of Common Prayer has been superseded by a proverbial liturgical buffet in the service of 21st-century consumerism. The capacity to apply ecclesiastical law across the Anglican Communion no longer exists, if indeed it ever did. As an internal regulative constitutional framework, ecclesiastical law protrudes awkwardly and painfully within much stronger secular law on human rights, equality law and employment legislation.

In all of this, knowledge is power. But if knowledge is everywhere, then it follows that power is dispersed too. The bishops and their ecclesiocracies are at the mercy of local preferences and democratic choices. Robert Bellah was right to state that in modernity everyone now can, to some extent, determine their own faith.[4] Individualism reigns.

In the midst of this milieu for the Church of England, the burdensome 'imagined empire' (or community) of the Anglican Communion has become entrapped within its own webs of meaning. The narrative of a global Communion has metastasised over time and become a growth mass that is beyond the control of the Church of England or any Archbishop of Canterbury. The growth mass inhibits the constituent parts of the body from working together and, like a tumour or sarcoma, presents a localised threat to specific organs. The larger the growth mass looms, the worse it looks, though in actual fact the condition is unlikely to prove fatal. That said, reduction of the mass through therapies that treat the body cells and target the tumour is likely to be required. Surgery is unlikely to be of long-term help.

Post-Colonial Legacy

In Sharon Welch's remarkable essay on ethics, she puts her finger on the framework of power that has led to the present situation in the Church of England where many cannot escape the past and, at the same time, no one is prepared to take responsibility for it. She writes of the 'fundamental immorality of Euro-American ethics', and says there are three twists that lie 'at the heart of Western concepts of virtue'. These are 'too much power poisons virtue; the evil caused by whites refusing to see the consequences of their actions; and the passionate destruction by whites of anything that cannot be controlled'.[5]

Welch discusses the African American novels of Paule Marshall, and in particular *The Chosen Place, the Timeless People* (1969) and *Praisesong for the Widow* (1983).[6] While Marshall is a novelist, her works are rich fragments of memory, testimony, history and witness brought together in compelling narratives that are, of themselves, more real than the reality they reflect. On the matter of legacy, *The Chosen Place, the Timeless People* begins with a West African proverb: 'Once a great wrong has been done, it never dies. People speak the words of peace, but their hearts do not forgive. Generations perform ceremonies of reconciliation but there is no end.'

The chosen place which is the subject of Marshall's 1969 novel is Bourneville, a remote and devastated part of some Caribbean island. The inhabitants are the timeless people: black, poor, and inextricably linked to their past enslavement. The novel tells of a moment when time is disrupted by the arrival of an ambitious

American research project team, and the subsequent tense, ambivalent relationships that then evolve. The friction between natives and foreigners, black and white, the haves and have-nots, and the upper and lower class, highlights the vicissitudes and disparities of power.

Central to the novel is the premise that unless whites can identify and own their exploitation of black people here in previous generations, history is condemned to repeat itself. If there is no repentance, there is no conversion. For the most part, the white characters that Marshall introduces to us are caught up in a fog of their own oblivion. One such character, Harriet, is depicted as the embodiment of a certain kind of white righteousness that refuses to comprehend how control, class and privilege can cause her virtuous efforts to be distorting and alienating.

In one telling passage, Harriet cannot help herself responding to the immediate hunger she sees in the faces of the black children whom she visits one day. Their parents, Stinger and Gwen, are away cutting sugar cane—back-breaking work that does nothing to alleviate poverty. Harriet, having called at the house, realises that the children have not eaten all day, and it is now past 5 pm. She sees half-a-dozen eggs and offers to make the children an omelette. Yet the eldest child protests.

But Harriet is having none of it and ignores the protest. She makes the omelette and then leaves. Despite the children expressing no gratitude for this, Harriet reasons to herself that she has acted out of virtue and necessity, and the children's ingratitude is ill-mannered.

Only later is Harriet faced with the consequences of her (doubtless well-intentioned) intervention. Stinger and Gwen needed to sell the eggs—one of their very few sources of income—to make ends meet and to buy other food. Harriet is mortified, yet she cannot face up to the arrogant, cavalier disregard her action represented. She is even more devastated when she learns that the children did not even eat the omelette, as it would be selfish. She argues that the eggs were better for the children to eat than the 'awful' daily diet of rice and beans that sustains the family. She has no comprehension that the income from the eggs bought decent quantities of rice and beans.

Who gets to determine exactly how reparation is paid out? Surely not the unrepentant, who cannot see the degeneracy of those responsible who have inflicted such loss and trauma upon others but refuse to account for it in the present and the future? It is still too easy for white Euro-American people to assume that they bear no responsibility for the past and yet somehow presume to resolve the present and future for others.

Marshall's character of Harriet serves as a kind of exemplar of virtue gone wrong with inbred classism. As Welch notes, Harriet exhibits 'one of the most effective defence mechanisms of the upper class and of all those in power: the inability to tolerate the rage of those who they have oppressed and an inability to hear what is being expressed through that rage ... the self-righteous rejection of rage as a legitimate form of expression is itself a perpetuation of the cause of the rage'.[7]

The exporting of oppression by a (doubtless well-meaning) white, male, superior, imperial, upper-class culture across the Anglican Communion has produced a bitter harvest of comparable responses. Whether it is gender, sexuality, marriage and divorce, the victims of sexual abuse, racism and sexism, we see, time and time again, the same history repeating itself. Those in control presume that their virtue is superior, and that their position and power are inherent and conferred by some right not chosen by them. Their authority is, likewise, a gift they hold on to, for fear of losing control.

The culture of English episcopal entitlement and elitism is fundamentally resistant to democratic processes in all but name. The imperialism of the English—a structure and attitude, as Edward Said noted, that has 'the imagination of empire'—remains a vital 'myth' in the Church of England and is part of the 'serious fiction' that shapes its outlooks.[8] And yet the forces of revolution and independence that seeded early American democracy will continue slowly but surely to replace the unaccountable monarchical framework that continues to govern the Church of England. Though this persists, one can almost hear the final rasps and gasps for breath. It is dying.

As it is dying, it is fighting within itself to see what can survive, be salvaged and saved. Some believe that only the evangelicals have a future; others, that only a small remnant of faithful Orthodox and Roman Catholics will continue; others still, that some post-church future is all that remains. In truth, what all pretenders to the future crown lack is an honest account of the past and the present. None of those who presume to inherit the remnant of the Church of England (whatever that is) are faring well in late modernity. It has been unable to provide acceptable moral leadership at a national level, and on the international stage (i.e., the Communion) it has put all its energies into a fatal litany of expedient compromises on areas such as gender and sexuality—exactly as it did with slavery and racism, centuries before. The English ecclesial hierarchy will invest in keeping the union together at the expense of moral leadership.

The courtiers that serve at Lambeth Palace and Church House Westminster, who are in reality the real masters and custodians of the cult, are invested as acolytes in an English-sacral myth that cannot bear to face its post-colonial relativity. Such officers will forever be content to contemplate modest reforms, though they are unlikely to deliver a great deal in exchange for those demands. At all costs, the courtiers are most heavily invested in maintaining their own independent control, and avoiding democracy at all costs as well as any accountability or transparency. Modest reforms will be contemplated, discussed, diluted and eventually dismissed. This monarchical power will resist any whiff of revolution.

Similar English imperialist attitudes have been found in the hallowed cloisters of Lambeth Palace. Whether it is women petitioning for ordination, lesbian and gay Christians protesting for equality, or victims of sexual abuse at the hands of the Church of England demonstrating for reparation, all have been told to be quiet, disperse and go home. When they refused, they were given stones, not bread.[9] As the Civil Rights Movement in the United States found, just as the Anti-Apartheid Movement encountered, the powers that rule do not take kindly to having their positions and privileges questioned. External scrutiny of the operation of such power will always be fiercely resisted. There will be expressions of 'deep regret', which will be repeated next time. There is never an apology. This is, of course, a very contrary position for the church to hold when light and truth are, in theory at least, fundamental. But not if the light shines on the church, and the truth exposes the church.[10]

The Vocation of the Husk

As a polity, English Anglicanism, together with its exported forms, also lacks the requisite emotional intelligence to deal with the strong passions that arise through divisions and dissent. The manneredness of elitist muscular Christianity was unable to cope with a changing world and tended to shut down debate under the guise of maintaining peace and tranquil relations for the common good. In truth, however, the hierarchy, by virtue of their monarchical polity, are unable and unwilling to engage with strong passions aroused by classism, sexism, racism, elitism and oppression. As a result, feelings and emotions in the church that run high are left to fester, which then stymies the possibilities for truth and reconciliation in the Anglican Communion and across the Church of England. The moral reckoning is avoided, and a thick veneer of managerial process and mannered polity applied, thereby maintaining the status quo and Anglican-English-episcopal monarchical power.[11]

What a good, honest critical cultural study of English Anglicanism can open up is the hidden wiring that connects the centres and nodes of power and privilege. If justice and truth are fundamental to the identity of a church and nation—and I think it hard to argue the contrary—then exposing the anatomy of English Anglicanism is an urgent, ongoing task. To paraphrase the anthropologist Ruth Benedict, the purpose of anthropology and cultural-critical theory is to make the world a safer place for human differences to coexist. Otherwise, monarchy, autocracy, despotism and hegemonies prevail.

The purpose of such moral reckoning is not to sit in judgement so much as it is to suggest other creative and generative possibilities for being that do not depend on expended or near-extinct forms of order and governance. That requires us to develop a capacity which, at its simplest, involves separating the message from the messenger, or the glory of the Lord from the temple, ark or any vessel said to carry the presence of God. The messenger and the vessels do not endure forever. Only God is eternal. But why does this matter here?

The supposed four instruments of unity that are meant to enable the Anglican Communion to cohere no longer function. They lack authority, traction and buy-in. The instruments (i.e., Archbishop of Canterbury, Lambeth Conference, Anglican Consultative Council and the Meeting of the Primates) are novel claims advanced in the 20th century. Their very existence suggests that unity will struggle to be maintained through a self-constructed myth.[12]

The consecration of Samuel Seabury as the first US Episcopal bishop in 1784 demonstrates the redundancy of the four instruments of the Anglican Communion, before they were ever initiated. The instruments are wholly optional and not remotely essential, as Anglicans in Sydney and Africa will gleefully remind the Archbishop of Canterbury. Somewhere between a third and a half of the bishops in the Anglican Communion ignore them. In short, the four instruments of unity have as much claim to function as a force for unity as the Commonwealth Games. Nobody will deny these events are Good Things. But they do not of themselves resolve international disputes in other forums, let alone bring peace in the midst of war.

In the Gospel of John (12:24), Jesus claims that new life only comes through death. His life mirrors that, with surrender to death being the only door to resurrection. As is so often the case, however, even good Bible translations often fail to convey the richness and wisdom of what Jesus suggests. Most renditions of John 12:24 record Jesus saying that 'unless a grain of wheat dies' it will not bear fruit. But the Greek (*kokkos*) is 'husk', 'kernel' or 'corn'. Biologically, the 'grain' does not die, and never does; the grain remains dormant until it germinates. What the grain needs is for the husk to fall to the ground and rot, and only then can the grain germinate. The Greek word *apothane*, rendered as 'to die', is an agrarian term for the husk of any seed rotting to death, so that the seed springs to life.

The hearers of these words were being invited to ponder what must decay and rot in order to enhance some more abundant life. It could not be the job of the kernel to choose where it falls. And today, even a very casual audit of the ways in which the social gospel continues to yield fruit across the nations served by the Anglican Communion bears this out. In this emerging post-Communion, post-colonial era, the kernel of the 'church phase' of Anglicanism may be passing away. The age of the husk has passed. But what was sown has germinated and sprouted, and it has already fed and nurtured many millions.

In Australia, Anglicare reaches the most vulnerable in society with its comprehensive schemes of care, compassion and social action. In South Africa, the Anglican record on truth, justice, reconciliation and political change is matchless. In India and Japan, though there are minuscule numbers of Anglicans, their schools, universities and colleges with an Anglican foundation still provide some of the very best education known. Hospitals with Anglican foundations can be found in Palestine, Africa and America. In Hong Kong and Macau, the Anglican social welfare projects are so professional, essential and highly regarded that they receive significant state support. In England, Hong Kong and other countries, the number of schoolchildren educated through Anglican educational institutions is far greater than the numbers attending churches. The Episcopal Church of the United States has been a consistent beacon for justice, equality, reparation and social action across the globe. The Mothers' Union, one of England's finest global innovations and institutions, is one of the most significant agents of change in the developing world.

All empires turn into empty husks, eventually. The mighty Persian, Greek and Roman empires were all destined to fall and decay. But the seeds that these dead and decomposed empires carried are still germinating today. The British Empire is no different, and neither is the Commonwealth. The husk or kernel of the British Empire and the Anglican Communion is decaying and dying. It has been so since 1784.[13]

It is the action of death and decay that is inherently life-giving. It is possible to move an institution from one of 'cultured despair to one of learned hope'.[14] Ultimately, to follow the preacher from Galilee and to fashion the right kind of dangerous memory requires the recovery of love, justice and mutual service. Such values are often found at the heart of the very best revolutions. Yet death must be faced. As David Kynaston notes of Winston Churchill's funeral in January 1965, 'this was an act of mourning for the Imperial past ... the final act in Britain's greatness ... It was not Churchill the nation was burying, but a part of their own history, not a statesman but an Empire, not a hero but themselves, as they once were and would never be again.'[15]

Yet in death there is the possibility of more abundant life. The seeds of Anglicanism will continue to bear fruit. If Anglicans can look to a future that is divested of the desire to remain as some kind of eternal ecclesial empire, which instead comes to terms with being the husk it always was, perhaps they will be able to see that Jesus was right all along: 'except a corn of wheat fall into the ground and die, it abideth alone; but if it die, it bringeth forth much fruit'.

The grain of truth is this. In the centuries-long slow passing away of the Anglican Communion husk, there has always been the grace-filled potential for life, liberation, hope, blessing and living legacy, just waiting to germinate. Only when the church embraces the revolutions and radical changes embodied by its founder and rooted in its foundation can there be any kind of resurrection. Until then, this age of disintegration and decomposition will remain and continue to reign.

CONCLUSION

THE WRITING ON THE WALL

Madeline Grant, a parliamentary sketch-writer for the *Daily Telegraph*, succinctly captures the dichotomy within the Church of England:

> There is not one Church of England—but two. There's the Reverend Dr Jekyll, the one who performs invaluable work on the ground; burying the dead, visiting the sick, educating more than a quarter of our nation's schoolchildren to a much higher standard than the state normally achieves. This church manages the food banks, playgroups, dementia cafés and loneliness workshops. Its parish priests do this for little money; its thousands of volunteers do it for none at all.
>
> Then there is the other Church of England—the Reverend Mr Hyde. This is a church of unaccountable committees, upward failure ... and identikit managerial jargon ... It is increasingly clear that these two churches cannot both survive; that this second Church of England, which controls all of its money, runs its internal organisations, manages (read: stitches up) appointments, is doing its utmost to destroy the other one.[1]

While some may harbour a deep existential gloom for the loss of English pre-eminence, the reality is that this pre-eminence has been retracting and retreating for well over a century. The Church of England has been struggling for far longer and, alongside the wider Anglican Communion, is heading for an implosion. Some of the decline is self-inflicted. Some of it is the result of the hubris of English Anglicanism. Some of it is due to the failure of its leadership to adapt. The Church of England's hierarchy seem unable to read the signs of the times and have barely woken up to their blinking incomprehension of the 21st century. There certainly needs to be a reality check.

The post-colonial era is not a time to patch things up and move on, as though nothing serious had ever really happened. It is now time to face the past, pay the dues that are owed, so that all can move forward together with integrity and honesty, for the sake of all humanity. Reputations and institutions will continue to suffer despair until such moral reckoning. Empire and church must both account for their past, express their penitence, change their ways, and pay their dues to the present and future. The legacy of white supremacist Christo-authoritarianism imposed by European churches on populations across the world has yet to be reckoned with. The hierarchical and racist missiology and theology that was freighted within colonial propaganda and church teachings will continue to be resisted and rejected. This is beyond reform or some kind of re-set.[2]

Meanwhile, English Anglicanism has long been dogged by its own sense of self-importance. As one old quip suggests, its strapline should be 'Serving the nation since AD 587 with a slight sense of superiority'. With other denominations, it can appear smug, even haughty. Its leaders act as entitled, and the aura of establishment trappings doesn't help. Indeed, they hinder the Church of England from recognising its 21st-century marginality. If one puts this together with collapsing morale among clergy and congregations, and the near-total erosion of trust and confidence in the leadership and its ecclesiocrats, the recipe is there for death by hubris.[3]

English Anglicanism still likes to regard itself as the world's third-largest Christian denomination. But this is part of the dangerous myth-memory that it is captive to. Moreover, 'third-largest' is a highly contestable claim, when reckoned with Presbyterians (75 million), Methodists (70 million) and Lutherans (77 million). Anglicanism counts more than 25 million from the Church of England within the claimed global total of 80 million. In fact, only 0.5 million attend the Church of England on a normal Sunday. The truer number for Anglicans is probably around 50 million worldwide, similar to that of the Baptists. That said, Anglicanism has shifted from being a small, colonial denomination to having a strong presence elsewhere in the world. The Anglican churches in Nigeria, Uganda, Kenya and Rwanda represent the explosive growth of Anglicanism in the global South, in contrast to the steady decline in the developed world.

Population trends have decisively shifted the Anglican Communion's centre of gravity toward the global South, with approximately three out of four Anglicans living outside Europe and North America. This shift has led to an increasingly bitter inter-Communion feud, in which the global South has challenged 'liberal' moral outlooks of the developed world, with debate mainly focused on the Western church's growing acceptance of equality on LGBTQ+, gender and other issues. The shift of Anglicanism to the global South has led to a clash of values and identity within the Anglican Communion. The churches in the global West have embraced socially and culturally progressive values, while the global South has taken more culturally conservative stances on social issues, particularly on LGBTQ+ recognition. This has caused significant tension within the Communion, with accusations of liberal heresy and challenges to traditional Christian doctrines.

The global South is not a monolith: the Anglican Church of Southern Africa is relatively liberal compared with other African and global South churches. There are debates about the influence of wealthier, predominantly white Western churches on the traditional-leaning global South, with accusations of cultural imperialism and financial coercion. There are also discussions about the role of the Archbishop of Canterbury as the spiritual figurehead of the Communion, with some global South bishops declaring that they no longer consider the Archbishop *primus inter pares*. As a result, some Church of England evangelicals have encouraged conservative Anglicans to join the global South-backed Anglican Network in Europe. This new conservative alliance has taken more culturally conservative stances on social issues, particularly on LGBTQ+ recognition.

Conservative Anglicans now have new networks that enshrine their values, and these are outside the control of the Archbishop of Canterbury and the Church of England. The new alliances include the Diocese of the Southern Cross (Sydney, Australia), Anglican Churches in North America (ACNA), the Global South Fellowship of Confessing Anglicans (GSFA), and the Global Anglican Future Conference (GAFCON). There are increasing indications that there may soon be a New Wine Network for conservative charismatic evangelical Anglicans. The Church of England Evangelical Council is also in the process of breaking away from the wider church on LGBTQ+ issues and proposed prayers of blessing for same-sex couples.

While they overlap, they have distinct goals and strategies. As of 2023, several global South primates announced a state of impaired or broken communion with global Western churches, including the Church of England, as a response to what the global South sees as straying from the 'Anglican way'. Some conservative Anglicans have said that the global South must create an orthodox 'Global Anglican Communion' and leave the Western 'Canterbury Communion' behind. This includes replacing the office of the Archbishop of Canterbury with a new spiritual head and global centre for Anglicanism, breaking away from Anglicanism's colonial, Anglocentric past.

Lambeth Conferences have never really worked, and have been dominated by discord, boycotts and dissent. The 2008 Lambeth Conference was dominated by strife regarding the rise of GAFCON, now seen by some as an alternative Lambeth. It was boycotted by the primates of Nigeria, Uganda, Kenya and Rwanda over their opposition to the Episcopal Church of the USA (TEC). At the 2022 Lambeth Conference, global South bishops refused to take Holy Communion with gay and lesbian bishops, and both the global South and West camps produced rival statements articulating their positions on homosexuality. The GAFCON-aligned bishops made clear their desire to have the TEC sanctioned and to reaffirm the Anglican Communion's condemnation of homosexuality.[4] Conservative Anglican splinter denominations and dioceses have also emerged in the UK and Europe, including the Free Church of England (FCE) and the global South-endorsed Anglican Network in Europe (ANiE).

The post-colonial era has been a slow train coming. But it actually arrived quite some time ago, and it has gradually removed the power, prestige and mystique from monarchical authority. The revolution is now well under way, and the Church of England has tried its utmost to contain, ignore or appease it. It knows it cannot oppose it. At the same time, the English continue to resist any perceived threat to their pre-eminence. Recent research showed that 66% of English Anglicans voted to leave the European Union (compared to 53% of the English population as a whole), and a similar number in the Church of England think that spending on welfare in the UK and overseas is too high. English Anglicans are by majority pro-Brexit and anti-immigration.[5] Andrew Hindmoor notes that

Roman Catholics are twice as likely to vote Labour than their Anglican counterparts. Even as Britain becomes less Christian, Anglicans remain by sheer instinct pro-union (in terms of the United Kingdom), anti-immigration and conservative. In 2013, opposition to same-sex marriage was twice as high among Anglicans as among the wider English population.[6]

The Church of England clergy may be centre-left in their politics, but their congregations are invariably rather more right-leaning. As some commentators observe, every Sunday sees a *Guardian* reader in a dog collar preaching to a congregation who draw their opinions from the *Daily Telegraph* or *Daily Mail*. Yet imperialism is heading for the exit door. What this will mean for the future of Anglicanism is hard to say, but all the signs point to it becoming a more explicit federation of autonomous Protestant churches that maintain the appearance of Catholicism in aesthetics and liturgy but not in doctrine. Thus was it ever so.

With a federation of autonomous churches emerging as the likely default structure, imperialism will continue to compete with democracy and accountability across the episcopate of Anglicanism. However, the imperialism will eventually collapse under its own weight of expectation. Things fall apart, and people do too. The Church of England is already close to crisis on clergy numbers, with too few recruited and too many taking early retirement, citing the church itself as the cause of the deterioration in their well-being and mental health. When all the people know the emperor has no clothes on, and see that in broad daylight, it is time to find a different narrative. Otherwise, nobody can bear the ongoing spectacle of embarrassment and humiliation, which pomp and ceremony cannot overcome.

In terms of that future, the age of crisis for the Anglican Communion and the Church of England has yet to dawn. Looking ahead, 2034 will mark the 250th anniversary of Seabury's consecration (1784). It also marks the 500th anniversary of the Act of Supremacy (1534), in which Henry VIII formally severed England's links with Rome, and established himself as Supreme Head of the English national church. For half a millennium, the Church of England has enjoyed its established status and claims to be leading a vast global Communion. Yet few Anglicans in the global South will ever know or care about the English politics and foreign affairs that gave rise to the Anglican Communion. Few will ever swear any kind of fealty to some distant spiritual potentate residing in some ancient palace in Canterbury.

The story of the writing on the wall marks the end of an empire. In the Book of Daniel (chapter 5), the writer tells of a sumptuous banquet hosted by Belshazzar, the great king of the Babylonians. At the feast, Belshazzar drinks from the sacred vessels he had looted from the temple in Jerusalem. The story records the appearance of a miraculous hand that writes in Aramaic on the wall. The king, fearful and deeply perturbed and unable to comprehend the writing, calls for his astrologers and diviners to translate, but they cannot. Presently, Daniel, a highly regarded Jewish exile and prophet, is summoned. He translates what is essentially graffiti from God: 'numbered and weighed, they are divided'. [7] Your days are numbered; you have been weighed and found wanting; your empire will be divided.

The saga of the Anglican Communion has also reached a natural end. The details of the post-colonial relationships are still to be worked out, as they are between the warring factions internally. In the meantime, the Church of England will continue its gentle slide into becoming a normal, national Protestant denomination but free of the veneers, trappings and baubles conferred by virtue of establishment. In a democracy and meritocracy, an elitist, entitled and established church is not a good look and no longer a tenable proposition to market. The Church of England, forever concerned with its *appearance* in public, and still hankering for popularity, will eventually figure this out. The writing is on the wall.

Collapse: The End of the Anglican Via Media

If the end is nigh for global Anglicanism, how was this not seen earlier? In part, the answer lies within the eye of the beholder. Churches are inclined to only see what they want to see. In this, the Church of England and broader Anglican polity has invested hugely in narrating itself as the ultimate blend of Catholic and Protestant and has imagined that in having the best of both worlds, it somehow enjoys not only superiority, but also an uncanny capacity for resilient survivability.

If Anglicanism really is some kind of tough ecclesial hybrid, how might we characterise the distinctive features found within the culture of Roman Catholicism? That would comprise seven sacraments, with saints, priests, religious orders (i.e., monks and nuns), Marian devotion, the Papacy, law and a high view of doctrine. Virtually any characterisation of Protestantism would be lacking most of those elements. There would be a minister, liturgy, the preaching of the scriptures, and although there could be doctrines (but often contested) and rites for baptism and the eucharist, their understanding and performance would fluctuate considerably in style and content across the denominational penumbra.

So in what sense, if any, is Anglicanism some authentic *via media* of these Catholic and Protestant attributes? Little, it seems to me. Hybridity and breadth are not to be confused with catholicity. True, spiritually, Anglicanism is somewhat magpie-like in that it borrows freely from other traditions. It has also produced its own rich spirituality for around 500 years, with an abundant blend of poetic, aesthetic, mystical and disciplined schoolings. In terms of *appearances* – especially those found in liturgy – apparent hybridity is apparently manifest. For example, some Anglican clergy dress like Catholic clergy; some may even adopt courtesy nomenclature such as 'father'. Yet others decline to use the title 'Revd' at all and avoid wearing clerical attire.

However, on closer inspection we can see that such *appearances* are deceptive, since the actual theology of Anglicanism is Reformed and Protestant, not Catholic. It would be odd if that were not so, since this is what Anglicans have consistently claimed since the mid-sixteenth century.[8] Formally, Anglicans believe that there are only two sacraments: baptism and eucharist. Ordination and marriage do not 'make the cut', so to speak.[9] Anglicans do not need their marriages to be "annulled" by the church. Within reason, they can divorce and remarry, if they so wish. They do not need to seek the permission of Rome, or even their local bishop.

Thus, when conservative Anglicans protest about same-sex couples marrying as a "change to the doctrine of marriage", they are reaching for a Roman Catholic doctrine, and not some Protestant view of marriage. Some Anglicans believe in ordination as a sacrament and as a matter of ontological change. However, most Anglicans do not share this view, and regard ordination as something more akin to the public authorisation of ministry. Until very recently, that was the standard Anglican theological understanding of ordained ministry.[10]

The *via media* is, of course, a generic Latin phrase meaning "the middle road" or the "way between (and avoiding or reconciling) two extremes". It has become a philosophical maxim somewhat akin to the Golden Mean which advocated moderation in all thoughts and actions. It originated from an earlier Delphic maxim (i.e., "nothing to excess") that was aligned with Aristotle's (384-322 BCE) advocacy of moderation in all things, finding a pathway between extremities. Augustine's early fifth-century *City of God* (i.e., *De civitate Dei contra paganos,* ch 11) used the idea of *via media* to *connect* two extremes, rather than avoid either. Later, theologians came to see the *via media* as a divine principle. Jesus was, after all, both fully human and fully divine.

However, the proper historical roots of the Anglican *via media* lie in its balance between Reformed theology (e.g., Zurich and Calvinism) and that of German Lutherans. The theological outlook of early Anglicans was essentially closer to Calvinism than Lutheranism, and the thirty-nine articles expresses that. It was only in the nineteenth century that Anglicans began to talk about themselves as some *via media* between Protestantism and Catholicism. Here, it was the Tractarians within the Oxford Movement who espoused this new interpretation. The Oxford Movement had its own cultural genesis rooted in conservative reactions to the trauma of the American and French Revolutions (1776-83 and 1789), the eventual collapse of the Holy Roman Empire in the 1830s, and the 1829 Catholic Emancipation Act in Britain, together with the Church Temporalities Act of the Church of Ireland (1833). By the late 1820s, European national churches were no longer secure in their identity and positions and began searching for deeper roots and older personalities.

It is therefore no surprise that from the 1830s, some in the Church of England began to "rediscover" their Catholic origins – an idea that would have seemed dangerously "foreign" and anti-English when Napoleon was defeated at the battle of Waterloo (1815), or Nelson lost his life at Trafalgar (1805) barely a few decades before the Oxford Movement. Yet for the Tractarians, by the late 1820s, this new romantic conservatism had begun to reimagine the Church of England as the "English Branch" of the true Catholic Church, yet one that was free from "Roman error" and infused with hitherto lost Reformed orthodoxy. The Church of England was now to be understood as a true branch of the Church Universal, yet withal preserved it free from doctrinal error. It is Catholic and Apostolic, yet not Papatistical.[11]

This huge leap of faith and reason required a whole set of presumptions to be swallowed that just a few decades earlier were unarticulated and mostly unknown, including that the "apostolic descent and continuity" of the Church of England was in line with the true Catholic faith, before the latter had erred through its (so-called) "Papistical corruptions" and become heretical.

In 1834, John Henry Newman argued in a series of tracts entitled *Via Media* that the Anglican Church could be regarded as Catholic because it had kept an episcopal hierarchy (so remained apostolic), retained the central sacraments, continued to follow ancient liturgy, and followed a Reformed theology that was free of (allegedly late-developed) Catholic accretions.[12] Newman repositioned the Church of England as the authentic middle way between the extremes of Catholicism and Protestantism. It was a kind of sacralised Goldilocks ecclesiology – a perfect balance of hot and cold, and yet without falling into the error of Laodicean spirituality.[13]

At the time, Newman's argument seemed compelling, and it resonates with some modern-day outlooks still found in other denominations, such as the Church of Sweden, which sees itself as an evangelical-catholic hybrid created through a process of reforming purification. The Church of Sweden, much like the Church of England, does not see itself as a new church, but rather as a hybrid continuum faithfully incorporating both Catholic and Protestant tradition and orthodoxy.

The fabrication was not to last. Newman became a Roman Catholic in 1845. Yet 1834 bequeaths yet another awkward anniversary for the Church of England to face up to in 2034, namely the bicentennial of Newman's classic *Via Media* argument, which he ultimately rejected. Newman came to see that his own argument for *via media* had collapsed. There was no "middle-way" between Catholic apostolic dogma and the rationalist relativism of Protestants. Newman abandoned the *via media* hypothesis because he saw it as a false antinomy. The Church of England had to make its mind up as to whether it was the ancient church of the first millennium or some new creation of the second millennium. What it could not claim, authentically and honestly, was to be the legitimate child of both. Newman's epiphany gradually crystallised, but once it did, his conversion to Roman Catholicism was only a question of time.[14]

Part of the problem facing the Church of England and the wider Anglican Communion in moving forward is that Newman's version of *Via Media* has been rendered redundant. It has effectively imploded; it has collapsed from within. It has taken some while, but Anglicans have eventually figured out that just as there is no credible middle moral ground between racism and racial equality, it is hard to find the Golden Mean between the dogmatic and the democratic. Thus, it is challenging to run a church that is trying to affirm the equality of all on the grounds of gender, sexuality, ethnicity and disability, and yet also at the same time affirm and equally privilege those who still object to such equality.

Put plainly in English idiom, it is hard to have your cake and eat it. A small percentage of Anglicans oppose the ordination of women. However, in the Church of England, such views enjoy being protected characters in ecclesiastical law, effectively enshrining discrimination. This is provenly a recipe for moral compromise and ecclesial incoherence. It is not advanced on disability and ethnicity – although, please note, it once was. Yet the Church of England still valorises compromising policies and practices on gender and sexuality.

One can perhaps imagine some parallel universe, in which the Church of England seeks to protect a small minority of people who want to smoke in enclosed public places, so insist that non-smokers accommodate smokers, reserve public spaces and places for smokers, always stipulate that provision be made for them, and brand those who advocate no-smoking spaces as being intolerant. In some cases, it will be argued that smokers should be allowed to light up and express their preference in non-smoking spaces, as though this amounted to equitable treatment. All of this is done in the name of "mutual flourishing".[15] But just as there is no *via media* on smoking or racism, nor can there be on sexism or sexuality.

The internecine wars now taking place within the Anglican Communion on equal marriage are still to be fought out over money, sex and power. These battles are increasingly bitter, and they hold up a dim mirror to the Church of England's monarchical polity. In essence, because no bishop can be wrong, and they all presume that they possess thin ancient Greek or Roman god-like characteristics of being omnipotent, omniscient, omnicompetent and omnipresent, no bishop can ever back down. So, when the bishops, provinces and dioceses squabble amongst themselves, it becomes a kind of dystopian Homeric saga. Worse still, it is quite apparent that bishops do not know very much, have few powers apart from quasi-regal coercion and their enshrined unaccountability, and are mostly only all-present by virtue of social media.

The dark farce is that most quasi-regal bishops cannot really fathom how anyone can call them to account or disagree with them. And when it is one of their own, they call upon a proverbial Zeus to arbitrate and rule in their favour. The problem goes all the way back to the English episcopal culture. One that protects bullying episcopal demi-gods, who, even when dreadfully capricious and browbeating, but then occasionally acting with kindness and sincerity, cannot and will not be held to account.[16]

With the collapse of the fabled *Via Media* schema devised under Newman and the Tractarians, the Church of England and wider Anglican Communion are now retreating to their roots. Namely, what has become a collation of post-colonial national, regional, and local Protestant churches, with varying views on theology, culture and church discipline, struggling to find common ground and work out how to resolve their differences. No *via media* can manage this; the middle way is a fabrication and self-deception.

The Church of England and the wider Anglican Communion will have to cultivate a different mindset and develop new leadership and collegiality structures if it is to survive. But there is no indication that this will be forthcoming from Lambeth Palace or the Church of England anytime soon. They will not want to be their own gravedigger, and so will cling to the *via media* myth for as long as possible. However, sustaining the pious fiction of some middle-way Protestant-Catholic hybrid-global Communion is no longer possible. In its stead, what has finally emerged is another over-expansive trans-national Protestant denomination in terminal decline, unable to exorcise the ghosts of its past, deal with its present, or face its end.

Since 1534 English Anglicanism has primarily been a expansive national and colonial project. This rapidly petered out in the post-war era and has ceased to be tenable in the twenty-first century. The Church of England now needs to relinquish its empire of the mind. It needs to adjust to its reduced support and position at a national level if it is to retain any future credibility. As for disestablishment, if it continues in refusing to jump, it will have to be pushed. That writing is already on the wall.

Meanwhile, Newman came to the realisation that he could not be half Protestant and half Catholic. Nobody could. There was no hybrid, and Anglicanism was not some *via media* after all. You are either a Roman Catholic or you are not. Anglicans, concluded Newman, were not. It was that simple. Newman converted to Rome, and the rest is history.

Elegy—the Decline and Fall of English Anglicanism and its Elitism

'Too late' are probably the saddest two words in the English language, as many an elegy can echo. Evelyn Waugh's satirical novel Decline and Fall, in which the phrase appears, was a contraction of Edward Gibbon's *The History of the Decline and Fall of the Roman Empire* (published between 1776-1789 by Strahan & Cadell, London) and also an allusion to Oswald Spengler's *The Decline of the West* (published between 1918–1922), which first appeared in an English translation in 1926. Both authors argued that the rise of empires and their cultures is inevitably followed by their fall.

The publication dates of these books chime with our primary concerns. 1776 marked the beginning of a revolution against the English pattern of monarchical authority over America. By 1926, Britain and the Dominions had agreed all were equal members of a community within the British Empire. Whilst all owed allegiance to the British monarch the United Kingdom no longer ruled over them. This community was called the 'British Commonwealth of Nations'. Even then, change was slow. The British Empire Games first held in 1930 only adjusted its nomenclature to being the British Empire and Commonwealth Games from 1954 to 1966, and then the British Commonwealth Games from 1970 to 1974. Only after that date was 'British' reluctantly dropped.

The Church of England has been playing a reluctant game of catch-up for almost a century. The empire is over, and the Anglican Communion had barely caught on as an idea before it started to unravel. At the same time, the Church of England has been struggling to make sense of its identity as the spiritual arm of an English enterprise in empire-building for almost 500 years, and is unable to critically deconstruct its reliance upon quasi-regal forms of governance. Its bishops now only function as confused and conflated versions of ancient demi-gods—partially omniscient, omnipresent and omnipotent—yet demonstrably lacking in knowledge, power and presence. By the time 2034 arrives, the Anglican Communion will be over, and the Church of England as it is currently configured, kaputt.

The slide from gradual-to-sudden collapse is a very English story—and one of blinking incomprehension to those still trying to run some version of a post-colonial ecclesial empire. Anthony Sampson's classic *Anatomy of Britain* portrayed an English elite of gentleman amateurs running institutions that now require highly specialised and professional expertise.[17] True, there is a new elite of well-qualified liberal cosmopolitans who are culturally progressive now in place, but few look to the churches as a career pathway. Were they to do so, the resistance from the Old Guard would quickly become apparent.

This leaves the Church of England's elite playing at what Leonore Davidoff dubbed 'status theatre',[18] with bishops and ecclesiocrats drawing symbolic and governance boundaries around themselves in ever-decreasing circles. There are still a few who want to be a part of that circle, and it is still the case that the learned accents, inflections and manners of leadership will suffice as a passport. The complexion of the Church of England's autocracy therefore remains male, white and right—conservative with a small 'c', and prepared to tinker with inclusivity provided the balance of power is not unduly perturbed. The post-war decline of deference which might impact other privileged elites has little traction in the upper echelons of the Church of England's leadership, as it remains aloof and unaccountable. The clergy and laity, meanwhile, despite being better-equipped to perform their tasks and serve the church than ever before, have seen their power and financial conditions significantly reduced by the entitled elites. The resulting ennui now encountered at grass-root parish levels is only set to only accelerate. Waugh and Hemingway were right. It is probably now far too late to stop a gradual decline becoming something very sudden.

***

On the morning I completed this book, I also took myself down to St Andrew's Episcopal Cathedral in the city of Aberdeen, next to the building where Samuel Seabury had been consecrated on a chilly November day in 1784. I presided at the Eucharist on that Sunday—another cold November morning—on the same day that the Episcopal Church remembers Seabury. It was a christening, and my wife (also an Anglican priest) preached and baptised. While the congregation is mostly Nigerian, there is an international flavour to each and every Sunday. The Provost is from India. We were joined by a small trickle of American visitors and a steady stream of ever-present Eastern Europeans. The only flag to be seen in the cathedral is the Stars and Stripes of the United States, which was donated by President Eisenhower.

This is not an established church, nor does it need to be. Such things would not matter to the congregation, and it is a fair guess that establishment matters little to any congregation—cosmopolitan and multicultural—outside England. It is only the leaders of English Anglicanism who have a problem with their identity and status. The rest of the world moved on long ago. That Sunday in Aberdeen, the joyous prayers and songs of the people coursed through the congregation, and I marvelled at this gathering—something Seabury could never have envisaged, yet it celebrated a far richer kind of communion open to all.

CODA

NOBODY'S FRIENDS AND THE END OF HIERARCHY

On the appointment of George Carey to the See of Canterbury in 1991, a senior Cathedral Dean was invited by a journalist to comment on the elevation of his former colleague to the throne of St Augustine. Plainly underwhelmed by the appointment, the Dean sighed that this "was just a sign of the times", only to then add "and I don't much care for these times." Whatever those times were, history has a habit of repeating itself. First as irony, second as tragedy, and finally as farce.

On November 12 2024, it was announced that the 105th Archbishop of Canterbury, the Most Reverend and Right Honourable Justin Welby, had resigned over his handling of the case of John Smyth QC. This was without precedent in the near 500-year history of the Church of England. Two Church of England archbishops had been executed: in the reign of Mary Tudor, Thomas Cranmer was burnt at the stake in 1556; while William Laud was beheaded in 1645, after the defeat of Charles I by the New Model Army.[1] But no Archbishop has ever before had to resign in disgrace. The archbishops were executed after dubious legal proceedings, with the outcome lying somewhere between irony and tragedy. Welby's resignation, preceded by no legal process, was one of farce. For sure, a sign of the times.

John Smyth was one of the most prolific sexual abusers in recent Church of England history, yet with substantial evidence of cover-ups and inaction protecting him at the very highest levels. The report into the abuse was conducted by Keith Makin,[2] and despite being subjected to lengthy delays by lawyers acting for Lambeth Palace, Justin Welby's position quickly became untenable. The *Makin Report* was published on November 7 2024, providing forensic accounts of the failures and coverups, if not systemic corruption in the culture within the ecclesial hierarchy. Welby resigned on November 12.[3]

As mainstream media commentators were quick to note, Welby's ten-year tenure had failed to create a culture of transparency and accountability in the upper echelons of ecclesial governance.[4] This is the protruding tip of a smouldering volcano. John Smyth QC, who died in 2018 without ever being brought to justice, represents "the Church of England's Jimmy Savile crisis". Smyth hailed from an impeccable elite public school and upper-class Oxbridge pedigree, and had been a prominent mover and shaker in the conservative evangelical world from the 1970s. That culture had played a substantial part in forming Justin Welby's Christian faith, his eventual arch-episcopal governance, and a whole generation of English bishops.

Smyth had been deeply entwined with Nobody's Friends, a Private Dining Club in London that meets at Lambeth Palace. Founded in 1800, Nobody's Friends is one of the oldest dining clubs in London, with the membership largely comprising Tory, High Church and Freemasons, split 50-50 between ordained Church of England clergy and senior ecclesiocrats and ecclesiastical lawyers, many of whom work at Lambeth Palace.[5] These links appear to have been especially problematic in the field of safeguarding, governance and other spheres which eventually saw the sudden demise of Welby's tenure.[6]

Welby himself heralded from the Holy Trinity Brompton network of churches (i.e., middle-upper-class 'happy-clappy'), and had a background in the oil industry prior to ordination training. He also had a somewhat eclectic background in mediation work. Educated at Eton and Cambridge, he was steeped in Tory ancestry with an elitist upper-class pedigree. Those who chose him must have assumed that his background in business, a short stretch in reconciliation work, and being steeped in the upper echelons of the English establishment, rendered him a safe pair of hands. However, the ecclesiocrats who brought in Welby failed to factor in the unconscious bias of English upper-class elitism. Namely, one that believes in its own effortless superiority, never thinks for even a second that it owes an explanation to the public and need never account for its actions.

Welby's brief for the role would have come straight from the English post-colonial playbook. This is one which presumes that on balance, English imperialism made the world a better place. The brief would be to Make Anglicanism Great Again (MAGA); to restore its reputation through numerical church growth, good public relations, unlimited upper-class charm combined with effortless, beneficent, superior imperialistic governance, with grand ecclesiastical status theatre. In other words, keep calm and carry on.

Yet by 2024 this no longer worked and had effectively imploded. There are doubtless many reasons, and historians will pick over the ecclesial carcass in the generations to come. As we have already indicated in this book, imperialism – whether national, international or local-episcopal – is no longer a trusted mode of governance for most Anglicans. Bishops and their senior advisors have no accountability, are aloof from democratic mandate and averse to external regulatory oversight. They will lecture the rest of the world on democracy and equality but are under no obligation to be subject to the laws that govern everyone else. Bishops think they are experts on anything they speak of by virtue of their office. Like demi-gods, they invest in their own omniscient and omnicompetent myth-presumptions, as though by being a bishop they have gained sufficient expertise and knowledge to lecture the world on anything they might hold a view on.

Our times are different. The people in the pews expect democratic accountability and transparency. They might consent to being under authority, but only provided it is subject to independent external scrutiny and regulation. It remains the case that most Anglican bishops would prefer the hot fires of hell to any egalitarian answerability. In that sense, Welby's resignation might be seen as a repeat episode in the Church of England's "1776 and all that" moment: no taxation without representation. Why should any punter in the pew fund governance rooted in autocracy with pretentions towards theocracy? Increasingly, the indications are that they won't put up with some distant authority they did not elect yet presumes to instruct and assumes can be compliantly taxed.[7] The people in the pew have also discovered that they have some power. Over 15,000 of them signing a petition calling for Welby to step down. As this is a revolutionary act, without precedent in the 500 year history of the Church of England, we have arrived at a point where the public will hold the episcopacy to account, and if ignored, protest and withdraw their funding. No taxation without representation.

Welby is arguably a representative harbinger of an ecclesial revolution. It has been coming for some while. As the former Labour Party MP Tony Benn (1925-2014) repeatedly asked of those in authority, "What power have you got? Where did you get it from? In whose interests do you exercise it? To whom are you accountable? And how can we get rid of you?"[8] If the answer to every one of those questions from the bishops and senior ecclesiocrats is "only God, or possibly the reigning monarch", then the stage is fully set for open revolt by those in the pews.

In many respects, the story of global Anglicanism – not yet 500 years old – is one of a Protestant democratic polity vying with faux-catholic quasi-regal notions of autocracy and theocracy. The latter, when blended with monarchical imperialism, presumes it does not need to give an account of itself or even consult. It just rules and reigns, and when subjected to questions, ignores its stakeholders and the media as though they were insolent and unruly serfs. It will spurn democratic accountability and treat congregations as medieval monarchs might once have regarded subjects.[9]

This has not always been an English problem. Let us not forget that Samuel Seabury, the first Anglican bishop to be consecrated (1784) without the approval of the Church of England, wore a specially made mitre fashioned from beaver-pelt and gold filigree wherever he went, in order to signal his self-proclaimed divine authority over a bemused American citizenry. Seabury believed his cathedral was wherever he happened to be celebrating the eucharist, which amounts to a kind of spiritual narcissism and demand for monarchical deference. He thought the laity should have no say at all in the governance of the church, and his diocese, Connecticut, did not change that until later in the twentieth century. Seabury's lofty regal outlook matched his pro-slavery and high Tory leanings.

Yet these quasi-quaint eclectic views have not prevailed. American Episcopalians are assiduously pro-democratic, and their ecclesial polity is progressively Protestant, albeit with some catholic accents. The Church of England and wider Anglican Communion will be drawn inexorably to that same pole in the coming decades, and that spells the end for English Anglican imperialism at home and abroad. Its time is up, and the resignation of the 105th Archbishop of Canterbury demonstrated that the public have little appetite for an institution that does not practice what it preaches. If democracy, egalitarianism and accountability are good for the rest of the world, then English Anglicanism will have to re-model itself.

Until it does, dismissal by the public and decline will continue. To paraphrase Ernest Hemingway, bankruptcy happens in two ways: first very slowly, then all of a sudden.[10] Leading the Church of England from hereon will be like trying to ascend the proverbial glass cliff. Falling further and faster is the most likely result. But staying put is hardly an option. The only future left for Anglicanism lies at ground level. The leadership needs to climb down, and as fast as possible.[11]

As we have indicated, by 2034 there may not be much of an Anglican Communion to argue over, or barely a remnant of the Church of England to debate. At local levels it will undoubtedly and deservedly endure. But as a national, let alone established church, its future is far from secure. Disestablishment, in one form or another, surely beckons. What this critical-cultural theological history and ecclesiology has sought to signal is that, difficult though facing the past and present is, the future does not have to be quite so bleak.[12]

Put simply, if the Anglican hierarchy were to treat their clergy, people and the rest of the world as respected equals, and be fully immersed in relationships shaped by transparency, mutual accountability and trust, as well as being subject to proper external regulation, they might discover that they had quite a lot of friends. Until then, 'Nobody's Friends' will become a self-fulfilling prophecy. Indeed, unless there is a revolution, 'Nobody's Friends' will become the unsought epitaph inscribed on a tomb for the entitled hierarchy of English Anglicanism.

GLOSSARY OF TERMS AND LIST OF ORGANISATIONS

ACNA (Anglican Church in North America). In 2008, the churches of Nigeria, Rwanda, Uganda and the Anglican Church of South America launched ACNA. Though numerically small (100,000?), their influence is considerable.

Anglican Quadrilateral—sometimes known as the Lambeth or Chicago-Lambeth Quadrilateral—constitutes the basis for inner coherence in Anglican polity and order and moderate external ecumenical discussion. The four are: the Holy Scripture as the rule of faith; the Apostles' and the Nicene creeds; the two sacraments of Baptism and Holy Communion; and the historic episcopate. Declared by the General Convention of the Protestant Episcopal Church in Chicago in 1886, they were amended and adopted by the Anglican Communion's Lambeth Conference of 1888. The four are sometimes regarded as a reflection of Richard Hooker's threefold proposition of scripture, tradition and reason, with some also arguing that tradition or culture is a fourth implicit pillar within Hooker's Anglican ecclesiology. The Quadrilateral is not binding on Anglican churches.

Archbishop. A bishop presiding over a larger group of dioceses.

Book of Common Prayer (BCP). The established rite of the Church of England since 1662 (and earlier versions in the 16th century) by which its worship and teaching is regulated.

Church House, Westminster. Headquarters of the Church of England.

Diocese of the Southern Cross. An extra-territorial Australasian offshoot of the conservative Diocese of Sydney.

Four Instruments of Unity. The Archbishop of Canterbury (1867), the Lambeth Conference (1867), Anglican Consultative Council (1971) and Anglican Primates (1979)—the dates indicate when their transnational authority was first proposed. The Church of England began to appoint colonial bishops after Samuel Seabury's consecration by the American Episcopalians. In 1787 Charles Inglis (Bishop of Nova Scotia) was appointed with jurisdiction over all of British North America. In 1814 a bishop of Calcutta was made; in 1824 the first bishop was sent to the West Indies and in 1836 to Australia. By 1840, there were still only ten colonial bishops for the Church of England, but even this small beginning greatly facilitated the growth of Anglicanism around the world. In 1841 a Colonial Bishoprics Council was set up, and soon, many more dioceses were created.

Free Church of England (FCE). Founded in Totnes in 1844 when a number of Reformed Protestant congregations separated from the established Church of England. The doctrinal basis of the FCE and ethos is Anglican although it is not a member of the Anglican Communion. It is a Reformed conservative evangelical denomination in ethos, follows the Book of Common Prayer and uses conservative modern-language forms that belong to the Anglican tradition. The Church of England acknowledges the FCE as a church with valid orders, like the Church of England in South Africa (Reformed and pro-Apartheid, and quite separate from the Anglican Church of Southern Africa, which is in full communion with the wider Anglican Church).

GAFCON (Global Anglican Future Conference). Existing since 2008, GAFCON comprises a large group of conservative Anglican bishops, who met in Jerusalem ahead of the Lambeth Conference. GAFCON stresses its anti-colonial stance against a neo-imperial global West on matters of sexuality, HIV/AIDS and other issues.

GSFA (Global South Fellowship of Confessing Anglicans). The GSFA arose around 2003 in opposition to Gene Robinson's consecration as a bishop in the TEC. It eventually formed GAFCON in 2008. GAFCON/GSFA claims around 40 million adherents, which, discounting European, North American, Australasian and South African Anglicans (perhaps 10 million, maximum), is a reasonably fair estimate.

Lambeth Palace. London home and headquarters of the Archbishop of Canterbury.

Primate. An archbishop presiding over national or provincial dioceses.

Primus inter pares. Latin for 'first among equals', and applied to the office and function of the Archbishop of Canterbury.

TEC. The Episcopal Church of the United States of America.

Thirty-Nine Articles. Finalised in 1571 during the reign of Elizabeth I, these are the Protestant articles of faith that mark out the Protestant identity of the Church of England in its separation from Roman Catholicism. Within the Provinces of the Anglican Communion, the status of the Thirty-nine Articles varies in the several churches of the Anglican Communion. Very few of the Anglican Provinces now use, require or acknowledge them. Since 1865 Church of England clergy have had to 'affirm' the doctrine in the articles is 'agreeable to the Word of God'. In the United States of America the articles were revised in 1801 to remove references to royal supremacy.

Via media. It is commonplace to see the *via media* as a complementary amalgam of Catholic and Protestant. But suppose for a moment that this is only partly true? What if the polity is a fundamental tension between Episcopal and Presbyterian polity? I would venture it is. Indeed, across the provinces of the Anglican Communion, the vast majority of local churches have high degrees of autonomy. They are self-funding and self-directing, needing bishops only for occasional rites and visitations. That is a model of Presbyterian governance, but one that makes room for bishops as teachers, pastors and symbols of unity regarding the faith. They have little, if any, executive power. This was how the Episcopal Church in the United States was established, drawing on the inchoate crypto-Presbyterian polity of the Scottish Episcopal Church with the consecration of Samuel Seabury in 1784 at Aberdeen.

APPENDIX 1

THE WORLDWIDE ANGLICAN COMMUNION

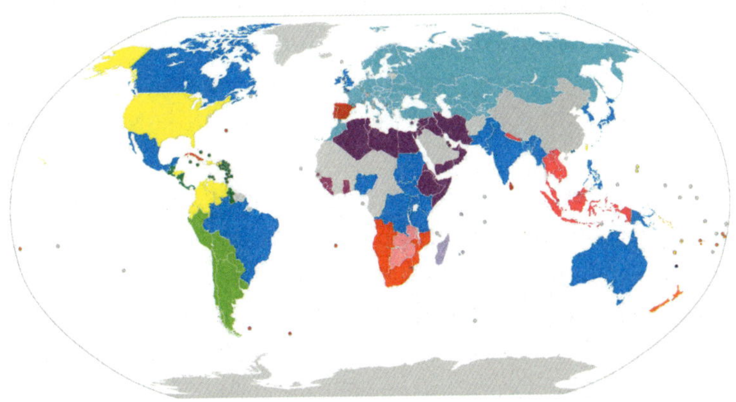

A world map showing the provinces of the Anglican Communion:

Autonomous churches Episcopal Church of the United States Church in the Province of the West Indies Anglican Church in Central America	Episcopal Church in Jerusalem and the Middle East Church of the Province of the Indian Ocean Anglican Church in Aotearoa, New Zealand and Polynesia

Anglican Church of South America	Church of the Province of Melanesia
Anglican Church of Southern Africa	Diocese in Europe of the Church of England
Church of the Province of Central Africa	Extra-provincial to the Archbishop of Canterbury
Church of the Province of West Africa	Church of the Province of South East Asia
	No organised Anglican presence

The Church of Ireland serves both Northern Ireland and the Republic of Ireland; and the Anglican Church of Korea serves South Korea and, theoretically, North Korea.

Indian Anglicanism is currently divided into the Church of North India, the Church of South India and the Mar Thoma Church.

The Diocese in Europe (formally the Diocese of Gibraltar in Europe), in the Province of Canterbury, is also present in Portugal and Spain.

The Episcopal Church (United States)-affiliated Convocation of Episcopal Churches in Europe has affiliates in Austria, Belgium, France, Georgia, Germany and Italy.

APPENDIX 2

COUNTRIES INVADED BY GREAT BRITAIN

Created with Datawrapper

Great Britain (or, rather, England), with its significant military and trading power, carried out unrivalled invasions and colonisation across the globe. Only 22 countries have not been invaded by the British, as highlighted on the accompanying map: Andorra, Belarus, Bolivia, Burundi, Central African Republic, Chad, Congo, Guatemala, Ivory Coast, Kyrgyzstan, Liechtenstein, Luxembourg, Mali, Marshall Islands, Monaco, Mongolia, Paraguay, São Tomé and Príncipe, Sweden, Tajikistan, Uzbekistan, and Vatican City. Invading 171 out of 193 countries worldwide is no small feat. In contrast, the United States has only invaded 68 countries. This map tells a story about the long-standing worldwide power of Great Britain, and explains how the Church of England became 'universal'—through territorial conquest, commerce and colonisation.

APPENDIX 3

PROVINCES OF THE ANGLICAN COMMUNION

The Anglican Communion consists of 42 autonomous provinces each with its own primate and governing structure. These provinces may take the form of national churches (such as in Canada, Uganda or Japan) or a collection of nations (such as the West Indies, Central Africa or South East Asia).

Provinces	**Territorial Jurisdiction**
Episcopal/Anglican Province of Alexandria	Algeria, Djibouti, Egypt, Eritrea, Ethiopia, Libya, Somalia, Tunisia
Anglican Church in Aotearoa, New Zealand and Polynesia	Cook Islands, Fiji, New Zealand, Samoa, Tonga
Anglican Church of Australia	Australia
Church of Bangladesh	Bangladesh
Anglican Episcopal Church of Brazil	Brazil
Province of the Anglican Church of Burundi	Burundi
Anglican Church of Canada	Canada

Provinces	Territorial Jurisdiction
Church of the Province of Central Africa	Botswana, Malawi, Zambia, Zimbabwe
Anglican Church in Central America	Costa Rica, El Salvador, Guatemala, Nicaragua, Panama
Anglican Church of Chile	Chile
Province of the Anglican Church of the Congo	Democratic Republic of Congo, Republic of Congo
Church of England	Crown Dependencies, England, Europe
Hong Kong Sheng Kung Hui (Hong Kong Anglican Church)	Hong Kong, Macau
Church of the Province of the Indian Ocean	Madagascar, Mauritius, Seychelles
Church of Ireland	Northern Ireland, Republic of Ireland
Anglican Church in Japan	Japan
Episcopal Church in Jerusalem and the Middle East	Bahrain, Cyprus, Iran, Iraq, Israel, Jordan, Kuwait, Lebanon, Oman, Palestine, Qatar, Saudi Arabia, Syria, United Arab Emirates, Yemen
Anglican Church of Kenya	Kenya
Anglican Church of Korea	North Korea, South Korea
Anglican Church of Melanesia	New Caledonia, Solomon Islands, Vanuatu
Anglican Church of Mexico	Mexico

APPENDIX 3

Provinces	**Territorial Jurisdiction**
Anglican Church of Mozambique and Angola	Angola, Mozambique
Church of the Province of Myanmar	Myanmar
Church of Nigeria	Nigeria
Church of North India	Bhutan, India
Church of Pakistan	Pakistan
Anglican Church of Papua New Guinea	Papua New Guinea
Episcopal Church in the Philippines	Philippines
Anglican Church of Rwanda	Rwanda
Scottish Episcopal Church	Scotland
Anglican Church of South America	Argentina, Bolivia, Paraguay, Peru, Uruguay
Church of the Province of South East Asia	Brunei, Cambodia, Indonesia, Laos, Malaysia, Nepal, Singapore, Thailand, Vietnam
Church of South India	India, Sri Lanka
Province of the Episcopal Church of South Sudan	South Sudan
Anglican Church of Southern Africa	Eswatini, Lesotho, Namibia, St Helena, South Africa
Province of the Episcopal Church of Sudan	Sudan
Anglican Church of Tanzania	Tanzania
Church of Uganda	Uganda

Provinces	**Territorial Jurisdiction**
Episcopal Church	British Virgin Islands, Colombia, Cuba, Dominican Republic, Ecuador, Europe, Guam, Haiti, Honduras, Northern Mariana Islands, Puerto Rico, Taiwan, United States, United States Virgin Islands, Venezuela
Church in Wales	Wales
Church of the Province of West Africa	Cameroon, Cape Verde, Gambia, Ghana, Guinea, Liberia, Senegal, Sierra Leone
Church in the Province of the West Indies	Anguilla, Antigua and Barbuda, Aruba, Bahamas, Barbados, Belize, Cayman Islands, Dominica, Grenada, Guyana, Jamaica, Montserrat, Saba, Saint-Barthélemy, St Kitts and Nevis, St Lucia, St Martin, St Vincent and the Grenadines, Sint Eustatius, Trinidad and Tobago, Turks and Caicos Islands

Extra-Provincial Churches

In addition to the 42 provinces, there are 5 extra-provincial churches under the metropolitical authority of the Archbishop of Canterbury.

Extra-Provincial Church	Territorial Jurisdiction
Anglican Church of Bermuda	Bermuda
Church of Ceylon	Sri Lanka
Parish of the Falkland Islands	Falkland Islands
Lusitanian Catholic Apostolic Evangelical Church	Portugal
Spanish Reformed Episcopal Church	Spain

Anglican Provinces That Have Ceased to Exist

Province	Territorial Jurisdiction	Year Established	Year Dissolved
Chung Hua Sheng Kung Hui	China	1912	1949 (1958)
Church of Hawaii	Hawaii	1862	1902
Church of India, Pakistan, Burma and Ceylon	Bangladesh, India, Myanmar, Pakistan, Sri Lanka	1930	1970
Protestant Episcopal Church in the Confederate States of America	Confederate States of America	1861	1865
United Church of England and Ireland	England, Wales, Ireland	1800	1871

APPENDIX 4

THE TOP 100
ANGLICAN CHURCHES NOT FORMALLY CONNECTED TO THE GLOBAL ANGLICAN COMMUNION

This Top 100 highlights how fragmented global Anglicanism has become since the 19th century. The Churches listed below are not 'in communion' with the wider Anglican Communion. It is a complex field, since some are 'recognised', such as the Church of England in South Africa, whose ordinations are regarded as valid by the Church of England, yet deemed to be irregular. To be part of the Anglican Communion, a church must have a formal relation with the See of Canterbury. Many of these groups class themselves as 'continuing churches'. By this they claim to be continuing with orthodox and traditional beliefs and practices while the Anglican Communion is not. Some claims about origins are specious (e.g., 'founded by Joseph of Arimathea at Glastonbury in AD 36').

An Anglican church must be able to show apostolic succession, which requires at least one bishop to have had valid consecration through an Anglican rite. While that bishop may have been consecrated in the Anglican church, they are not obliged to remain legally part of it. Each of the churches listed below had at least one independent bishop who had his own compelling reasons for breaking away. (For further discussion, see Martyn Percy, 'Falling Out of Love: The Ordination of Women and Recent Anglo-American Anglican Schisms Explored', *Journal of Contemporary Religion*, vol. 12, no. 1, 1998, pp. 35–49).

Great Britain and Ireland

These include the Anglican Free Communion, established in England in 1897 by a union of several small British episcopates established in the 1870s, and the Free Church of England (also known as the Reformed Episcopal Church), formed in 1844. The Province of the Order of Christ the King claims to have been established by Joseph of Arimathea circa AD 36 at Glastonbury, so preceding Roman Catholicism. The Traditional Church of England, one of the original 'continuing' churches in England, was formed in 1994. The Anglican Mission in England (AMiE) and Church of Ireland (Traditional Rite) make up over a dozen British and Irish Continuing Anglican Churches.

Global, Extra-Territorial Provinces

The oldest of these is the Anglican Rite Roman Catholic Church, an autonomous Old Roman Catholic Patriarchate with Anglican patrimony, descended from the Roman Catholic See of Utrecht. The See of Utrecht has been independent since 1145, after the Pope granted autonomy. The Charismatic Episcopal Church was founded in 1992 by independent Pentecostal congregations. Bodies such as the Anglican Church Worldwide claim they are not in communion with Canterbury administratively but are spiritually. Together with bodies such as the Episcopal Catholic Church (founded in 1897) and the Worldwide Anglican Church (but note, *not* the Anglican Communion), there are more than three dozen such federations.

Hispanic, Caribbean, Central and South America

There are approximately two dozen Anglican-style dioceses, provinces, networks and federations not in a formal relationship with the Anglican Communion. They include the Iglesia Anglicana Ortodoxa del Perú, a Peruvian branch of the Anglican Orthodox Church, the Provincia Iglesia Anglicana Reformada, based in Colombia, and the Iglesia Episcopal Anglicana de Chile.

Europe

The Anglican Catholic Diocese of Christ the Redeemer has congregations in England, Italy, Spain, France, Malta, Germany and Russia. There are also churches claiming to be Anglican such as the Italian Mission King Charles the Martyr (Missione Anglicana Tradizionalista Carlo I Stuart), which is part of the Anglican Catholic Diocese of Christ the Redeemer, and the Reformierte Episkopalkirche in Deutschland, which is part of the Reformed Episcopal Church in Germany. There are at least a dozen Anglican networks in Europe that are not officially part of the Anglican Communion.

North America

With at least sixty different Anglican networks, dioceses and federations not officially part of the Anglican Communion, the United States and Canada have the most of any continent. The Anglican Church in North America (ACNA, whose ordinations are recognised by the Archbishop of Canterbury, but not by American Episcopalians) has an estimated membership of 100,000 and claims two dozen dioceses. Some of the churches claiming Anglican parentage are fusions with other traditions. These include the Anglican Orthodox Church (AOC), founded in 1963 in Statesville, North Carolina; the Reformed Anglican Church (Florida), which is traditionalist and evangelical; the Free Protestant Episcopal Church (Saskatchewan); the Anglican Mission in America (AMiA); the Charismatic Episcopal Church; the Anglican Rite Old Catholic Church, based in Texas; and the Progressive Episcopal Diocese of the South. The Church of England, Cayman Islands, still disputes the legality of the Bishop of Jamaica and the Primate of the West Indies.

Africa

There are over half-a-dozen networks and federations including the Anglican Catholic Church of Kenya, founded in 2006, and the Reformed Evangelical Anglican Churches of Namibia. The Church of England in South Africa (CESA) was founded in 1938. The Reformed Evangelical Anglican Church of South Africa (REACH-SA) is the official operating name. Pro-apartheid for much of their history, they now relate to the Diocese of Sydney. Unusually, their ordinations are recognised by the Archbishop of Canterbury.

Asia

There are at least a dozen different Anglican-style bodies, including the Church of India, affiliated to the Worldwide Traditional Anglican Communion with about 42 Anglican churches. This is separate from the Anglican Episcopal Churches of India and the Anglican Orthodox Church in India. The India Christian Mission Church (Episcopal) was established in 1897 by an Anglican priest from Bicester in England and ministers in Andhra Pradesh State.

South-east Asia, Australasia

The Anglican Independent Communion Australia was founded in 2006. The Anglican Orthodox Church of the Fiji Islands, the Anglican Church in the Philippines (Traditional), the Episcopal Church of the Solomon Islands, The Filipino Communion of Evangelical Episcopal Churches, the Nippon Kirisuto Seikokai (Traditional Rite, Japan), The Traditional Anglican Communion in New Zealand, and the Diocese of the Southern Cross (Sydney) constitute more than a dozen networks and federations of Anglican-style churches not in any formal relationship with the official Anglican Communion.

APPENDIX 5

TIMELINE OF THE CHURCH OF ENGLAND AND ANGLICAN COMMUNION SINCE 1534

Monarchy	Church of England	Europe and Beyond
TUDOR		
Henry VIII (1509–47)	**1521** Henry opposes Luther in writing *Assertio septem sacramentorum*, or Defence of the Seven Sacraments. Pope Leo X rewards Henry by granting him the title *Fidei Defensor*, or Defender of the Faith. **1526** William Tyndale publishes a translation of the New Testament in English. **1533** The marriage of Henry and Catherine of Aragon is declared null and void by Thomas Cranmer, Archbishop of Canterbury, in defiance of the Catholic Church. Henry marries Anne Boleyn.	**1517** Luther writes his *Ninety-Five Theses*. This document criticises the selling of indulgences. Protestants consider publication of the theses the beginning of the Reformation. **1521** The Pope excommunicates Luther. Luther begins to translate the Bible into German. **1528** First Scottish Protestant martyr burned at St Andrews.

Monarchy	Church of England	Europe and Beyond
	1534 Act of Supremacy: the English monarch becomes Supreme Head of the Church in England, which separates from the Roman Catholic Church. **1535–6** Thomas More is executed for refusing to support the English Reformation. William Tyndale burnt at the stake for heresy. **1539** The Six Articles condemn Lutheranism. Hugh Latimer, Bishop of Winchester, resigns in protest. Henry continues to execute Lutherans and Roman Catholics. **1536–40** The dissolution of the monasteries in England, Wales and Ireland leads to the largest state-sponsored sequestration of religious assets ever.	**1534** Ignatius of Loyola founds the Jesuit order as part of the Catholic Counter-Reformation. Parts of Poland, Hungary and Germany are reconverted from Protestantism to Catholicism. **1536** Protestant reformer John Calvin publishes his work of systematic theology, *Institutes of the Christian Religion*. **1546** Death of Martin Luther.
Edward VI (1547–53)	**1549** Publication of the first version of the Book of Common Prayer in the Church of England. A second (revised) edition follows in 1552. It is more Protestant in tone.	**1545–63** Catholic Reformation. The Council at Trent reforms and clarifies Catholic doctrine.
Mary I (1553–8)	Catholicism restored in England. Persecution of Protestants begins. New bishops are appointed and all married priests are removed. Protestant martyrs include Thomas Cranmer, burnt at the stake in Oxford.	**1555** Peace of Augsburg grants toleration to Lutherans within the Holy Roman Empire, using the principle of *cuius regio, eius religio* (lit., whose realm, his religion).

Monarchy	Church of England	Europe and Beyond
	1528–60 The Scottish Reformation takes place, eventually culminating in Catholicism being outlawed and the Reformed Presbyterian Kirk becoming the legally recognised form of Christianity in Scotland.	Cardinal Pole (Mary's archbishop) tries to re-establish monasteries and convents. Only 100 of 1,500 monks and nuns return.
Elizabeth I (1558–1603)	**1563** The 39 Articles of the Church of England produced as a doctrinal statement of faith. **1560** Publication of the Geneva Bible, the first English translation with chapter and verse divisions. Richard Hooker writes *The Lawes of Ecclesiastical Polity*, and Anglicanism's *via media* ethos evolves. **1563** Foxe's *Book of Martyrs* published, describing the Pope as the antichrist. **1568** The Bishops' Bible authorised and published. **1579** Sir Francis Drake reaches San Francisco Bay, California—the first Church of England service said and sermon preached in America. English adventurism engages in piracy, trade and early territorial claims.	**1554** English privateer captures hundreds of slaves from Spanish merchants and re-sells them. Profiteering through adventurism and piracy becomes rife. **1563** Death of John Knox, leader of the Reformation in Scotland. **1564** Death of John Calvin. **1598** French Protestants (Huguenots) are granted toleration by Henry IV in the Edict of Nantes.

Monarchy	Church of England	Europe and Beyond
STUART		
James I (1603–25)	**1605** 'Gunpowder Plot' by alleged Roman Catholic fanatics seeking to destroy Parliament. **1611** Publication of the (Authorised) King James Version of the Bible. **1612** First Church of England church outside Great Britain is built on Bermuda. This was unintended, but it marks another date for the start of global Anglicanism. **1620** Puritans leave for America on the *Mayflower*. Plymouth Bay colony founded in America.	**1601** East India Company founded and begins trading in earnest. **1607** Jamestown in Virginia is established as a colony. **1618** Start of Thirty Years War between Protestants and Catholics. **1624** Virginia becomes a Royal colony, with Anglican liturgy mandatory.
Charles I (1625–49)	**1628** Charles is heavily influenced by continental Roman Catholicism. Married to Henrietta, a Roman Catholic. William Laud is made archbishop and oversees the persecution of Puritans. Charles attempts to reintroduce Anglican bishops to Scotland, but this is resisted. Parliament declines to support Charles going to war over the issues. **1645** William Laud beheaded.	**1630** Massachusetts Bay colony founded by Puritans on a Calvinist model for a Christian commonwealth. **1637** The Scottish Prayer Book is published. It calls priests 'presbyters'. It becomes the basis for the future American Prayer Book. **1638** Scotland removes its bishops.

Monarchy	Church of England	Europe and Beyond
	1642–49 English Civil War also envelops Wales, Scotland and Ireland. This is primarily a religious war fought on the principle of the 'divine right' to rule versus a more presbyterial 'will of the people' polity. The war ends with the trial and execution of Charles I in 1649.	**1640** Westminster Assembly drafts its Confession. **1648** Thirty Years War ends.
Protectorate (1649–60) under Oliver Cromwell	Cromwell's experiment with early democratic republican ideals strips the Church of England of its bishops and powers. Former Royalists flee to Virginia to settle the colony.	'Diggers', 'Levellers' and 'Ranters' cause problems for Cromwell's Puritan regime.
Charles II (1660–85)	**1662** Act of Uniformity reimposes the Church of England. Revised Book of Common Prayer makes many practices optional and reintroduces many saints' days. The publication is a compromise, with prayers for the dead, reserved sacrament and other Catholic practices still outlawed. However, the surplice is established as legal clerical garb.	Charles II dies a Roman Catholic, and is succeeded by his brother, James II, an ardent Roman Catholic. **1684** Massachusetts Bay colony's charter as a Puritan state is revoked by England.
James II (1685–88)	The king's prosecution of Archbishop Sancroft and colleagues ends with the Glorious Revolution, and James II flees.	**1685** Revocation of the Edict of Nantes by Louis XIV. Exodus of Protestants from France.

Monarchy	Church of England	Europe and Beyond
William III and Mary II (1689–1702)	Parliament replaces James II with a Protestant monarch, William of Orange. The Church of Scotland is officially Presbyterian as part of the settlement. Bishop Thomas Ken and others refuse allegiance to King William and become 'non-jurors'. **1688** Act of Toleration partly restores civil rights to Roman Catholics and Dissenters. The events since the Reformation have finally convinced most Anglicans of the virtues of tolerance and mutual forbearance. **1689** Bill of Rights establishes a constitutional monarchy ruling over England, Scotland and Ireland (in 1690). Scottish Episcopalian bishops refuse to recognise the monarchy and are deprived of their sees (until 1788). **1692** Persecution of Jacobites in Scotland continues. Jacobite leaders of the MacDonald clan are massacred at Glencoe by the Campbells. **1697** Thomas Bray, Church of England clergyman, founds Society for Promoting Christian Knowledge.	**1689** William establishes control of Scotland with victory at the Battle of Dunkeld. **1690** William establishes rule over all of Ireland with victory against James II at the Battle of the Boyne. **1696** William III of England survives a kidnap and assassination attempt by Jacobite sympathisers. **1697** Freedom of worship guaranteed in New England and New York for all Protestants. **1697** The Civil List Act passed, which sets the funds available to the British monarchy. **1707** Act of Union unites England and Scotland. An increasingly united Britain flexes its trading and military muscle across the world.

Monarchy	Church of England	Europe and Beyond
	1701 Bray founds Society for the Propagation of the Gospel, which sponsors over 300 missionaries in the colonies over the next century.	
Anne (1702–14)	Anne reigns as Queen of England, Scotland and Ireland from 1702 and then, following the 1707 Act of Union, over a united kingdom as Queen of Great Britain until her death in 1714. **1713–15** Treaty of Utrecht ends War of Spanish Succession and gains Britain more territories and a monopoly to supply slaves to the Spanish Empire.	**1704** Duke of Marlborough defeats Spanish at Battle of Blenheim. Queen Anne's Bounty established through slavery-related income to support poorer clergy.
HANOVERIAN		
George I (1714–27)	Britain consolidates its overseas power and trade. First inklings of industrial revolution and early signs of the Enlightenment. Slave plantations now firmly established in the Caribbean and North America. **1715–19** Jacobite rebellions in Scotland put down.	**1733** James Oglethorpe, British Army officer, founds a colony in Georgia for the relief of debtors.

Monarchy	Church of England	Europe and Beyond
George II (1727–60)	**1738** John and Charles Wesley and George Whitefield, all Anglican priests, have religious experiences in Georgia. In Britain, Methodism is a movement on the cusp of becoming a church. **1745** Second Jacobite Rebellion fails.	Anglicans, being rationalists or even deists, oppose the Great Awakening. Liberal opposition is called 'Old Light'.
George III (1760–1820)	**1784** Methodist Episcopal Church founded in Baltimore by leaders designated by John Wesley. Methodism now a separate denomination. **1784** Samuel Seabury becomes the first bishop of the nascent Episcopal Church. Episcopalians begin to organise as an entity. **1800–1** The Acts of Union unite England, Ireland, Scotland and Wales as Great Britain. **1804** Absalom Jones, the first black American Episcopalian priest, is ordained. **1807** Slave trade abolished in England (but not across the British Empire).	**1776–83** American War of Independence results in the formation of Episcopal Church. Colonisation of Australia begins. **1789** French Revolution. **1798** Irish Revolution under Wolfe Tone brutally put down. **1803** More territories begin to join the US. The French sell Louisiana to the Americans. American settlers begin to press westward to the Pacific.

Monarchy	Church of England	Europe and Beyond
George IV (1820–30)	Massive urbanisation in the wake of the industrial revolution leads to the unprecedented building of new churches in slum areas and emerging cities. **1829** Catholic Emancipation Act allows Catholics to sit in British Parliament.	**1812** Britain re-invades the US as part of a trade war. Invaders defeated. **1815** British and Prussian forces defeat Napoleon at the Battle of Waterloo.
William IV (1830–37)	**1832** First Reform Act enfranchises large numbers of the English poor. The Act is opposed by the bishops; the Archbishop of Canterbury is almost struck by a dead cat during anti-clerical riots. **1833** Beginnings of the Oxford Movement with John Keble, John Henry Newman and others. The Tractarians are anti-modernist and anti-liberal, and call for a return to a more Roman Catholic ethos, and less control on church affairs by Parliament. **1833** Slave trade finally abolished across the British Empire. But slave-owners are compensated for their loss of assets and income. **1835** Jackson Kemper ordained bishop and is the first missionary bishop to the American frontier.	Advances in science and technology begin to challenge religious authority and Christian hegemony in all spheres of public life. Charles Lyell, a devout Anglican, researches his *Elements of Geology* (published in 1839), which forms the foundation of modern earth science. Evangelicals are appalled by Lyell's rejection of a literal reading of Genesis.

Monarchy	Church of England	Europe and Beyond
Victoria (1837–1901)	**1844** George Augustus Selwyn becomes first Bishop of New Zealand. **1853** William Colenso becomes Bishop of Natal. Colenso (influenced by the teaching F.D. Maurice) had been introduced to his wife by Samuel Taylor Coleridge. Colenso translated the Bible into Zulu, and empathised with their custom of polygamy. **1854** Cuddesdon is the first purpose-built Church of England seminary established in Oxford by Bishop Samuel Wilberforce (and opponent of Darwin). **1858** Jewish citizens allowed to become MPs. **1863** Attempts to remove Colenso as Bishop of Natal on charges of heresy initially succeed but eventually fail. **1864** Samuel Crowther, former black slave, made Bishop on the Niger. **1866** Channing Moore Williams made Bishop of China and Japan.	**1859** Charles Darwin's *Origin of Species* published. **1860** *Essays and Reviews* is published, favourable to science and modernism. It pleads for tolerance and common sense in doctrinal matters, instead of 'godless orthodoxy', so that the church can retain credibility. Benjamin Jowett popularises historical and literary criticism of the Bible. **1865** Thomas Huxley humiliates Bishop Samuel Wilberforce in an evolution debate. Wilberforce eventually apologises to Darwin. **1870** First Vatican Council. Roman Catholics affirm Papal infallibility. **1890** Charles Gore writes *Lux Mundi*, suggesting Anglo-Catholics can accept historical and literary criticism of the Bible. Response is favourable.

Monarchy	Church of England	Europe and Beyond
	1867 In response to the Colenso affair, the first Lambeth Conference is convened; of 144 bishops, 76 bishops are in attendance. The Archbishop of York has misgivings and declines to attend. There is no censure of Colenso. **1869** Church of Ireland disestablished. **1878** Second Lambeth Conference tries to focus on missionary work and its organisation. **1888** Third Lambeth Conference struggles with issues of maintaining unity and order. **1890** Christian Student Movement founded.	**1896** Pope Leo XIII declares Anglican orders 'absolutely null and void'. **1901** onwards. The sun begins to set on the British Empire.
WINDSOR		
Edward VII (1901–10)	**1910** First World Missionary Conference, held in Edinburgh. It anticipates the triumphant global spread of Christianity by the end of the 20th century. **1906** *The English Hymnal*, the product of the Oxford Movement, enriches worship.	**1910** *The Fundamentals* series begins publication in the US. Emphasis placed on literal inerrancy of the Bible, and rejection of historical and literary criticism of scripture and modern understandings of the natural world.

Monarchy	Church of England	Europe and Beyond
	1900 onwards Revivals take place in Scotland, Wales and Northeast England (e.g., from 1907, Sunderland Pentecostalism in Monkwermouth under Smith Wigglesworth, Alexander Boddy, and others).	**1906–8** The Azusa Street Revival in California is the harbinger of Pentecostalism, which will become the largest 20th-century movement within the Christian churches.
George V (1910–36)	**1920** Church of Wales disestablished. **1928** Revised Book of Common Prayer published, but Parliament declines to approve it, leading to major church–state tensions.	**1914–18** First World War. Across Europe, Christianity is far less influential thereafter.
Edward VIII (1936)	**1936** Edward abdicates, leading to a significant crisis in the constitution of church and state.	The rise of secular fascism and communism begins to threaten world peace.
George VI (1936–52)	**1944** First Anglican woman (Li Tim Oi) ordained priest in China. She ministers in Macao. **1944** William Temple publishes *Christianity and Social Order*, heralding the advent of the NHS.	**1939–45** Second World War. The post-war years were marked by the Cold War, rapid secularisation, and the post-colonial era.
Elizabeth II (1952–2022)	**1952** Revised Standard Version of the Bible is published and proves enormously popular. The Episcopal Church, with the National Council of Churches, is responsible. **1963** John A.T. Robinson's *Honest to God* is published. Welcomed by many, it is perceived by some as an attack on 'traditional' teaching.	**1960** onwards. Charismatic revival impacts on Anglicans. Riots and revolutions across Europe, including church's involvement in anti-war movements and campaigns for nuclear disarmament (CND).

Monarchy	Church of England	Europe and Beyond
	1971 Hong Kong ordains two women priests. **1974** Eleven women ordained as priests in Philadelphia, US. Widely welcomed, the action nonetheless lacked official approval. **1988–2008** Disastrous Lambeth Conferences fail to find resolution on gender and LGBTQ+ issues, leading to significant fragmentation, new schisms and calls for alternative episcopal oversight.	**1970** onwards. American Episcopalians approve ordination of women to orders of deacon, priest and bishop (**1976**). Liturgical relaxation and reform gives more choice to congregations, but reduces unity across the Anglican Communion. **1980** onwards. Growing and seemingly irreparable splits on sexuality, gender, authority and power.
Charles III (2022–)	The Church of England is unable to reach a point of decision on issues that divide it and the wider Anglican Communion. The bishops in the House of Lords make speeches advocating greater public trust in institutions and calling for renewed faith in democracy. Meanwhile, democratic accountability, proper governance, transparency, access to basic legal rights and honest reparation remain hard to secure within the Church of England itself. Like some medieval monarchical state, it remains a law unto itself.	Continued global schism and national ecclesial fragmentation occur, and formalising these divisions appears to be only a matter of time.

ACKNOWLEDGEMENTS

I am deeply and profoundly grateful to the Dean of Virginia Theological Seminary, Dr. Ian Markham for setting me on the road to engage with this work. Particular thanks also go to Suzanne Clackson, Angela Berlis, Bridget Nichols, Rainer Hirsch-Luipold, Kate Quarry, Stephen Pickard, Peter Selby, Gareth Jones, Tim Larsen, Daniel Pedersen, Anthony Bash, Johnny Douglas, Anthony Reddie, Laura Mair, Joseph Thompson, Katherine Grieb, Jarel Robinson-Brown, Maurice Elliott, Clive Billeness, Carlton Turner, Barney Crockett, Graham Sawyer, Leslie Herrmann, Tom Greggs and Mark Strange for conversations and perceptive comments on earlier drafts of the text. I thank the publisher especially for unstinting support.

Friends and colleagues have been a rich source of constant nourishment—in particular, Henry, Nigel, Deborah, Sue, Mark, Jonathan, Robin and Stephen. My immediate family, as ever, have sustained the writing and thinking with their usual blend of TLC—Time, Lyra (running our beloved hound) and plentiful Coffee—and here I owe the greatest debt of all to Emma for her love, support and unfailing fortitude.

NOTES

FRONTMATTER

1. Quoted in *The Economist*, 16 November 2002, p. 11.

INTRODUCTION

1. For an account of resistance to the British Empire, see David Veevers, *The Great Defiance: How the World Took On the British Empire*, Ebury Press, 2023.
2. Akala, *Natives: Race and Class in the Ruins of Empire*, John Murray, 2018. For a recent discussion of the issues, see Aaron Reeves and Sam Friedman, *Born to Rule: The making and Remaking of the British Elite*, Harvard UP, 2024.
3. Edward Said, *Culture and Imperialism*, Vintage, 1994, pp. 7–9.
4. Said, *Culture and Imperialism*, p. 12. As we will argue, the Church of England only came into being as an entity in 1534, after Henry VIII assumed headship under the Act of Supremacy. The break with Rome was legal and political before it was theological. C.f. Benedict Anderson, *Imagined Communities: The Origins and Spread of Nationalism*, Verso, 1983.
5. Between 1873 and 1876 Nietzsche published his four *Untimely Meditations*. The second essay is titled 'The Use and Abuse of History for Life' (1874; German '*Vom Nutzen und Nachtheil der Historie für das Leben*'—literally, '*On the Uses and Disadvantages of*

History for Life'). See Friedrich Nietzsche, *Untimely Meditations*, trans. R.J. Hollingdale, Cambridge UP, 1997.

6. See for example Nigel Biggar, *Colonialism: A Moral Reckoning*, HarperCollins, 2022. See also Alan Lester (ed.), *The Truth about Empire: Real Histories of British Colonialism*, Hurst, 2024. The contributors have provided a substantial response to Biggar's work.
7. Nietzsche's work is well discussed in relation to history and culture in two books by Roger Scruton: *An Intelligent Person's Guide to Modern Culture*, Duckworth, 1998, and *An Intelligent Person's Guide to Philosophy*, Duckworth, 1996.
8. Mark C. Taylor, *About Religion: Economies of Faith in Virtual Culture*, Chicago UP, 1999.
9. George Lindbeck, *Nature of Doctrine: Religion and Theology in a Postliberal Age*, Westminster John Knox Press, 1984.
10. See Mike Powell, *Amglish: Two Nations Divided by a Common Language*, Infinity Venture Publishing, 2015; Terry Eagleton, *Across the Pond: An Englishman's View of America*, W.W. Norton and Co., 2013; and David Dimbleby and David Reynolds, *An Ocean Apart: The Relationship between Britain and America*, Hodder and Stoughton, 1988.

1. THE RISE AND FALL OF A GLOBAL CHURCH

1. Daniel Muñoz, 'North to South: A Reappraisal of Anglican Communion Membership Figures', *Journal of Anglican Studies*, vol. 14, 2016, pp. 71–95. The true number of Anglicans, globally, is more likely to be 45–50 million.
2. Peter Frankopan, *The Silk Roads: A New History of the World*, Bloomsbury, 2015, pp. 215–16.
3. Frankopan, *The Silk Roads*, p. 277. See also *India and the End of the Empire: Selected Writings of Daniel O'Connor*, eds. Ann Loades & David Jasper, Sacristy Press, 2023.
4. Penelope Carson, *The East India Company and Religion, 1698–1858*, Boydell and Brewer, 2012.
5. See Walter Reid, *Fighting Retreat: Churchill and India*, Hurst Publishing, 2024.

6. H. Richard Niebuhr's *The Social Sources of Denominationalism*, Meridian Books, 1957 [1929] is an unsurpassed study of class, race and hierarchy in churches.
7. Readers wishing to examine specific studies of the history of classism in English Anglicanism are referred to John Shelton Reed, *Glorious Battle: The Cultural Politics of Victorian Anglo-Catholicism*, Vanderbilt UP, 1996; and W.S.F. Pickering, *Anglo-Catholicism: A Study in Religious Ambiguity*, Routledge, 1980.
8. William Faulkner, *Requiem for a Nun*, Chatto and Windus, 1919.
9. George Orwell, *Nineteen Eighty-Four*, Secker and Warburg, 1949, p. 162.
10. For an analogical and Darwinian approach to ecclesiology, see Martyn Percy, *Clergy: The Origin of Species*, Bloomsbury, 2008.
11. The relationship between increasingly extreme right-wing nationalism in government and opposition to equality and freedom regarding sexuality and gender is explored in Gionathan Lo Mascolo (ed.), *The Christian Right in Europe: Movements, Networks and Denominations*, Transcript Publications, 2023.
12. See M. Percy, 'Richard Hooker', in I. Markham (ed.), *The Blackwell Student's Companion to the Theologians*, Blackwell, 2013, pp. 204–7.

2. FAITH IN AN AGE OF CRISIS

1. See Lee Gatiss, *The Tragedy of 1662: The Ejection and Persecution of the Puritans*, Latimer Trust, 2007.
2. See David Runciman, *The History of Ideas: Equality, Justice and Revolution*, Profile Books, 2024.
3. See Dan Davies, *The Unaccountability Machine*, Profile, 2024; and see also Stafford Beer, *Brain of the Firm*, John Wiley and Sons, 1972.
4. Such Presbyterian polity is often snidely dismissed as 'congregationalism', as though the alternative was the whole catholic unit of the wider parish. Again, this is now hard-wired into the myth-made memory of many Church of England clergy.
5. Agnes Arnold-Forster, *Nostalgia: A History of a Dangerous Emotion*, Picador, 2024.
6. See Henry Reece, *The Fall: Last Days of the English Republic*, Yale UP, 2023.

7. GS 2354, General Synod, 'Trust and Trustworthiness within the Church of England'.
8. See Nick Montgomery and Carla Bergman, *Joyful Militancy: Building Thriving Resistance in Modern Times*, AK Press and Institute for Anarchist Studies, 2017. The authors discuss the problems inherent in rigid radicalism, and commend kinship, friends, trust and kindness as the basis for social revolution. See also Italo Calvino, *Six Memos for the Next Millennium*, translated by Geoffrey Brock, Penguin, 1988, especially the discussions on lightness and multiplicity.

3. EMPIRE, CHURCH AND MORAL GEOGRAPHY

1. The field of moral geography was established by David Smith. Rather like David Voas's later work on religious geography, Smith saw that distinct social, political and environmental conditions directly shaped ethical norms. On moral geography, see David Smith, *Moral Geographies: Ethics in a World of Difference*, Edinburgh UP, 2000, and *Geography and Social Justice: Social Justice in a Changing World*, John Wiley and Co., 1994; see also David Smith and Roger Lee (eds.), *Geographies and Moralities*, Wiley-Blackwell, 2004, and David Smith and James Proctor (eds.), *Geography and Ethics: Journeys in a Moral Terrain*, Routledge, 1999. For a more specific discussion of English-island identity and moral landscape, see Charlotte Lydia Riley, *Imperial Island: A History of Empire in Modern Britain*, Bodley Head, 2023.
2. For two interesting alternative perspectives based on reality, see Ian Wright, *Brilliant Maps: An Atlas for Curious Minds*, Granta, 2019; and Gideon Defoe, *An Atlas of Extinct Countries*, HarperCollins, 2020.
3. Official figures claimed by the Anglican Communion: https://www.anglicancommunion.org/. For a discussion of the problematic moral nature of Anglican geography, see *India and the End of the Empire: Selected Writings of Daniel O'Connor*, eds. Ann Loades & David Jasper, Sacristy Press, 2023, pp. 161ff, op cit. Martyn Percy (et al, eds.), *The Oxford Handbook of Anglican Studies*, Oxford UP, 2016, pp. 271–84.

4. Daniel Muñoz, 'North to South: A Reappraisal of Anglican Communion Membership Figures', *Journal of Anglican Studies*, vol. 14, 2016, pp. 71–95.
5. On China, see Richard R. Cook and David W. Pao (eds.), *After Imperialism: Christian Identity in China and the Global Evangelical Movement*, Lutterworth, 2012; G. Wright Doyle (ed.), *Builders of the Chinese Church: Pioneer Protestant Missionaries and Chinese Church Leaders*, Lutterworth, 2015, and Eunice V. Johnson and Carol Lee (eds.) *Hamrin Timothy Richard's Vision: Education and Reform in China, 1880–1910*, Lutterworth, 2015.
6. Amy DeRogartis, *Moral Geography: Maps, Missionaries and the American Frontier*, Columbia UP, 2003.
7. Hong Kong provides an interesting case study. The port of Aberdeen in the Special Autonomous Region of China inevitably reflects the Scottish legacy of the territory, and that is reflected in the establishment of a specific kind of culture in banking and financing. The English appropriation of that culture, much later, has bequeathed to Hong Kong an interesting blend of Scottish conservatism and English adventurism. On this, see Chris Blackhurst, *Too Big To Jail*, Macmillan, 2022, pp. 16ff, which details the Aberdonian origins of the banking giant HSBC from 1864, including its role in profiting from the opium trade. Thomas Sutherland (b. 1834, Aberdeen) formed the fledgling HSBC that worked with the British government in the aftermath of the Second Opium War (1856-60) that saw merchants and investors make enormous profits from the narcotics trade. In Cantonese, HSBC was given a new name by Chinese investors: 'abundance of remittances' or 'focus of wealth'. Sutherland became an MP in 1884, and was later knighted. He died in 1922.
8. Anna Johnston, *Missionary Writing and Empire, 1800–1860*, Cambridge UP, 2003.
9. The valorisation of such missionary endeavour is expressed in numerous stained glass windows in Anglican churches across the British Empire. See G.A. Bremner, 'Colonial Themes in Stained Glass, Home and Abroad: A Visual Survey', *Journal of Interdisciplinary Studies in the Long Nineteenth Century*, vol. 30, 2020. Bremner also notes another stained glass window at St Ebbe's Oxford, depicting a cowering native Aboriginal as the gospel is preached.

10. John Darch, *Missionary Imperialists? Missionaries, Government, and the Growth of the British Empire in the Tropics, 1860–1885*, Wipf and Stock, 2009.
11. For a different kind of critical approach, see Nigel Biggar, *Colonialism: A Moral Reckoning*, HarperCollins, 2022.
12. Recent attempts at reparation should be noted—see *Revive* (USPG magazine, Winter 2023/2024, vol. 2, pp. 12–13), noting the Codrington Reparations Project which sets aside £7 million for taking reparative action in Barbados. However, it is unclear how or if any of the communities in Africa from which the slaves were forcibly drawn and then shipped to Barbados have been invited into similar reparative processes. See Michael Banner, *Britain's Slavery Debt: Reparations Now!*, Oxford UP, 2024.
13. For further reading, see Emilia Viotta da Costa, *Crowns of Glory, Tears of Blood: The Demerara Slave Rebellion of 1823*, Oxford UP, 1997; and Christian Høgsbjerg, *Atlantic History in Fifteen Slave Revolts: Resistance, Rebellion and Abolition from Below*, Bloomsbury, 2023.
14. Ambrose Mong, *Guns and Gospel: Imperialism and Evangelism in China*, James Clarke and Co., 2016.
15. See Vaudine England, *Fortune's Bazaar: The Making of Hong Kong*, Corsair, 2023; and Ho-Fung Hung, *City on the Edge: Hong Kong under Chinese Rule*, Cambridge UP, 2022.
16. Mark O'Neill, *Frederick: The Life of My Missionary Grandfather in Manchuria*, JFC Publishing, 2012.
17. O'Neill, 2012, p. 49.
18. O'Neill, 2012, pp. 112-121.

4. TIPPING POINTS

1. Richard Hooker, *Of the Laws of Ecclesiastical Polity*, vol. I, books I–IV and VII, Everyman Library, 1963. Richard Hooker (1554–1600) wrote his book from 1594, a work regarded as the quintessential distillation of Anglican polity, virtues and character, and an apologia for the *via media*.
2. David Hackett Fischer, *Albion's Seed: Four British Folkways in America*, Oxford UP, 1992.

3. The literature on this is only now becoming apparent, detailing the genocide and the casual, almost recreational culling of Aboriginal people across Australia, including the detention centres and 'resettlement initiatives'. On the sustained campaign of aboriginal genocide in Australia, see David Marr, *Killing for Country: A Family Story*, Black Inc. Publishing, 2023.
4. See Philip Turner, *Christian Socialism: The Promise of an Almost Forgotten Tradition*, James Clarke and Co., 2022.
5. Lest we valorise Dearmer too much, it must be remembered that he was pointedly anti-Catholic. Like many in his day, Dearmer regarded Catholicism as the religion of the poor, foreign and criminal degenerates.
6. See Martin Klauber, Scott Manetsch and Erwin Lutzer, *The Great Commission: Evangelicals and the History of World Missions*, B&H Publishing Group, 2008.
7. Emilia Viotta da Costa, *Crowns of Glory, Tears of Blood: The Demerara Slave Rebellion of 1823, Oxford UP, 1997*, p. 14.

5. SLAVERY, CHURCH AND COLONIAL RACISM

1. See Padraic X. Scanlon, *Slave Empire: How Slavery Built Modern Britain*, Little, Brown Book Group and Robinson Publishers, 2020.
2. See Desirée Baptiste, 'Incidents in the Life of an Anglican Slave', a dramatic poem written and performed in 2024 at Jesus College Cambridge. The poem was inspired by a rare document: a 1723 letter written by an anonymous enslaved Anglican Virginian to the 'Lord Arch Bishop of London'. The letter is housed at Lambeth Palace library.
3. Rich Barr, 'Church of England Urged to Target £1bn for Legacy of Slavery Fund', *Financial Times*, 4 March 2024.
4. William Moore, *The Spectator*, 15 March 2024, https://www.spectator.co.uk/article/is-the-c-of-e-about-to-say-sorry-for-christianity.
5. See the Sam Sharpe Lectures, edited by Rosemarie Davidson and E.P. Louis, *History, Rebellion and Reform*, SCM Press, 2023.
6. Alex Renton, *Blood Legacy: Reckoning with a Family's Story of Slavery*, Canongate, 2021.

7. Readers interested in the background to such interventions in social evolution and the role of English Anglicanism are referred to Simon Szreter, *Fertility, Class and Gender in Britain, 1860–1940*, Cambridge UP, 2010, and *The Hidden Affliction: Sexually Transmitted Infections and Infertility in History*, Rochester UP, 2019.
8. Sherwin Bailey, *Eugenics Review*, vol. 50, no. 4, January 1959, pp. 239–45.
9. Sherwin Bailey, *Eugenics Review*, January 1959, p. 242.
10. For example, see current pastoral guidance for ministers, which largely talks about growth and worship, and assumes that pastoral care amounts to little more than empathetic listening skills: https://dioceseofyork.org.uk/uploads/attachment/34/training-for-lay-people.pdf.
11. See Douglas Lorimer, *Science, Race Relations and Resistance: Britain, 1870–1914*, Manchester UP, 2013. Underpinning the pseudo-science of eugenics were early 18th-century naturalists, who tended to reinforce gender stereotypes and presumptions. In the 21st century science is only just beginning to rewire gendered assumptions, including the female of species – plant, animal, etc. – being inherently and naturally passive, receptive and maternal. English 'race theory' across the empire during the 18th–20th centuries was hardly different. See also Tim McInerney, *Nobility and the Making of Race in Eighteenth-Century Britain*, Bloomsbury, 2023.

6. CROWNING GLORY

1. For a polemical critique, see John Crace, *Depraved New World*, Guardian Faber, 2023, pp. 329–33. Crace characterises the coronation with his customary bite, and highlights how the ceremony remained a Protestant rite that enshrined the power and privilege of the Church of England.
2. David Nicholls, *Deity and Domination: Images of God and the State in the 19th and 20th Centuries*, Routledge, 1989. See also Tom Holland, *Dominion: The Making of the Western Mind*, Abacus Books, 2019.
3. Doubt was cast over the lineage of Edward, whose birth was not witnessed by close family or attended by ministers of state and

religion. Edward was widely suspected of being a changeling in order to establish and impose a future Catholic monarchy in succession to James II.

4. Emile Durkheim, *The Elementary Forms of the Religious Life*, trans. by J.W. Swain, George Allen and Unwin, 1964 [1912]; Edward Shils, *Tradition*, Chicago UP, 1981; and Shils, *The Constitution of Society*, Chicago UP, 1982.
5. See William Ramp, 'Paradoxes of sovereignty: Toward a Durkheimian analysis of monarchy', *Journal of Classical Sociology*, vol. 14, no. 2, May 2014, pp. 222–46.
6. See the discussion on the future of nostalgia in Anne Applebaum, *Twilight of Democracy*, Allen Lane, 2020, pp. 55–105, and her discussion of democracy being undermined in *Autocracy Inc.*, Allen Lane, 2024, pp. 122ff.
7. See David Runciman, *Confronting Leviathan*, Profile Books, 2021.
8. See Simon Jenkins, 'Prince William Should Finish What Charles Started—and Sever the Ridiculous Ties of Church and State', *Guardian*, 19 January 2024, p. 23.

7. TO BE OR NOT TO BE?

1. Torsten Bell, *Great Britain? How We Get Our Future Back*, Bodley Head, 2024, p. 69.
2. https://www.churchtimes.co.uk/articles/2024/19-july/news/uk/evangelicals-play-down-the-commissioning-of-20-overseers.
3. For interest, readers are referred to Heather Streets, *Martial Races: The Military, Race and Masculinity in British Imperial Culture, 1857–1914*, Manchester UP, 2004; Harry Goulbourne, *Race Relations in Britain since 1945*, Red Globe Press 1998; Erik Bleich, *Race Politics in Britain and France: Ideas and Policymaking since the 1960s*, Cambridge UP, 2003; Simon Peplow, *Race and Riots in Thatcher's Britain*, Manchester UP, 2019; Shailja Sharma and Daniel Livesay, *Children of Uncertain Fortune: Mixed-Race Jamaicans in Britain and the Atlantic Family, 1733–1833*, North Carolina UP, 2019; Jerome Gay, *The Whitewashing of Christianity*, 13th and Joan, 2021.

4. Citing the lack of investment in infrastructure, Torsten Bell (*Great Britain?*, pp. 8ff) identifies the building of reservoirs as a key indicator of decline. Between 1850 and 1992, over 200 reservoirs were built to provide clean water to Britain's growing population. Despite the population of the UK having increased by over 10 million since 1992, no new reservoir has been built, and the quality of water and the infrastructures supplying it have mostly declined.
5. Mary Wills and Madge Dresser, *The Transatlantic Slave Economy and England's Built Environment: A Research Audit*, Historic England, August 2020.
6. Hans Kundnani, *Eurowhiteness: Culture, Empire and Race in the European Project*, Hurst, 2023.
7. See Nicholas Rankin, *Trapped in History: Kenya, Mau Mau and Me*, Faber, 2023.
8. See Jennifer Kavanagh and Michael Rich, *Truth Decay: An Initial Exploration of the Diminishing Role of Facts and Analysis in American Public Life*, RAND Corporation, 2018.
9. See Walter Ong, *Orality and Literacy*, Routledge, 1982.
10. Or, for that matter, just forgotten. Few studies of Cardinal John Henry Newman ever dwell on his defence of slavery and reluctance to condemn it, even after the American Civil War.

8. ANGLICANISM: A MORAL RECKONING

1. Maxine Berg and Pat Hudson, *Slavery, Capitalism and the Industrial Revolution*, Polity Press, 2023.
2. Emilia Viotta da Costa, *Crowns of Glory, Tears of Blood: The Demerara Slave Rebellion of 1823*, Oxford UP, 1994, p. 80.
3. See Act of Appeals (also called The Ecclesiastical Appeals Act 1532 [24 Hen 8 c 12] and Statute in Restraint of Appeals).
4. Similar problems are extant with suicide. It was repealed as a criminal offence in England in 1961 (section 2 of the Suicide Act) but remains a crime in several former colonies.
5. On this see Katharine Jenkins, *Ontology and Oppression: Race, Gender, and Social Reality*, Oxford UP, 2023.
6. On English attitudes to sex and sexuality, see Mike Rendell, *Sex and*

Sexuality in Georgian Britain, Pen and Sword History, 2020; Carol McGrath, *Sex and Sexuality in Tudor England*, Pen and Sword History, 2022; and Andrea Zuvich, *Sex and Sexuality in Stuart Britain*, Pen and Sword History, 2020. See also Violet Fenn, *Sex and Sexuality in Victorian Britain*, Pen and Sword History, 2025 (forthcoming).

7. See https://www.opendemocracy.net/en/beyond-liddism-towards-real-global-security/. Paul Rogers: 'Much of modern politics is concerned with what I call "lidism", measures aimed not to address the underlying issues but to keep the lid on'; cited in Huw Richards, 'Peace Studies in Our Time', *The Guardian*, 3 January 2006, p. 17. The lid probably came off for Britain when Ireland became a Free State in 1922, with 26 of the 32 counties breaking away from British rule. Or perhaps over Suez in 1956. See Matthew Parker, *One Fine Day: Britain's Empire on the Brink*, Abacus, 2023.
8. See https://www.anao.gov.au/work/corporate/anao-integrity-framework-and-report-2022-23; and Seumas Miller, *Moral Foundations of Social Institutions*, Cambridge UP, 2010; and Carl Dahlström and Victor Lapuente, *Organizing Leviathan: Politicians, Bureaucrats, and the Making of Good Government*, Cambridge UP, 2017; and analysis on institutional failings, https://www.premierchristianity.com/opinion/uccf-its-time-for-me-to-say-sorry/17095.article; and in regard to cover-ups on policing, the military and later in churches, see https://www.apsreview.gov.au/sites/default/files/resources/being-trusted-respected-partner-aps-integrity-framework.pdf and https://transparency.org.au/wp-content/uploads/2020/11/NIS_FULL_REPORT_Web.pdf.
9. One can trace this liturgically too. The 1662 Book of Common Prayer contains no prayers for the dead and the practice was deemed to be unlawful in *The Homily on Prayer* (chapter 3). However, Non-jurors did use prayers for the dead, and these became popularised in the wake of military fatalities, beginning in 1900 with the Boer War, and becoming even more universal during and after the First World War. Yet another example of pastoral and liturgical expediency and pragmatism finding some way past (hitherto) doctrinal reservations.

9. COMMUNION AND COMMONWEALTH

1. Daniel O'Connor, *The Chaplains of the East India Company, 1601–1858,* Bloomsbury, 2011.
2. *Treatise*, book III, part III, section III. See https://www.gutenberg.org/files/4705/4705-h/4705-h.htm.
3. Luis Bermejo SJ, *The Spirit of Life*, Loyola UP, 1988.
4. Jim Davis and Michael Graham, *The Great Dechurching*, Zondervan, 2023.
5. Style and substance are often in an uneasy relationship within Anglican polity and practice at the best of times. The resource https://anglicansonline.org/communion/nic.html lists over 140 breakaway 'Anglican Provinces' across the world that are not part of the official Anglican Communion. These provinces have their own clergy, bishops and archbishops, thousands of churches, hundreds of dioceses, and several dozen institutions delivering training and education for clergy and laity. The vast majority claim to be 'traditional' and 'orthodox', and assert that the wider Anglican Communion is to be regarded as the apostate body. A significant number of these para-Anglican Provinces have adopted evangelical, Reformed, Orthodox, Catholic, Pentecostal and Charismatic characteristics as part of their identity and ongoing differentiation. The vast majority are not recognised by the Anglican Communion, and, similarly, the para-Anglican Provinces do not look to Canterbury for recognition.
6. I have in mind the explicit struggles with racism and extremism in the New World, though these are implicit and latent in Old World paradigms too. See Tim Alberta, *The Kingdom, the Power and the Glory: American Evangelicals in an Age of Extremism*, HarperCollins 2023; and Jim Wallis, *The False White Gospel: Rejecting Christian Nationalism, Reclaiming True Faith, and Refounding Democracy*, St Martin's Press, 2024.

10. THE ENGLISH ENIGMA

1. Ekaterina Kolpinskaya and Stuart Fox, *Religion and Euroscepticism in Brexit Britain*, Routledge, 2021.

2. Alex Renton, *Blood Legacy: Reckoning with a Family's Story of Slavery*, Canongate, 2021.
3. See Martyn Percy, *The Future Shapes of Anglicanism: Currents, Contours, Charts*, Routledge, 2017.
4. On this, see Andrew Brown and Linda Woodhead, *That Was the Church That Was: How the Church of England Lost the English People*, Bloomsbury, 2016.
5. See Martyn Percy, 'Conflict in Congregations: Power, Polity and Peace in the Church', in Jolyon Mitchell, Francesca Po, Suzanna Millar and Martyn Percy (eds.), *The Wiley Blackwell Companion to Religion and Peace*, Wiley Blackwell, 2022, pp. 364–72.
6. Thomas Dixon, *Weeping Britannia: Portrait of a Nation in Tears*, Oxford UP, 2015.
7. For further discussion, see Cornel West, *Democracy Matters: Winning the Fight against Imperialism*, Penguin, 2004.
8. See Philip Selznick, *Leadership in Administration: A Sociological Interpretation*, 3rd edn, California UP, 1984, and *The Moral Commonwealth: Social Theory and the Promise of Community*, California UP, 1992. Like Selznick, Charles Handy distinguishes between leadership in organisations and that of institutions (*Understanding Organizations*, 4th edn, Penguin, 1993, and *Understanding Voluntary Organizations: How To Make Them Function Effectively*, 2nd edn, Penguin, 2000. See also Lyndon Shakespeare, *Being the Body of Christ in the Age of Management*, Cascade Books, 2016.
9. For further discussion of these attempts at reform and renewal, see Martyn Percy, *The Future Shapes of Anglicanism: Currents, Contours, Charts*, Routledge, 2017.
10. That Vennells was considered for London must be in part due to the influence of the Green Report of 2014: https://www.churchofengland.org/sites/default/files/2017-12/gs_2026_-_nurturing_and_discerning_senior_leaders.pdf. The work was amongst the 'first fruits' of the new Welby primacy. Opinions about the Green Report were divided in 2014–15, and a slew of articles criticised the work for its lack of theology, and also the glaring absence of academic research and writing on management and leadership.
11. The irony is that Lord Green was commissioned to prepare the Green

Report in the wake of his leadership of HSBC. While Green was not himself accused of any wrongdoing, City opinion was critical of an unwieldy financial conglomerate (which is effectively what HSBC had become) that was not functioning optimally.

12. Justin Welby, *Reimagining Britain*, Bloomsbury, 2018, pp. ix and 292. See also Chris Blackhurst, *Too Big to Jail: Inside HSBC, the Mexican Drug Cartels and the Greatest Banking Scandal of the Century*, Macmillan, 2022. See also Nick Wallis, *The Great Post Office Scandal: The Story of the Fight to Expose a Multimillion Pound IT Disaster which put Innocent People in Jail*, Bath Publishing, 2012.
13. See the *Church Times* leader comment on Paula Vennells and the Post Office, 12 January 2024, p. 12: 'Post Office traumatic stress and disorder'; and Angela Tilby, 'Church of England should heed lessons of Post Office saga', *Church Times*, 12 January 2024, p. 16.
14. Thus, the composition and discharge of safeguarding policy and practice in the Church of England is unsurprising. In safeguarding, for example, there are no means for addressing incompetence and corruption. Officials are unregulated, unaccountable, unlicensed and often untrained. The processes are unprofessional, unjust, unsafe and untrustworthy. Victims find the processes to be abusive and traumatising, amounting to little more than a self-protection scheme designed to preserve the reputation of the church.

11. CHURCH, COMMUNION AND CLASSISM

1. Derek Scally, *The Best Catholics in the World*, Penguin, 2021.
2. There are numerous studies focusing on the scandals in Ireland relating to the notorious Magdalen Laundries (funded by the state), and the plight of young unmarried pregnant women and their babies. One of the best recent works is Clair Wills, *Missing Persons, or, My Grandmother's Secrets*, Allen Lane, 2023.
3. This premise rests on the observations made by Hannah Arendt, *Eichman in Jerusalem: A Report on the Banality of Evil*, Penguin Modern Classics, 2022 [1963]. However, the Nuremberg trials of Nazi war criminals were handled quite differently and arguably much more poorly than their Tokyo counterparts. The Tokyo International

Tribunals were peppered with racist and colonialist bias against the Japanese defendants, including by British judges and those representing the Empire and Commonwealth. See Gary Rees, *Judgment at Tokyo: World War II on Trial and the Making of Modern Asia*, Picador, 2023.

4. 1960; written by Dalton Trumbo and directed by Stanley Kubrick.
5. Howard Fast, *Spartacus*, Blue Heron Press, 1951.
6. See Martyn Percy, 'Class, Ethnicity and Education: Leadership, Congregations and the Sociology of Anglicanism', in Jeremy Morris (ed.), *The Oxford History of the Anglican Church in the Twentieth Century*, Oxford UP, 2017, pp. 137–59, and Martyn Percy, 'Context, Character and Challenges: The Shaping of Ordination Training in the Anglican Communion' and 'Introduction' (with S. Clarke and M. Chapman), in Mark Chapman and Sathi Clarke (eds.), *Oxford Handbook of Anglican Studies*, Oxford UP, 2015, pp. 490–504, 1–18.
7. For a fuller discussion of accountability, operating at a distance from responsibility, see Sharon Welch, *A Feminist Ethic of Risk*, Fortress Press, 2000.
8. See Michael Banner, *Britain's Slavery Debt: Reparations Now!*, Oxford University Press, 2024.
9. Travis Glasson, *Mastering Christianity: Missionary Anglicanism and Slavery in the Atlantic World*, Oxford UP, 2017.
10. On this, see Noam Chomsky, *The Precipice: Neoliberalism, the Pandemic and the Urgent Need for Social Change*, Penguin, pp. 194ff.
11. The Collect begins, 'Stir up, we beseech thee, O Lord, the wills of thy faithful people; that they, bringing forth the fruit of good works, may of thee be plenteously rewarded ...' The prayer, besides being semi-Pelagian, was in common use for the mixing of Christmas pudding ingredients five weeks before 25 December.
12. Some may point out that this was during the Labour government of Ramsay MacDonald. However, the Labour Party was a minority in the House of Commons with less than a third of the seats, not even the largest party. The Unionists were a larger party, but not united and so unable to function in government. This meant the Labour Party, though in office, was not in power.
13. On this, see Pen Vogler, *Stuffed: A History of Good Food and Hard Times in Britain,* Atlantic Books, 2023, pp. 167–9.

14. See Martyn Percy, 'Christmas in the Anglican Tradition', in Timothy Larsen (ed.), *The Oxford Handbook of Christmas*, Oxford UP, 2020, pp. 153–66.

12. CULTURAL WEATHER FORECASTS

1. Jim Davis and Michael Graham *The Great Dechurching*, Zondervan, 2023, p. 31.
2. See Karen Swallow Prior, *The Evangelical Imagination: How Stories, Images and Metaphors Created a Culture in Crisis*, Brazos Press, 2023.
3. On this, see Martyn Percy, *Clergy: The Origin of Species*, Bloomsbury and T&T Clark, 2006.
4. See: https://en.wikipedia.org/wiki/Eastern_Orthodoxy_by_country
5. For further discussion, see Chistopher Clark and Wolfram Kaiser (eds.), *Culture Wars: Secular–Catholic Conflict in Nineteenth Century Europe*, Cambridge UP, 2003.
6. The emergence of an 'information society' laid the foundations for the French Revolution. See Robert Darnton, *The Revolutionary Temper: Paris, 1748–1789*, Allen Lane, 2023.
7. C.S. Lewis, *Mere Christianity*, HarperCollins, 1952, p. 28.
8. On this, see the discussion by Cornel West in *Democracy Matters: Winning the Fight against Imperialism*, Penguin 2004, pp. 145–72. West highlights examples from the US—Dorothy Day, Martin Luther King Jr, Sojourners, etc.—which have led the struggle for equality and democracy against denominations and churches in the civic, social, political as well as spiritual realm that have sought to uphold imperialist world-views and practices in the name of Christianity, yet have been oppressive and hierarchical in character.

13. THINGS FALL APART

1. Even in the Church of England, the Channel Islands, Sodor and Man, and the Diocese in Europe are all subject to competing civil laws, and canon law is different.

2. See Theo Honson, https://www.spectator.co.uk/article/the-c-of-e-needs-to-talk-about-sex/, 13 July 2024, for an excellent discussion of the inherent Anglican fudginess on sexuality.
3. For a theological reflection, see Joe Aldred, *Flourishing in Babylon: Black British Agency and Self-Determination*, SCM–Canterbury Press, 2024.
4. Chinua Achebe, *Things Fall Apart*, Bantam, Doubleday and Dell, 1958.
5. Jean-François Lyotard, *The Postmodern Condition: A Report on Knowledge*, Manchester UP, 1984, p. 5.
6. Jennifer Kavanagh and Michael Rich, *Truth Decay: An Initial Exploration of the Diminishing Role of Facts and Analysis in American Public Life*, RAND Publishing, 2018.
7. University College London Policy Laboratory, Sept. 2023, https://www.moreincommon.org.uk/our-work/research/the-respect-agenda/.
8. See Martyn Percy, *The Precarious Church: Redeeming the Body of Christ*, SCM–Canterbury Press, 2023.
9. The Committee on Standards in Public Life was established by UK prime minister John Major in 1994 to advise on ethical standards of public life. It promotes the Seven Principles of Public Life, also known as the Nolan Principles, named after the first chairman of the committee, Lord Nolan. They are Selflessness, Integrity, Objectivity, Accountability, Openness, Honesty and Leadership. The Seven Principles apply to anyone who works as a public office holder. Despite clergy being public office holders, the Church of England has declined to adopt the Nolan Principles.
10. It is not as if studies of socio-cultural changes had not predicted this. See Kenneth Thompson, *Bureaucracy and Church Reform: The Organizational Response of the Church of England to Social Change, 1800–1965*, Oxford UP, 1970. See also Martyn Percy, 'It's not an organisation: It's the Body of Christ', *Church Times*, 22 November 2013, p. 11, https://www.churchtimes.co.uk/articles/2013/22-november/comment/opinion/it-s-not-an-organisation-it-s-the-body-of-christ.
11. The background to the distinction between organisation and institution lies in the writings of Philip Selznick. For a discussion of

his work in this field, see Martin Krygier, *Philip Selznick: Ideals in the World*, Stanford UP, 2012.

12. On this, see Paul Avis (ed.), *The Journey of Christian Initiation: Theological and Pastoral Perspectives*, Church House Publishing, 2011.
13. Charles Handy, *The Gods of Management: The Four Cultures of Leadership*, Souvenir Press, 1978. See also Charles Handy, *Understanding Organisations*, Penguin, 1976; and *Understanding Voluntary Organisations*, Penguin, 1986. I note that most bishops have read the 1976 book and expect to be able to manage the organisation of the Church of England, but have not read the 1986 follow-up, which clarifies the difficulty of leading a voluntary body, which is largely what the Church of England is.
14. Handy, *The Gods of Management*, pp. 193ff. See also James Hopewell, *Congregation: Stories and Structures*, Fortress Press, 1987, for an illuminating discussion of the Zeus myth at work in a specifically church-based context: 'an arbitrary and dictatorial rule ... punish[ing] those who dared to oppose him ... a one-man show who got his way ... [by] the acquiescence of corporation-minded members ... [and ridiculed opponents]' (pp. 187ff).
15. Murray Bowen, *Family Therapy in Clinical Practice*, Jason Aronson Publishers, 1990.
16. This has become especially apparent over the debates on sexuality and the blessing or marriage of same-sex couples, *Living in Love and Faith*, 2020–2024, where the hierarchy consistently undermines the democratic will of Synod. It is worth noting that many writers in business management and leadership have attended to this. For example, Patrick Lencioni, *The Five Dysfunctions of a Team: A Leadership Fable*, Jossey-Bass, 2002 and *The Advantage*, Jossey-Bass, 2012, where the author analyses organisational health, and we can see that his Five Dysfunctions are now being played out in the Church of England. They are Absence of Trust; Fear of Conflict; Lack of Commitment; Avoidance of Accountability; and Inattention to Results.
17. See https://www.thinkinganglicans.org.uk/llf-over-130-general-synod-members-oppose-reset-and-settlement/ and https://www.thinkinganglicans.org.uk/llf-statement-from-the-bishop-of-newcastle/.

18. See also Catherine M. Rakow, *Making Sense of Human Life: Murray Bowen's Determined Effort Toward Family Systems Theory*, Routledge, 2022.
19. Mady Thung, *The Precarious Organisation: Sociological Explorations of the Church's Mission and Structure*, Mouton and Co., 1976.
20. Thung, *The Precarious Organisation*, p. 193.
21. See Gary Magee and Andrew Thompson, *Empire and Globalisation: Networks of People, Goods and Capital in the British World, c.1850–1914*, Cambridge UP, 2010, pp. 117–26 and 154–66.

14. BEYOND CONTROL

1. Joseph Nye's *Understanding International Conflicts: An Introduction to Theory and History*, Pearson, 1997, paved the way for several reflections on the uses of hard and soft power, including *The Paradox of American Power* (Oxford UP, 2003) and *The Powers to Lead* (Oxford UP, 2008).
2. See Martyn Percy, *The Humble Church: Becoming the Body of Christ*, SCM-Canterbury Press, 2021, and *The Precarious Church: Redeeming the Body of Christ*, SCM–Canterbury Press, 2023.
3. See Gideon Defoe, *An Atlas of Extinct Countries*, Fourth Estate, 2020.
4. See Michael Jinkins, *The Church Faces Death: Ecclesiology in a Post-Modern Context*, Oxford UP, 2002.
5. Sarah Wilkinson Report on the closure of the ISB, https://www.churchofengland.org/sites/default/files/2023-12/isb-review-report-30-november-2023.pdf.
6. For further discussion, see commentary on 'Thinking Anglicans', https://www.thinkinganglicans.org.uk/isb-phase-1-wilkinson-report-published/.
7. Oligarchies tend to protect or promote religious monopolies, a point not lost on Peter Berger, *The Sacred Canopy*, Doubleday 1969, pp. 144, where he notes that the tendency of such nations and rulers is to reproduce 'oligopolistic' faiths that are hierarchical in character, and dominate any other rivals or alternatives. The Church of England would qualify as an oligopolistic denomination (in effect the head of a religious cartel), presuming to rule on behalf of others nationally

and internationally. See Torkel Brekke, *Faithonomics*, Hurst and Co., 2016, pp. 202–3, which also discusses how this legitimates discrimination.

8. For a fine and penetrating study focusing on one country, see Michael Gross, *The War against Catholicism: Liberalism and the Anti-Catholic Imagination in Nineteenth Century Germany*, Michigan UP, 2005.
9. Carrie Tirado Bramen, *American Niceness: A Cultural History*, Harvard UP, 2017.
10. Bramen, *American Niceness*, pp. 251–3.
11. G.A. Bremner, 'Colonial Themes in Stained Glass, Home and Abroad: A Visual Survey', *Journal of Interdisciplinary Studies in the Long Nineteenth Century*, vol. 30, 2020.
12. Bramen, *American Niceness*, pp. 40–95.
13. For an illuminating discussion, see Bruce Bueno de Mesquita, *The Invention of Power: Popes, Kings, and the Birth of the West*, Hachette Publishing, 2022.
14. Henry Whipple, *Lights and Shadows of a Long Episcopate*, Macmillan, 1900.
15. See his full account in Horace Greeley, *An Overland Journey, from New York to San Francisco, in the Summer of 1859*, C.M. Saxton, Barker and Co., 1860, ch. 13. See also Tzvetan Todorov, *The Conquest of America*, trans. Richard Howard, Harper and Row, Perennial Library, 1985; and obviously Edward W. Said, *Orientalism*, Routledge and Kegan Paul, 1978.
16. Madeleine Davies, 'Report Uncovered Church House "Turf Wars" Concerns', *Church Times*, 19 January 2024, p. 5.
17. Mark Harrison, *Secret Leviathan: Secrecy and State Capacity Under Soviet Communism*, Stanford UP, 2023.
18. See Clive Field, *Counting Religion in Britain, 1970–2020: Secularization in Statistical Context*, Oxford UP, 2022, and Church of England Statistics for Mission, 2022.
19. Paul Thomas, *Church Times*, quoting *The Guardian*, 15 December 2023.
20. Matthew Guest, *Christianity and the University Experience*, Bloomsbury, 2013. The study surveyed 4,500 undergraduate students and conducted 100 interviews. The research team found that most

Christian students were typically moderate in their religious beliefs, tolerant toward others, and liberal in their morality.

21. Conservative-Evangelical and Anglo-Catholic parish churches withholding funding from dioceses and seeking alternative episcopal oversight to complement their theological outlooks are already widespread in the Church of England. Recent quasi-ordinations characterised as "commissioning for ministry" in two London churches did not result in any disciplinary or legal action against the clergy involved. See: https://www.churchtimes.co.uk/articles/2024/19- july/news/uk/evangelicals-play-down-the-commissioning-of-20-overseers. On the bishop-designate of Wolverhampton, see: Francis Martin, https://www.churchtimes.co.uk/articles/2024/6-september/news/uk/next-bishop-of-wolverhampton-regrets-part-in-non-canonical-ordination See also Ruth Peacock, 'Sofa Governance of Church of England Criticised', Religion and Media, July 24th 2023 (https://religionmediacentre.org.uk/news/church-of-englands-sofa-governmenthas-led-to-collapse-of-trust/; https://www.churchofengland.org/sites/default/files/2024-06/gs2354-trust-and-trustworthiness-within-the-church-of-england-a-preliminary-report.pdf; and https://www.moreincommon.org.uk/our-work/research/the-respect-agenda/ from the University College London Policy Laboratory, September 2023).

15. GRAINS OF TRUTH

1. Norman Doe, *A New History of the Church in Wales: Governance and Ministry, Theology and Society*, Cambridge UP, 2020.
2. See Glanmor Williams, *The Welsh Church from Reformation to Disestablishment, 1603–1920*, University of Wales Press, 2007.
3. See Martyn Percy, *The Humble Church* (2021), *The Precarious Church* (2023) and *The Exiled Church* (2025), SCM–Canterbury Press.
4. Robert Bellah, *Habits of the Heart: Individualism and Commitment in American Life*, HarperCollins, 1988.
5. Sharon Welch, *A Feminist Ethic of Risk*, Fortress Press, 2000, p. 51.
6. Paule Marshall, *The Chosen Place, the Timeless People*, Random House, 1969; and *Praisesong for the Widow*, Random House, 1983.
7. Welch, *A Feminist Ethic of Risk*, p. 57.

8. Edward Said, *Culture and Imperialism*, Vintage, 1994, p. 12.
9. See Una Kroll, *Bread, Not Stones*, Christian Awareness Press, 2014; and Andrew Graystone, 'We Asked for Bread, but You Gave Us Stones', https://www.thinkinganglicans.org.uk/wp-content/uploads/2018/06/Stones-not-Bread.compressed.pdf. The biblical reference is to Matthew 7:9.
10. John 3:21 (KJV): 'But he that doeth *truth* cometh to the *light*, that his deeds may be made manifest, that they are wrought in God'.
11. This is currently most evident in safeguarding policy and process, where the Church of England hierarchy have been found to cover up for neglect, partiality or mistakes made by senior officers and bishops, or actual acts perpetrated by bishops. The tactic adopted by the Secretariat is to ensure all complaints are managed by a succession of inconclusive and anodyne reviews, thereby ensuring that victims of abuse and miscarriages of justice rarely if ever receive closure, compensation or compassion. For a timeline on the scale and extent of recent cases of abuse, see https://houseofsurvivors.org/.
12. Nor is the unity with the Thirty-Nine Articles, or a common liturgy. The Anglican Communion is effectively a fiction of unity, without a common narrative, binding law or agreed fundamentals.
13. Growth has its limits, and this is set out admirably in Mancur Olson, *The Rise and Decline of Nations: Economic Growth, Stagflation, and Social Rigidities*, Yale UP, 1984. See also his *Power and Prosperity: Outgrowing Communist and Capitalist Dictatorships*, Basic Books, 2000.
14. Welch, *A Feminist Ethic of Risk*, p. 169. See also 'The Future of Anglican Studies' (special edition) of the *Journal of Anglican Studies*, September 2021, ed. Daniel Joslyn-Siemiatkoski.
15. David Kynaston, *A Northern Wind: Britain, 1962–6*, Bloomsbury, 2023, p. 841.

CONCLUSION

1. Madeline Grant, 'Church Leadership Is Destroying the Church of England I Love', *Daily Telegraph*, 5 March 2024.
2. For a treatment of the roots of such concerns in contemporary evangelicalism and its opposition to equal rights and democracy,

and its promotion of racial hierarchies, see Scott M. Coley, *Ministers of Propaganda: Truth, Power and the Ideology of the Religious Right*, Eerdmans, 2024.

3. At the time of writing, the Church of England has been unable to come up with a definition of independence for the oversight and regulation of its safeguarding work, financial auditing and other key areas. Where possible, it will outsource such work to trusted insiders, and claim that the semi-detached arrangement is independent (i.e., akin to stating that the Isle of Wight is 'independent' from the rest of the UK).
4. Dominic Nozzarella, 'The Anti-Colonial, Conservative Revolution in the Anglican Communion', London School of Economics, 11 December 2023.
5. See Linda Woodhead and Greg Smith, https://blogs.lse.ac.uk/brexit/2018/09/20/how-anglicans-tipped-the-brexit-vote/.
6. Andrew Hindmoor, *Haywire: A Political History of Britain since 2000*, Allen Lane, 2024, pp. 304–6.
7. The words—'Mene, Mene, Tekel, Peres'—are interpreted to predict the fall of the Babylonian empire. The Book of Daniel draws a contrast between the hubris exhibited by Belshazzar, and the humility of his father, Nebuchadnezzar, who acknowledged the kingship of the God of Israel. Daniel is rewarded for his translation at the feast, but Belshazzar dies that night, and his kingdom is immediately divided between the Medes and the Persians.
8. The 39 Articles of Religion were adopted by Convocation of the Church of England in 1563 and finalised in 1571. Since 1662 they have been published in the *Book of Common Prayer*. These articles are the Protestant and Reformed formularies for the Church of England.
9. For example, ordination is not a sacrament. That is why ordaining women as deacons, priests and bishops was not a change to doctrine. Articles XXIII, XXV and XXXVI only require ministers to be publicly recognised, and the ordinal follows that line. This is a Protestant theology of authorised ministry, not a Roman Catholic sacramental one. No doctrinal change took place to ordain women.
10. The recent development of new and faddish clergy cultures in Anglican ordinations – prostration before the bishop, anointing of the priestly hands, etc – were rarely seen before the 21st century. As

the Church of England has become more otiose to ordinary public life and declined in cultural value, ordination ceremonies have developed an ecclesial eccentricity bordering on the specious.

11. John Henry Newman, *Tract 20: the Visible Church*, Letter III., London: J & G. Rivington, 1833, p. 3.
12. See especially Tract 38 and Tract 41, both written and circulated in 1834. See John Henry Newman, *The Via Media of the Anglican Church: Letters and Tracts from 1830-1836*, London: J.F and G. Rivington, 1836.
13. C.f., *Revelation* 3:14–22, and the warning to the 'lukewarm church' that is neither hot nor cold – just slightly warm. The classic church of the *via media* is often critiqued as Laodicean and tepid. Anglicanism. born of England, mirrors its climate, which eschews extremes. The preference is for a temperate polity and spirituality; cloudy, occasional sunny spells with the odd shower. The outlook: mild.
14. This conversion was due in no small measure to the correspondence between Newman and the French theologian Abbé Jager. See Stephen Morgan, *John Henry Newman and the Development of Doctrine*, Washington DC: catholic University Press of America, 2021, pp. 118–132.
15. Mutual Flourishing, although ethically oxymoronic, is the official position of the Church of England in relation to the small minority who cannot accept women clergy and wish to perpetrate their ongoing exclusions and discriminatory conduct. Under this position, the rights of the dissenting minority are said to be fully recognised, accepted and protected by the church; and that acting on the will of the majority would be, de facto, discriminatory against the minority. This inevitably results in ethical immobility and ecclesial paralysis.
16. At the time of writing, it is estimated that there are complaints procedures against around 40% of the bishops in the Church of England, yet no sign of a single procedure resulting in any sanction. The bishops sit above the laws that govern their clergy, and essentially enjoy immunity from accountability or disciplinary procedures.
17. Anthony Sampson, *Anatomy of Britain*, Hodder & Stoughton, 1962. See also David Canadine, *The Decline and Fall of the British Aristocracy*, Vintage, 1999; Matthew Goodwin, *Values, Voice and Virtue*, Penguin,

2023; Owen Jones, *The Establishment: And How They Get Away With It*, Penguin, 2015; Philip Stanworth & Anthny Giddens, *Elites and Power in British Society*, Cambridge UP, 1974; and Aeron Davis, *Reckless Opportunists: The End of the Establishment*, Manchester UP, 2018.

18. Leonore Davidoff, *The Best Circles*, Ebury Press, 1986.

CODA

1. We date the Church of England from Thomas Cranmer, the first Protestant Archbishop of Canterbury from 1533/34. Prior to Cranmer, several Archbishops had their appointments vetoed by papal authority, several candidates chosen declined the See, some had their elections quashed or disputed by the monarch, one died of plague before consecration, another was excommunicated, one fled accused of high treason, and one resigned on being promoted to cardinal. Thomas Becket was assassinated in 1170, and Simon Sudbury beheaded by a mob during the Peasant's Revolt on 1381. Such archbishops and events all predated the birth of the Church of England.
2. https://www.churchofengland.org/sites/default/files/2024-11/independent-learning-lessons-review-john-smyth-qc-november-2024.pdf
3. See: https://www.churchtimes.co.uk/articles/2024/8-november/news/uk/prolific-brutal-and-horrific-makin-report-calls-out-the-smyth-abuse-and-the-cover-up
4. See Stephen Cherry, 'Welby Must Resign Now', *New Statesman*, 11 November 20124 https://www.newstatesman.com/comment/2024/11/justin-welby-must-resign-now and Martyn Percy, 'Welby is gone—but trust in the Church is broken beyond repair', *Prospect Magazine*, November 12 2024: https://www.prospectmagazine.co.uk/ideas/religion/church-of-england/68523/welby-is-gonebut-trust-in-the-church-is-broken-beyond-repair
5. https://en.wikipedia.org/wiki/Nobody%27s_Friends).
6. The likely links between Lambeth Palace and the hierarchy of the Church of England are discussed in *The Journal of Anglican Studies*, vol. 22, issue 2., November 2024. Lambeth Palace has not denied the links or contradicted the supporting evidence.

7. Some members of General Synod are now advocating stuffing the collection plates at Sunday worship as a sign of protest. See @ martinsewell, 14/12/24, 0843 am: "Put an empty envelope in the CofE collection plate as a protest at the lack of resignations".
8. See David Nichol, 'Tony Benn and the Five Essential Questions of Democracy', *The Nation*, 14 March 2014: https://www.thenation.com/article/archive/tony-benn-and-five-essential-questions-democracy/ See also: Stephen Nugent & Cris Shore, *Elite Cultures: Anthropological Perspectives*, Routledge, 2002.
9. Requests for sight of Conflicts of Interest Policies and Registers of Interests for members of the Archbishops' Council and senior ecclesiastical lawyers and officers have regularly been tabled at the Church of England's General Synod. Attempts were made in July 2020 2022, February 2023, July 2023 and November 2023, and were all rebuffed.
10. Ernest Hemingway, *The Sun Also Rises*, Scribner's, 1926.
11. See Martyn Percy, 'The Church of England in a Time of Crisis: Towards a Deconstruction of Normativity', *Anglican Theological Review*, winter 2024, vol. 106, issue 1. As we saw in the discussion of eugenics in chapter 5, normativity and regulative control of other people's bodies, relationships, desires and passions consumed the episcopal mindset from the 19th century onwards. Homosexuality and gender are currently the main concerns, and have preoccupied the Church of England's agenda since the 1960s. It was not always so. As late as 1866 the Archbishops of Canterbury and York were supportive of the surgical procedure of clitoridectomy as a means of controlling 'unruly female passions'. Likewise, many senior Anglican clergy and both archbishops openly endorsed tracts written on the evils and degeneration of masturbation well into the Edwardian period and beyond. See Diarmaid MacCulloch, *Lower than the Angels: A History of Sex and Christianity*, Allen Lane, 2024; and Helen King, *Immaculate Forms: Uncovering the History of Women's Bodies*, Wellcome Foundation, 2024.
12. As noted at the beginning of this book, we have adopted the post-liberal approach to doctrine taken by the likes of George Lindbeck (*The Nature of Doctrine*, 1984), Peter Berger (*The Heretical Imperative*, 1979) and contextual theologians such as James Hopewell (*Congregation: Stories and Structures*, 1987).

INDEX